Britain and Norway
in the
Second World War

SCANDINAVIA AND THE BALTIC 1939

North Cape
Zapadnaya Litsa
Kola Inlet
Neiden • Kirkenes
Banak
Alta • Petsamo • Murmansk
Skibotn Lake Inari Nautsi
Tromsø *Kola Peninsula*
Lofoten Islands FINNMARK
Harstad • Kandalaksha
TROMS
Ofoten
Narvik
Muonio
Vest Fjord Kiruna
NORDLAND Gällivara Rovaniemi
Boden Tornio
Træna • Mo-i-Rana Luleå Kemi
Mosjøen Oulu
TRØNDELAG SWEDEN FINLAND
Namsos
Bud
Ålesund
Stadlandet
Bremanger Åndalsnes
Vågsøy Trondheim
Høyanger Järvsö L. Ladoga
Bergen Lillehammer HELSINKI Viipuri
Stord *Åland* Leningrad
NORWAY *Islands*
TELEMARK OSLO Tallinn SOVIET
Rjukan *ØSTFOLD* Västerås ESTONIA UNION
VESTFOLD STOCKHOLM
Stavanger Södertälje
Egersund Oxelösund
Kristiansand Riga
Jøssing Fjord Arendal LATVIA
Göteborg
Skagerrak LITHUANIA
Kattegat Memel
DENMARK Kaunas
COPENHAGEN Königsberg
BALTIC SEA
Kiel Danzig EAST
Rostock PRUSSIA
Hamburg Swinemünde
Emden POLAND
GERMANY

Atlantic Ocean
GUDBRANDSDAL
Oslo Fjord
Gulf of Bothnia
Gulf of Finland

• Place names
• CAPITALS
DISTRICTS
COUNTRIES

Geographical features
Narvik - Luleå Railway ╂╂╂╂╂╂╂╂
International boundaries 1.9.39 - - - -
0   100   200   300

Britain and Norway in the Second World War

Edited by Patrick Salmon

LONDON : HMSO

ISBN 0 11 701232 7

Contents

Preface

THIS book is based on the proceedings of a conference organised by the British Committee for the History of the Second World War and held at St Antony's College, Oxford, from 25 to 27 September 1991.

The Committee wishes to record its thanks for the support and encouragement of the Cabinet Office, the Gerald Holdsworth Trust, the Foreign and Commonwealth Office, the British Academy and HE the British Ambassador in Oslo, and on the Norwegian side Professor Olav Riste, co-organiser with Sir William Deakin, the Norwegian Institute for Defence Studies and the Norwegian Resistance Museum, without which the meeting could not have taken place. The conference participants were also grateful for the kind hospitality of the Warden and the Bursar of St Antony's College, Oxford, and the efficient and friendly services of their staff and those of St Anne's College. Such events cannot take place successfully without a great deal of meticulous and thoughtful preparation of arrangements and their monitoring on the spot. On this occasion the Committee and all participants were indebted to Mr Richard Bone, Head of the Library and Records Department, Foreign and Commonwealth Office, who lent the excellent services of Dr Ann Lane of his Historical Section as conference secretary; to Dr Alan Borg, Director-General of the Imperial War Museum, who lent the services of Mr Jonathan Chadwick as Secretary of the Committee; and to those who served on the academic Planning Sub-Committee chaired by Sir William Deakin, namely Professor Riste, Miss Andrews, Mr Brown, Professor Dilks, Air Commodore Harvey, Mr Mackintosh, Group Captain Madelin, Dr Salmon and Miss Ward.

The editor is grateful to Dr Mats Berdal, who translated the chapter by Ragnar Ulstein and helped to prepare a number of other chapters for publication. He also wishes to thank Professor Olav Riste for his advice, Mrs Eleanor Cunningham of the Department of History, University of Newcastle upon Tyne, for secretarial support, and Tom Kristiansen of the Norwegian Institute for Defence Studies for technical assistance.

The chapter by Sir Peter Thorne was first published in *Intelligence and National Security*, volume 7 (1992), and is reprinted by permission of Frank Cass and Co Ltd, London.

Notes on the contributors

Clive Archer is Professor in the Department of Politics and International Relations at the University of Aberdeen. He is Chairman of the Northern Waters and Arctic Study Group and of the Royal Institute of International Affairs Scottish Branch. He is the author of *Organizing Western Europe* and of *Uncertain Trust: The British-Norwegian Defence Relationship*, and editor of *Northern Waters* and *The Soviet Union and Northern Waters*.

David Brown has been Head of the Naval Historical Branch, Ministry of Defence, since 1977. He is a Fellow of the Royal Historical Society.

Paal Frisvold is a retired Lieutenant General of the Norwegian Army. He graduated from the Military Academy in 1932, served with the General Staff during the Norwegian Campaign, and joined the Norwegian Army in the UK in 1941. He was Chief, Advance Element, Norwegian Military Mission at General Thorne's HQ Force 134 1944–5, and Lieutenant General and Chief of the Norwegian Army 1961–6.

Sir Alexander Glen visited Spitsbergen in 1932, 1933 and 1934 and his leadership of the Oxford University 1935–6 Expedition won him the Patrons Gold Medal from the Royal Geographical Society. During the first years of the war he was posted, as an RNVR Officer, as Assistant Naval Attaché in Belgrade. Following his escape from Yugoslavia in 1941 he accompanied the operations in Spitsbergen in 1941 and 1942 for which he was awarded the British DSC, the Norwegian War Cross and the Chevalier (1st Class), Order of St Olav. He served later in Albania and Yugoslavia. After the war he moved into shipping and travel and served as Deputy Chairman (1960–4) and later as Chairman (1964–6) of the Export Council for Europe. His publications include *Young Men in the Arctic* (1935) and his autobiography *Footholds against a Whirlwind*.

Einar Grannes is a retired forest manager. He saw active service in the Norwegian Military Resistance (Milorg) 1941–2. In 1943 he joined the Linge Company in the UK, and returned to Norway with the Falcon group in 1944. He was severely wounded and captured by the Germans, being held as a prisoner of war in 1944–5. He is the author of the recent book *I skyggen av Jupiter 1941–1944* (In the Shadow of *Jupiter* 1941–1944).

Air Commodore Maurice Harvey retired from the Royal Air Force in 1991 after 35 years' service. He has been a student of military history for many years and is a graduate of the Royal College of Defence Studies. He has written several articles on military and political history and his first book, *Scandinavian Misadventure: The Campaign in Norway, 1940*, was published in 1990. He now writes full time and his most recent work, *The Allied Bomber War 1939–1945*, appeared at the end of 1992.

Rear Admiral Baard Helle was active in the underground movement in occupied Norway from 1942 to 1944, when he had to flee the country to avoid arrest by the Gestapo. He joined the Royal Norwegian Navy in late 1944 and served on H Nor MS *Stord* for the rest of the war. He was appointed Director of the Norwegian Naval Academy in 1975. After a period as Chief of Staff to the Inspector General of the Navy, he was promoted Rear Admiral in 1982 and appointed Commander of the Naval District Western Norway. He retired in 1985.

Tønne Huitfeldt is a retired Lieutenant General of the Norwegian Army. He joined the Norwegian Army in the UK and served as Lieutenant in a Norwegian Independent Mountain Company during the liberation of Finnmark in 1944-5. He was Lieutenant General and C-in-C North Norway 1977–81 and Director, International Military Staff of NATO 1981-5. From 1985 to 1991 he was Strategic Studies Coordinator at the Norwegian Institute for Defence Studies.

Malcolm Mackintosh was Assistant Secretary in the Cabinet Office, dealing with Soviet and East European affairs. He has been Hon Senior Research Fellow, Kings College, London, since 1987, and was a Senior Fellow in Soviet Studies at the International Institute for Strategic Studies in London from 1989 to 1991. Since 1991 he has been Hon Lecturer in International Relations at the University of St Andrews. He served in the army from 1941 to 1946 in the Middle East, Italy and the Balkans, and was a member of the British Military Mission in the Allied Control Commission in Bulgaria from 1944 to 1946. He is the author of *Strategy and Tactics of Soviet Foreign Policy*, *Juggernaut: A History of the Soviet Armed Forces*, and chapters on Soviet and Warsaw pact affairs.

Wilhelm Mohr is a retired Lieutenant General of the Royal Norwegian Air Force. He served as a pilot during the Norwegian Campaign, and in the Royal Norwegian Air Force within the RAF, where he commanded 332 (N) Fighter Squadron. He was C-in-C of the RNAF 1964–9, Vice-Chief and Chief of Allied Air Forces at AFNORTH 1969–72, and Director, National Defence College 1972-5. Following his retirement he was Director for 11 years of the Norwegian Accident Investigation Board for Civil Aviation.

Arnfinn Moland is a history graduate from Oslo University, and Research Fellow/Lecturer at the Norwegian Resistance Museum. He is co-author of the volume on the Norwegian Resistance in the series *Norge i krig* (Norway at War) published in 1987.

Sir Brooks Richards served with the Royal Navy 1939-45 in para-naval clandestine operations between England and occupied France, and later as

x

head of the Special Operations Executive's Country Section working from North Africa to southern France. He is currently conducting research into clandestine sea transport operations as an Official Historian, and his book on wartime communications with France will be published as an Official History by HMSO. Now retired from HM Diplomatic Service, he formerly served as Ambassador to Saigon and Greece.

Olav Riste is Director of the Norwegian Institute for Defence Studies, Adjunct Professor of History at Bergen University, and Fellow of the Norwegian Academy of Science and Letters. He was Senior Scholar, St Antony's College 1959–62 and obtained his DPhil at Oxford in 1963. His published works include a two-volume work in Norway in the wartime alliance.

Joachim Rønneberg is a retired editor in the Norwegian Broadcasting Corporation. He joined the Linge Company in the UK in 1941. After special training he was selected to lead the *Gunnerside* operation which carried out the successful sabotage of the heavy water plant at Rjukan in February 1943.

Patrick Salmon is a senior lecturer in History at the University of Newcastle upon Tyne. He was a visiting fellow at the Norwegian Institute for Defence Studies in 1991. He is the author of *Foreign Policy and National Identity: The Norwegian Integrity Treaty 1907–24* and (with John Hiden) of *The Baltic Nations and Europe: Estonia, Latvia and Lithuania in the Twentieth Century*.

Øivind Schau is a retired Commodore of the Royal Norwegian Navy. After graduating from the Naval Academy in 1938, he served with the Norwegian Navy in the UK throughout the war, on MTBs and destroyers. He held various senior command posts after the war, and retired as CO of the Navy's Administrative Corps.

Mark Seaman is a member of the Research and Information Office at the Imperial War Museum, London, and is currently engaged in the creation of a Special Forces archive. He is a contributor to a number of journals and publications, including *Brassey's Defence Analysis*, *Intelligence and National Security* and the *Times Atlas of the Second World War*.

Magne Skodvin is Professor Emeritus of History at the University of Oslo, and Fellow of the Norwegian Academy of Science and Letters. He is the author of several books and articles on Norway and the Second World War and on Norwegian foreign policy, of which the most recent one is *Krig og okkupasjon 1939–1945* (War and Occupation 1939–1945).

Sir Peter Tennant was a Fellow of Queens' College, Cambridge, and University lecturer in Scandinavian languages, 1933–47. He was Press Attaché in the British legation, Stockholm, 1939–45, and served there with SOE. Immediately after the war he served in the British Embassy in Paris and was Deputy Commandant, British Sector, Berlin, 1950–2. He resigned from the Foreign

Service to take up a position with the Federation of British Industries. He then took up directorships in the City until he retired in 1975. He is the author of *Ibsen's Dramatic Technique*, *The Scandinavian Book*, *Amelia Posse's Letters from Prague in 1948* (in Czech) and *Touchlines of War* (in Swedish and English).

Edward Thomas (nephew of the First World War poet Edward Thomas) studied German and music. He was in the Naval Intelligence Division during the Second World War, serving in Iceland, at Bletchley Park and as Staff Officer (Intelligence) to Admiral Sir Bruce Fraser in HMS *Duke of York*, Flagship of the Home Fleet. After the war he served with various joint intelligence staffs in Singapore, the Ministry of Defence and the Cabinet Office. In 1967 he was a student at the Imperial Defence College. His publications include, with Professor Sir Harry Hinsley, *British Intelligence in the Second World War*, Volumes 1–4, translations of books by the former German Chancellor, Helmut Schmidt, and a contribution to Sir Harry Hinsley (ed.), *Codebreakers* (1993).

Sir Peter Thorne served in The Grenadier Guards and as a Staff Officer during the war and was for 34 years a senior official of the House of Commons. He is the son of the late General Sir Andrew Thorne who was GOC in C Scottish Command, 1941–5, and GOC in C Allied Land Forces, Norway, and Head of the SHAEF mission to Norway in 1945. He has maintained his father's links with Norwegian friends, including the former head of Milorg, since 1945. He is author of *The Royal Mace in the House of Commons*, and of various HMSO pamphlets and articles in parliamentary and historical publications.

Atle Thowsen received his DPhil in History from Bergen University and is Assistant Director of the Bergen Maritime Museum. He is the author of several books on Norwegian maritime history, including a recently published volume on the Norwegian merchant navy at war 1939–43.

Ragnar Ulstein is a State Research Fellow. He served in the Linge Company 1941–5 and took part in several expeditions to occupied Norway including *Siskin* in 1944–5. He is the author of several books on Norwegian war history, including *Etterretningstjenesten* (The Intelligence Services) vols. I–III.

H.P. Willmott is Professor of Naval History, Department of Military Strategy and Operations, National War College, Washington DC. He was a lecturer with the Department of War Studies, Royal Military Academy Sandhurst, and was a visiting professor at Temple University, Philadelphia, and at Memphis State University in 1989–90. He is a Fellow of the Royal Historical Society. He has written extensively upon warfare in general and the Second World War in particular, his most important books being *Empires in the Balance* and *The Barrier and the Javelin* (the first two parts of a four-volume history of the Pacific war for the Naval Institute Press) and *The Great Crusade*, a military re-interpretation of the Second World War. The second volume of the Pacific history won the Lynam Book Award in 1983.

Herman Fredrik Zeiner Gundersen is a retired General of the Norwegian Army. He graduated from the Military Academy in 1936 and fought in the Norwegian Campaign. He served as Captain, then as Major in the Norwegian Army in the UK in 1940–5, and later as General and Chief of Defence in Norway 1972–7. He was Chairman, NATO Military Committee 1977–80.

Participants in the Conference

In addition to the paperwriters and commentators, among those who accepted invitations to attend all or part of the conference, as observers and to take part in the debates on the papers, were:

His Excellency Kjell Eliassen (Norwegian Ambassador in London), Miss Alyson Bailes (British Consul-General and Deputy Head of Mission in Oslo), Miss Patricia Andrews, Mr and Mrs Ralph Bennett, Mr Mats Berdal, Mr Richard Bone, Mr Jonathan Chadwick, Colonel Andrew Croft, Sir William Deakin (Chairman, British Committee), Professor David Dilks, Lieutenant-Colonel Lars Finstad, Dr Ann Lane, Group Captain Ian Madelin, Sir Robin Maxwell-Hyslop, Professor Robert O'Neill, Mr Leonard Pagliero, Professor Adam Roberts, Mrs Joachim Rønneberg, Mr Arthur Sclater, Colonel H Sundstrøm, Lady Anne Thorne and Mrs Ragnar Ulstein.

Abbreviations

ACE	Allied Command Europe
ANCC	Anglo-Norwegian Collaboration Committee
AOK	Armeeoberkommando (German Army High Command)
BOAC	British Overseas Airways Corporation
C-in-C	Commander-in-Chief
CAB	Cabinet
CCS	Combined Chiefs of Staff
CID	Committee of Imperial Defence
CIGS	Chief of the Imperial General Staff
CO	Commanding Officer
COS	Chiefs of Staff
COSSAC	Chief of Staff to the Supreme Allied Commander Designate
DCO	Directorate of Combined Operations
DEMS	Defensively Equipped Merchant Ships
FO	Depending on context, *either*: (1) Foreign Office, *or* (2) Forsvarets Oberkommando (Norwegian Defence Command)
HMS	His Majesty's Ship
HNMS	His Norwegian Majesty's Ship
JIC	Joint Intelligence Sub-Committee
JPS	Joint Planning Staff
MEW	Ministry of Economic Warfare
Milorg	Militær Organisasjonen (Norwegian Home Army)
MTB	Motor torpedo boat
Nortraship	Norwegian Shipping and Trade Mission
NRM	Norway's Resistance Museum
OSS	Office of Strategic Services (United States)
POW	Prisoner of war
PRO	Public Record Office
RAF	Royal Air Force
RN	Royal Navy
RNAF	Royal Norwegian Air Forces
SCAEF	Supreme Commander Allied Expeditionary Force
Scotco	Scottish Command
SD	Sicherheitsdienst (German Security Service)

SHAEF	Supreme Headquarters Allied Expeditionary Force
SIS	Secret Intelligence Service
Sivorg	Sivil Organisasjonen (civilian arm of Norwegian resistance)
SOE	Special Operations Executive
UD	Utenriksdepartementet (Norwegian Foreign Ministry)
USAAF	United States Army Air Force
WBN	Wehrmachtsbefehlshaber Norwegen (German C-in-C Norway)
WO	War Office
WSA	War Shipping Administration

Introduction

IT is now fifty years since Norwegian territory was liberated from German occupation. The Liberation began in October 1944 with the advance of the Red Army into North Norway and ended in May 1945 with the surrender of all German forces in the country to Milorg, the Norwegian underground army, and to a British military mission headed by General Sir Andrew Thorne. The surrender was followed by the return from London of Crown Prince Olav, commander in chief of the Norwegian armed forces, and of members of the Norwegian government in exile. On 7 June 1945, five years to the day after he had been forced to flee from North Norway on board a British cruiser, another British cruiser brought King Haakon VII back to Oslo.

The relationship between Great Britain and Norway from the summer of 1940 to the end of the war was a very close one. Britain was a place of refuge for the thousands of Norwegians who wished to carry on the fight against Germany both inside their country and overseas. British equipment and British training were of vital importance to the Norwegian resistance effort. Close and amicable relations were established between the British goverment and the Norwegian government in exile, as well as between the British and Norwegian armed forces. Even before the conclusion of the Anglo-Norwegian alliance in May 1941, the Norwegian government had become one of the most enthusiastic exponents of a new 'Atlantic' vision of wartime cooperation and post-war security. The Norwegian contribution to the Allied war effort encompassed some of the most heroic and celebrated actions of the Second World War, including the 'Shetland Bus' service and the destruction of Germany's supply of heavy water, first by the *Gunnerside* operation at Vemork in 1943, and later by the sinking of the remaining stocks on Lake Tinnsjø in 1944. Norwegian units serving overseas performed vital services at sea, on land and in the air. So too did the ships and seamen of the Norwegian merchant fleet.

But the Anglo-Norwegian relationship also contained tensions. Britain was a great power with wide-ranging burdens and responsibilities. Norway was a small power preoccupied with the liberation of its own territory. For Norway the relationship was everything: for Britain it was one among many. The Norwegian government in London suffered from the insecurities faced by all exiled governments, isolated from their own people and dependent on powerful friends. It is true that Norway's position was immeasurably strengthened by the financial independence resulting from its possession of one of the world's largest merchant fleets. Nevertheless it was obliged to bow to the dictates of an Allied strategy in which Norway occupied only a very minor place. Raids and sabotage actions that might be justified for their effect on Germany's war effort appeared in a very different light when they destroyed Norwegian property and led to reprisals and death for Norwegian citizens.

Much has been written on Anglo-Norwegian relations during the war, especially in Norway. Nevertheless there has been little available in English, except on some of the better known episodes, and there is nothing in the nature of an overview. The British Committee for the History of the Second World War, wishing to repair this deficiency, organised a colloquium at St Antony's College Oxford in September 1991.[1] The meeting brought together professional historians and veterans of the war from both Norway and Great Britain. Like the conference on Britain and European resistance held at St Antony's in 1962, it was in many ways a moving occasion. Some of the participants had been present at the earlier conference; others had not seen one another for fifty years or more.

The success of the 1991 colloquium derived from its mixture of historical analysis and personal experience. Nowhere was this more evident than in the animated discussions that continued for three days both in the formal sessions and in innumerable informal exchanges. A number of papers were followed by commentaries. These now appear as chapters in their own right. The formal sessions were tape-recorded in their entirety, and summaries of the discussion appear at various points in the book. The tapes, together with a transcript, have been deposited in the Imperial War Museum where they will be available for the use of other historians.

The book is divided into five sections. Part I deals with the period of Norwegian neutrality, from September 1939 to April 1940. Relations between Britain and Norway at the beginning of the war did not, on the face of it, provide a very promising background for the intimate political and military relationship that was to develop after Norway's entry into the war. Throughout this early period many Norwegians, notably the foreign minister Professor Halvdan Koht, felt that the chief threat to Norwegian neutrality came from Britain rather than Germany. *Patrick Salmon* and *Magne Skodvin* show that there was some basis for this belief in the obsession with Scandinavia that dominated the strategic thinking of British and French leaders in the first months of the war. Anglo-Norwegian relations were also subject to mutual misunderstandings and misconceptions. The British expected more cooperation from Norway than Norwegian leaders felt able to offer, despite their shared hostility to Nazism. In the end, the British lost patience. A spectacular violation of Norway's territorial integrity took place in February 1940 with the boarding of the *Altmark* (an event which decisively accelerated planning for Operation *Weserübung* in Germany); and in April a British minelaying operation was taking place in Norwegian waters at the same time as the German invasion forces were moving northward. *Maurice Harvey* reminds us how risky the operation was for Germany, and suggests some of the reasons that may have led Hitler to approve it. *David Brown* points out, however, that one thing the German forces did not have to put up with, unlike their British and French counterparts, was interference from their political superiors. *H.F. Zeiner Gundersen*, finally, provides a corrective to any tendency towards Anglocentrism in assessing the strategic balance of the Norwegian campaign.

Olav Riste's paper on the relationship between the British government and the Norwegian government in exile establishes the framework for Part II, which is devoted to the workings of the Anglo-Norwegian alliance. Professor

Riste shows that the Norwegian government in exile gained enormously by not standing on its dignity or insisting on its rights on every occasion, but instead showing the British that it was fully committed to the Allied cause and by establishing close working relationships with British politicians, diplomats and officers. Norway had one asset which was not possessed by any other exiled government: the immense Norwegian merchant fleet. In his paper on the origins and development of Nortraship, *Atle Thowsen* shows that Norwegian shipping sailing in Allied service was a source of revenue and prestige which assured the Norwegian government a large measure of autonomy. At the same time, it raised acute problems. How far could private profit be reconciled with the priority of winning the war? Should Norway try to devote its earnings to the tasks of post-war reconstruction, or subordinate its interests to those of the alliance as a whole? On the whole, cooperation between the British and Norwegian navies and air forces, discussed in the papers by *Øivind Schau*, *Baard Helle* and *Wilhelm Mohr*, was less problematical. The services in question managed to reconcile the Norwegian desire to establish independent naval and air units with the broader requirements of Allied strategy. The courage of the Norwegian forces and their operational successes are attested by the warm tributes from senior British officers quoted in all three papers.

There was, however, a fundamental difference of opinion between the British and Norwegian authorities, one that forms the subject of the last two papers in this section, by *H.P. Willmott* and *Einar Grannes*. It concerned planning for an Allied invasion of Western Europe. For the Norwegian government in exile, the priority was the liberation of their own country. For Britain (and for the United States) Norway was marginal – useful as a feint to divert German attention, but remote from the theatres where the outcome of the war would be decided. The discussion at the Oxford conference showed that the reverberations of that debate have not entirely died away. Whilst Dr Willmott took a thoroughly sceptical view of Operation *Jupiter*, the plan for an Allied invasion of Norway, and attributed its longevity mainly to Winston Churchill's obsession with Norway, Dr Grannes shared some of that scepticism but drew on the records of the German military authorities in Norway to show that in one respect *Jupiter* was of crucial importance. The Germans, at least, took Allied plans seriously. Hitler, moreover, was (like Churchill) preoccupied with Norway. His attention seems to have been further focused on that country by the fact that the commander of the notional forces detailed for one dummy operation, *Fortitude North*, was General Sir Andrew Thorne whom he had encountered as British military attaché in Berlin in 1934.[2]

There is naturally an overlap between Part III, which deals with intelligence and the Norwegian resistance, and Part IV, which is devoted to special operations. *Edward Thomas* draws on six wartime years with British naval intelligence, mostly to do with Norway, as well as on his work with Professor Sir Harry Hinsley on the official history of British intelligence in the Second World War.[3] Here the story starts with the lamentable failure of British intelligence assessment (*not* of intelligence gathering) before the German invasion of Norway but becomes one marked by notable successes: the first breaking of Enigma, the destruction of the *Bismarck* and the *Tirpitz*, and the close collaboration between the Norwegian and British intelligence services. Mr Thomas also reveals the intelligence dimension of the Lofoten and Vågsøy raids of March and December 1941 – an aspect which has not, perhaps, been fully known in Norway and which may be weighed in the balance against the reprisals exacted by the Germans on those communities. The paper by *Ragnar Ulstein*, author of a three-volume history of Norwegian intelligence during the Second World War, confirms the importance of the intelligence as 'probably the most significant contribution which the resistance movement made to the victory in 1945'.

The problems of organisation and coordination in the intelligence field discussed in Ulstein's paper were also present in the field of resistance proper (in so far as the two can be separated). *Arnfinn Moland* examines the relationship between Milorg, the Norwegian underground army, and SOE. He shows how difficult it was to establish effective cooperation between SOE and its Norwegian agents on the one hand, and the leaders of Milorg on the other. The year 1942 in particular was a disastrous one as a result, in part of conflicting priorities and poor communications. As in other spheres, however, 1943 seems to have marked a turning point after which the objectives of Milorg and SOE converged and real successes were scored. The paper by *Joachim Rønneberg*, leader of the *Gunnerside* operation of February 1943, reveals the frustrations felt by many young Norwegians who trained in the UK and were eager for action in Norway. Too often, it seemed, they were held back by the caution of Norwegian headquarters in London and Milorg in Norway. The RAF, moreover, persistently refused to accept advice from the agents whom it dropped into their own country. Nevertheless, the overwhelming impression was one of solidarity and of the feeling expressed by Mr Rønneberg at the Oxford colloquium that the Norwegians in Britain had 'two homelands'.

The paper by *Sir Brooks Richards* on clandestine sea transport between the British Isles and Norway begins Section IV. It amplifies, and in some respects corrects, the account given in David Howarth's famous book *The Shetland Bus* (London, 1951). In particular it reveals the importance not only of the services run by SOE – the subject of Howarth's book – but of those run by SIS, the Secret Intelligence Service. The year 1942 again emerges as one of crisis and tragedy – an impression confirmed by the contribution to the discussion of Mr Arthur Sclater, the last wartime commander of the Scalloway base. *Mark Seaman* places Norway in the context of clandestine air operations in occupied Europe and confirms Joachim Rønneberg's suspicions about the attitude of the RAF. Air chiefs such as Portal and Harris were deeply hostile towards special operations, and Norway posed particular difficulties and hazards for the air crews involved. Nevertheless, from 1943 onwards, special duty flights became an increasingly frequent and effective means of dropping agents and supplies into occupied Norway. *Sir Peter Tennant* suggested at the Oxford meeting that a better title for his paper might have been 'Revolver Harry's Private Army'. It is in fact an account of the activities of an extremely unneutral Swede, Harry Söderman. In his capacity as head of the Swedish State Criminological Institute, Söderman performed many services on behalf of the Allied cause in general and Norway in particular. His greatest contribution, perhaps, was in helping to organise the Norwegian police troops in Sweden, but he also undertook his own private liberation effort in May 1945. Indeed, as Sir Peter pointed out at Oxford, 'one of our participants here had his door in Møllergaten prison opened by Harry'. *Sir Alexander Glen's* paper reminds us of the strategic importance of Spitsbergen during the Second World War. For the Allies, accurate knowledge of ice conditions between north Norway and Spitsbergen was vital to the security of the Murmansk and Archangel convoys; for Germany, manned stations on Spitsbergen and other Arctic islands were essential for accurate weather forecasting. In 1942–3 control of Spitsbergen was contested between the British and Norwegians on the one hand, and the Germans on the other. The conflict was eventually won by the Allies, but at a heavy cost.

Part V is devoted to the liberation of Norway and its aftermath. *Paal Frisvold* and *Sir Peter Thorne* provide Norwegian and British perspectives on the planning for liberation. Considerable potential for conflict was inherent in a situation where Norway came low down on the scale of Allied priorities, and where the forces detailed for occupying the country at the end of the war were wholly inadequate to cope with serious German resistance. Clearly much of the success of the liberation was due to the excellent personal relations between Jens Christian Hauge, the head of Milorg, and General Sir Andrew Thorne, the commander of the Allied expeditionary force. Thorne's estimate of the likely behaviour of the German forces in Norway – that their fighting morale would break down but that their discipline would be maintained – was borne out in practice. There was much uncertainty, however, about the possibility of a last-ditch German stand in *Festung Norwegen*. The discussion at Oxford suggested that such fears had some substance. *Malcolm Mackintosh* and *Tønne Huitfeldt* discuss another important aspect of the liberation – the Soviet advance into North Norway towards the end of 1944. Once again, the Norwegian government in exile was faced with the dilemma of how to deal with a powerful ally. This time it was one which, though willing to accept a Norwegian contribution to the liberation, was thoroughly hostile to the presence of the Western Allies in the far north. *Clive Archer*, finally, discusses the extent to which wartime experience shaped post-war strategic thinking in Norway. He shows that, rather than bringing about a fundamental change of attitudes, the war confirmed pre-war assumptions about the need to secure Western assistance against potential aggressors, as well as to reassure the Soviet Union that Norway posed no threat to Soviet security. Norwegian membership of NATO after 1949 merely substituted an explicit Western guarantee of Norwegian security for the implicit British guarantee that had existed between 1905 and 1940, while the fact that Norway's membership was limited – most obviously by the ban on peacetime NATO bases in the country – was an expression of the policy of reassurance.

References

1   An account of the origins and work of the British Committee is given in the preface
    to a volume based on an earlier conference: William Deakin, Elisabeth Barker and
    Jonathan Chadwick (eds.), *British Political and Military Strategy in Central, Eastern
    and Southern Europe in 1944* (London, 1988).
2   Michael Howard, *Strategic Deception in the Second World War* (London, 1990), p.
    111.
3   F.H. Hinsley, E.E. Thomas, C.F.G. Ransom and R.C. Knight, *British Intelligence
    in the Second World War* (4 vols., London, 1979–88)

PART I

From Neutrality to War 1939–40

1 British strategy and Norway 1939–40

PATRICK SALMON

Introduction

ON 16 September 1939 the British minister to Norway, Sir Cecil Dormer, gave the Norwegian foreign minister a confidential assurance of British support in the event of a German attack. In the early hours of 8 April 1940 British naval forces laid a minefield in Norwegian territorial waters in the Vestfjord, controlling the approaches to Narvik. What had happened since the outbreak of war to persuade the British government that it was necessary to take this step? Why did Great Britain decide to violate the neutrality of a country which it had pledged itself to defend?

By the spring of 1940 Scandinavia had come to dominate the strategic deliberations of the British War Cabinet and their French colleagues. In the absence of the expected German assault on the western front, the Chamberlain and Daladier governments turned their attention to Scandinavia as a result of two developments. One was a growing belief in Swedish iron ore as the Achilles' heel of the German war economy. If Germany could be deprived of supplies from Sweden, the war might be brought to an end in a matter of months. The other development was the Soviet invasion of Finland on 30 November 1939. The Finns' unexpected success in halting the Soviet advance raised the prospect of a prolonged conflict from which the Allies might profit. An Anglo-French expeditionary force, ostensibly going to Finland's assistance, could gain control of the northern Swedish iron ore fields and possibly even open up a new 'front of attrition' against Germany in the north. This vision was dispelled when Finland was obliged to sue for peace with the Soviet Union in March 1940, but the Allied leadership remained transfixed by Scandinavia. However, its next proposal for action, the minelaying operation in Norwegian waters authorised by the Supreme War Council on 28 March 1940, was to be overtaken by the far better prepared and far more ruthless operation which culminated in the German occupation of Denmark and Norway on the night of 8–9 April.

As long as British strategy was dominated by the idea of military intervention in Scandinavia, as it was between December 1939 and March 1940, Norway's role was a subordinate one. It figured mainly as the country through which an expeditionary force would have to pass *en route* for Finland and the Swedish ore fields. Norway was of much greater importance when iron ore alone occupied the attention of Allied leaders, since the Norwegian port of Narvik was one of the main export routes for Swedish ore, and the only one when the Baltic was frozen in winter. But Norway was also important in its own right. From the point of view of economic warfare it was the source of a number of strategic raw materials such as nitrates, ferro-alloys and non-ferrous metals, as well as fish products and whale oil, which Britain sought to deny to Germany. The Norwegian merchant fleet was the fourth largest and among the most modern in the world, and it was a vital necessity for Britain to be able to charter as much of this tonnage as possible in order to secure its own seaborne supplies. Finally, Norway occupied a key position in the naval war. The neutral corridor along the Norwegian coast constituted a major gap in the British blockade of Germany. It sheltered not only the iron ore traffic from Narvik but also enemy submarines, commerce raiders and auxiliaries on their journeys between the German ports and the North Atlantic. A further possibility, and one not entirely absent from British minds, was that Germany might seek to occupy territory in south-west Norway (further north was unthinkable) in order to establish bases for air and sea attacks on the United Kingdom.

Norway also had considerable political significance for British policy makers at a time – during the so-called Phoney War – when so much reliance was placed on influencing world opinion and convincing the Germans that they could not win. Norway was a small, democratic, peace-loving country with close links to the United Kingdom. It should, many felt, align itself openly with the Allied cause in combating Hitlerism, which threatened the whole of Europe. Norwegians were understandably reluctant to accept this simple argument. Norwegian attitudes were complex and often contradictory. Along with a widespread hatred of Nazism went a rejection of great-power politics which tended to brand all great powers as equally culpable. Fear of involvement in the war was accompanied by a belief that Norway was relatively free from the danger of attack owing to Great Britain's naval supremacy. Whilst the Royal Navy was Norway's ultimate line of defence, Britain was also thought – to some extent correctly – to have a greater interest than Germany in undermining Norwegian neutrality. All of these views (and many others) were held by the Norwegian foreign minister Halvdan Koht, the dogmatic intellectual who had dominated Norwegian foreign policy since the coming to power of the Labour Party in 1935. Throughout the early months of the war he defended Norwegian neutrality more vigorously against Allied violations – which tended to be few but conspicuous – than against those of Germany, which were more frequent but less visible.

The Norwegian attitude (together with that of neighbouring Sweden) crippled Allied strategy in the winter of 1939–40. Repeated requests for compliance in Allied attempts to deal with the iron ore traffic or to send assistance to Finland met with repeated refusals. The British were not prepared to ignore Scandinavian protests. The French would have done so but were overruled by the British, who had the upper hand in the northern theatre. Many considerations lay behind Britain's caution, but among the most important was the effect that a violation of Scandinavian neutrality would have had upon 'opinion', whether at home or in the Dominions or in influential neutral countries such as the United States and Italy. Ironically, however, it was opinion rather than strictly military considerations which finally proved decisive for Britain's action in Norwegian waters in April 1940. In the aftermath of the Finnish defeat the Allies felt obliged to demonstrate their resolve rather than their democratic scruples. It was typical of the Allied conduct of the Phoney War that this demonstration should have been executed on the territory of a friendly neutral and not on that of Germany.

Britain and Norway at the outbreak of war: the question of a British guarantee

For most of the inter-war period relations between Norway and Britain were friendly but distant. British policy makers neglected Norway on the assumption that the Norwegians were so sympathetic towards, and so dependent upon Great Britain that little attention needed to be paid to them. They failed to grasp the strength of Norwegian isolationism, or to recognise that Norwegians were beginning to question the degree to which Britain would be able to maintain in wartime the naval supremacy on which Norway's security depended. In 1938–9, with war against Germany in prospect, some British officials came to realise that Norway was a problem. Norwegian faith in Britain's resolve had been undermined by the Munich crisis and later by the German occupation of Prague in March 1939. The Northern Department of the Foreign Office believed that the Norwegians must be reassured on this point if there was to be any prospect of their cooperating in a British blockade. Laurence Collier, the head of the Department, wrote:

> The assumption of the 'defeatists' – that this country would not defend Norway against Germany – is of course wrong; and a glance at the map ought to show them that we could never allow so vital a strategic position for attack on Great Britain to fall into German hands without a fight.
>
> It is thus all the more significant, as a measure of the disrepute into which we have fallen, that even a German attack on Norway is not thought, in that country itself, to be enough to rouse us.'[1]

Some months earlier, immediately after Munich, the Foreign Office had been worried by a suggestion made by the head of the Norwegian military air service, Colonel Gulliksen, that if war had broken out the Germans might have seized the new aerodrome at Sola near Stavanger, which was within striking distance of the British Isles.[2] There was no anxiety about the possibility of a German seizure of naval bases in Norway. The Admiralty came to hear of Admiral Wegener's book on the subject, published in 1929 and discussed extensively by the Norwegian naval authorities in 1936–7, only when it was drawn to their attention by Sir Robert Vansittart in April 1939.[3] Nevertheless the Northern Department was able to persuade the foreign secretary, Lord Halifax, that the question of Norwegian morale and the danger of air attack were sufficiently serious to justify an approach to the Chiefs of Staff asking them to consider the advisability of giving Norway a formal assurance of defence against German attack.[4]

The matter was debated at such length in the Foreign Office that a request was not sent to the Chiefs of Staff until 24 August, and their report was presented only on 4 September, a day after the outbreak of war.[5] The Chiefs of Staff endorsed the Foreign Office's proposal with the proviso that 'no assistance as regards direct air attack can be given'.[6] Dormer duly gave this assurance to Koht on 16 September and reported: 'He made no remark but it will probably have had a good effect.'[7] Knowing Koht's views, this was a thoroughly dubious assumption. Koht's suspicions of Great Britain would have been powerfully reinforced had he known of the reaction of one junior Foreign Office official to the Chiefs of Staff report. Daniel Lascelles, a member of the Northern Department who was to become first secretary at the Oslo legation in January 1940, welcomed the prospect of German reprisals against Norway since they would enable Britain 'to intervene in a "protective" capacity':

> At present one of our main difficulties is to find the means of attacking Germany on relatively undefended sectors. Operations against her in Norway would enable us to exploit our immense naval superiority to the full; they would hamper her at a moment when she wished to concentrate her forces elsewhere; and as Germany would have been the first to infringe Norwegian neutrality, the reactions of the other Scandinavian States would be extremely unfavourable to her.
>
> The real moral of this report is, in fact, that we should do all in our power to provoke a German infringement of Norwegian neutrality and be prepared to intervene vigorously as soon as this is brought about.[8]

Winston Churchill and the Narvik traffic

Britain's principal interests in Norway after the outbreak of war were in negotiating a war trade agreement which would limit Norwegian exports to Germany, and an agreement with Norwegian shipowners which would secure as large an amount of tonnage as possible for Britain's needs. As long as these two agreements remained unsigned there was a strong incentive to avoid any actions likely to antagonise the Norwegians. At the same time, however, there was growing concern with the question of Swedish iron ore. In September 1939 Winston Churchill, the First Lord of the Admiralty, emerged as the leading advocate of direct action against Narvik traffic in Norwegian territorial waters.

There had been little official Admiralty interest in Norway before war. Churchill himself had always been more interested in the Baltic. Early in 1939, however, the problem of Norwegian waters was considered by a small unofficial planning staff was working at the Admiralty under the leadership of Admiral Drax, 'the ablest and most incisive of the navy's strategists'.[9] If the Norwegians did not cooperate in forcing German merchant ships out of their waters, Drax argued, 'the only course left to us would be (after protest against the neutral's failure to enforce his neutrality) to enter territorial waters and sink enemy ships.'[10] Drax was again at the Admiralty in September 1939. On the question of the Narvik traffic he recommended: 'Press for Cabinet approval without delay. Necessary naval plans to be got out.'[11]

This appears to have been the origin of Churchill's well known proposal to the War Cabinet on 19 September 1939 that mines should be laid inside Norwegian territorial waters in order to drive the ore-carrying vessels outside the three-mile limit. Churchill's espousal of this proposal and his preoccupation with it thereafter were not due to economic considerations alone. They reflected a long-standing interest – dating to before the First World War – in involving the smaller European neutrals in Britain's wars with Germany. He was convinced in both cases that since Britain was fighting *their* war, it had the right to expect these countries to abandon their neutrality and join wholeheartedly in the Allied cause. To an increasing extent, too, Churchill advocated direct action for the same reason as Lascelles: in order to provoke a violent German reaction.

The Cabinet shelved Churchill's proposal on 5 October. At that time shipments from Narvik had fallen drastically and the negotiations for a war trade agreement with Sweden offered the prospect that the Swedes themselves might reduce their deliveries to Germany. By late November it was clear that German fears of interception had diminished and that shipments were on the increase once again. On 30 November, the day on which the Soviet Union launched its attack on Finland, Churchill revived his minelaying proposal. The coincidence was significant. The Cabinet was now sufficiently impressed to subject the questions of naval interception and of Swedish iron ore as a whole to further study. But the outbreak of the Soviet-Finnish war meant that Narvik could not longer be considered in isolation. If Swedish iron ore was as vital to Germany as the economic experts claimed, was the closure of the Narvik route sufficient? Would not the Baltic route have to be dealt with as well, or the Swedish ore fields be brought under direct Allied control? As the idea of military intervention gained momentum, Churchill's scheme came increasingly to be relegated to the status of a 'minor' plan.

Norway and the question of Allied military intervention in Scandinavia

Military operations in the Scandinavian peninsula had never been considered seriously by the British authorities before the war. But as early as 31 October 1939, in a report on the possibility of 'Soviet aggression against Finland or other Scandinavian countries', the Chiefs of Staff suggested that 'A small British force, say a Brigade Group, based on the Narvik-Boden railway and operating in support of the Norwegians and Swedes, might have an effect out of all proportion to its size.'[12] There were still serious misgivings, not least on the part of the Chief of the Imperial General Staff, General Ironside. On 16 November he told his colleagues that he was not at all in favour of sending either a military mission or land forces to Norway in any circumstances. . . . To hold Narvik against any considerable attack would require a division at least. If it was essential to stop the export of iron ore from Narvik we should have to consider a full sized expedition.[13]

The Chiefs of Staff went on to recommend to the Cabinet that the British assurance to Norway of 16 September, already excluding defence against air attack, should be confined to a promise of naval support alone.[14] All this was changed by the outbreak of the Soviet-Finnish Winter War. Both the early Soviet advance, which aroused fears of a drive to the ports of northern Norway, and the subsequent success of Finnish resistance gave impetus to the ideas of large-scale military intervention in Scandinavia which were beginning to crystallise in the Allied camp by the end of December 1939. Ironside himself was the most notable convert, informing the Military Co-ordination Committee on 20 December that an expedition to northern Sweden was 'a legitimate side-show, unlike Salonika, Archangel and Mesopotamia'.[15]

Where did Norway fit into these elaborate schemes? In the short term the growing preoccupation with the 'larger scheme' took some of the pressure off Norway, though this was not how it seemed to Norwegian leaders at the time. On 27 December the War Cabinet decided to go ahead with the Narvik operation – now to be carried out by naval interception instead of minelaying – on condition that the Scandinavian attitude was known to be satisfactory. They decided to say nothing about the iron ore traffic but to claim that the action was in retaliation for the sinking of three merchant ships by a German submarine in Norwegian territorial waters early in December. The vehement reactions of Norway and Sweden to the British diplomatic notes of 6 January 1940 led, after intensive debate, to the abandonment of the operation on 12 January.

It is significant that the War Cabinet took the Swedish protest much more seriously than the Norwegian. This was due in part to a correct perception of Sweden as being pivotal both for the iron ore question and for that of assistance to Finland. It also reflected superior Swedish diplomacy. Swedish diplomats and businessmen like Erik Boheman and Marcus Wallenberg had the knack of speaking candidly and in an ostensibly straightforward manner to the British. Boheman, for example, told the British chargé d'affaires in Stockholm that 'It would be better for you to slip in and sink the ships on the quiet than for you to declare that you were justified in so doing.'[16] The British were unaware that the Swedes were speaking in much the same terms to the Germans. It was also a characteristic British habit to speak more frankly about their motives to the Swedes than to the Norwegians, apparently with no thought that the information might be passed on. Thus the Swedish minister was informed as early as 4 January that the Admiralty was considering the problem of the Narvik traffic, whilst the Norwegians laboured for several days under the misconception that they needed to counter the British legal arguments about the sinkings of early December. This is testimony, among other things, to the lack of communication between the Norwegian and Swedish governments at the time (though the situation improved subsequently). In fact the Norwegians learned on 11 January from a British source – Lascelles, newly arrived in Oslo – that iron ore lay behind the British *démarche*, and only the following day received the same information from the Swedes.[17] In contrast to the Swedes, the Norwegians were regarded as being 'obstinate' and 'legalistic'.[18] There was some justification for this view, given Koht's obstructive attitude since the outbreak of war, particularly on questions of war trade and shipping. But it also reflected a deep-seated prejudice among British officialdom which made it difficult to take Norwegian objections seriously even when they were valid and cogently expressed – as they were by Norway's experienced and principled representative in London, Erik Colban.[19]

The *Altmark* incident

The postponement of the 'minor' operation made Norwegian involvement in the larger one all the more likely. The Supreme War Council of 5 February 1940 authorised the larger plan but at the same time made it conditional on Scandinavian consent. The Finns were to issue an appeal for Allied assistance, and Norway and Sweden were then to be asked to allow the transit of Allied troops across their territories. Two Allied forces were detailed for Norway. *Avonmouth* was to be sent to Narvik and was then to move up the railway to occupy the Swedish ore fields and the port of Luleå. Operation *Stratford* would be carried out at the same time. Five territorial battalions would be landed at Stavanger, Bergen and Trondheim in order to forestall the Germans and to prepare the way for the much larger force which would eventually take up position in central Sweden in anticipation of a German invasion. After the experience of January, Scandinavian consent was unlikely to be forthcoming. Many British leaders privately acknowledged this but were reluctant to face the implications: either to abandon the expedition or to use force against the neutrals. To an increasing extent they appear to have felt that the operation would be made possible only if Germany made 'some false step' by 'bursting out and violating Scandinavian neutrality'.[20] This fatalistic reliance on the enemy was not shared by Churchill. He wanted to provoke German action and sought to exploit the *Altmark* incident to bring it about.

The dramatic boarding of the German auxiliary ship *Altmark* in a Norwegian fjord by a British destroyer on the night of 16 February 1940, followed by the release of 299 British prisoners, provided an opportunity – as it proved, the last before the end of the Winter War – to pull out of the larger operation and return to the smaller but more feasible operation of laying mines in Norwegian waters. It was immediately seized upon by Churchill, whose principal aim was now to provoke 'Germany into an imprudent action which would open the door for us'.[21] On 20 February he ordered the Admiralty to make urgent preparations for the operation which, 'being minor and innocent, may be called "Wilfred" '.[22] The Cabinet was in a receptive mood and Churchill had learnt from his earlier mistakes: he did not try to rush his colleagues into an immediate decision. However, after ten days of discussion the Cabinet decided once again, on 29 February, to do nothing.

The reasoning behind their decision was set out with unusual clarity: Churchill's opponents had also learnt from their mistakes. First, the legal arguments in favour of going ahead were not as strong as they had appeared at first. Secondly, both the Dominion prime ministers and the leaders of the Opposition had been consulted and had expressed their misgivings. The reactions of Italy and the United States were also expected to be unfavourable. Then there were economic consequences which might include the loss of supplies of Danish foodstuffs, Swedish iron ore and other products. The Ministry of Economic Warfare (MEW), hitherto among the leading supporters of action against the Narvik traffic, warned that the Norwegians were certain to react strongly against any further violations of their neutrality – perhaps by denouncing the shipping agreement. If, on the other hand, Britain cultivated their good will, they might be prepared to charter all their tonnage to Britain. Trygve Lie, the Norwegian minister of supply, had even raised the prospect of secret military and naval conversations with Great Britain once the war trade agreement had been signed. Chamberlain was particularly impressed by this hint, which would have horrified Lie's colleagues had they known of it.[23] Chamberlain confessed that 'My own mind varied as fresh considerations were brought to my attention.'[24] The decisive consideration was probably a last minute warning from the chairman of the Oil Control Board that without Norwegian tankers 'it would be impossible "to conserve and maintain adequate supplies of petroleum products" '.[25] The Cabinet's renunciation of drastic action against Norway was underlined when they went on, immediately afterwards, to approve the signature of the Anglo-Norwegian trade agreement. There is therefore much to be said for the view that the *Altmark* affair proved the strength rather than the weakness of Norwegian neutrality and was 'a warning not to take Norwegian submission for granted.'[26]

In the last resort, however, Norway could not afford to offer serious resistance should the Allies press ahead with their plan of military intervention. This was not due merely to the inadequacy of Norway's defence forces. On 2 March the Norwegian government was obliged to consider an Allied request to allow the passage of troops for the assistance of Finland. Koht advised his colleagues that Norway must satisfy itself with a protest: it could not under any circumstances allow itself to be drawn into the war 'on the wrong side'.[27] Here, rather than in his tiresome protests to the British, Koht showed where his true sympathies lay.

Would the Allies have gone ahead with the operation in defiance of Scandinavian protests? They knew nothing of the Norwegian cabinet's discussion and were aware that even passive resistance on the part of the Norwegians and Swedes (for example, cutting off the power supply to the Narvik-Luleå railway) would be sufficient to jeopardise the entire expedition. They apparently came close to going ahead regardless in mid-March 1940, at the point at which Finnish resistance was close to collapse and peace talks were already in progress in Moscow. This very fact lent an air of unreality to the Cabinet's discussions. Nevertheless Ironside was confident on 11 March that it had been decided 'to go on with the Narvik plan at all costs and to arrive off the port and make a demand for passage through to Finland. . . . which means that we must be prepared for some sort of opposed landing'.[28] Serious opposition was not expected. Churchill thought that the Allied force would be able to get ashore by means of a combination of 'persuasion and cajolery'.[29] Ironside boasted: 'I can see our great big Scots Guards shouldering the sleepy Norwegians out of the way at 5 a.m. in the morning.'[30]

Norway in the aftermath of the Winter War

The Allies were spared the necessity of putting either their own resolve or that of the Norwegians and Swedes to the test by the conclusion of the peace of Moscow on 12 March. It is probable that few if any Cabinet ministers had seriously believed that the operation would go ahead. But they now had to find some way of compensating for the political and psychological damage caused by Finland's defeat, particularly in France, where it led to the fall of the Daladier government on 19 March. The search for a means of regaining the initiative and demonstrating Allied resolve led once again to Scandinavia.

The Supreme War Council of 28 March 1940 agreed that two minelaying operations should be carried out simultaneously. One was *Royal Marine*, Churchill's scheme for dropping 'fluvial mines' in the Rhine. The other was *Wilfred*. Neither had any great military value: their main function was symbolic. MEW admitted that as far as the Narvik traffic was concerned, 'it would hardly be possible to choose a less useful moment for the carrying out of the operation'.[31] In contrast to previous occasions, when leakages had been mostly confined to the French side, every effort was made to prepare opinion at home and abroad – as good a sign as any that the Cabinet were taking the decision seriously. Indiscretion was essential to a programme whose main function was to bolster Allied prestige. The extensive press discussion of the iron ore problem and the abuse of Norwegian territorial waters was among the main reasons why the Cabinet felt obliged to go ahead with *Wilfred* after the French decided on 30 March to drop *Royal Marine* (though the operation was postponed from 5 to 8 April): there was a 'general expectation that we were about to take some drastic action'.[32] Chamberlain in particular, so cautious on previous occasions, declared on 3 April that 'matters had now gone too far for us not to take action'.[33]

In these circumstances nothing the Norwegians could do could have any effect on either the British or the Germans, whose own plan, Operation *Weserübung*, was approaching fruition. Koht tried desperately to deflect British interest from iron ore and to convince both sides that Norway was able and determined to defend its neutrality. He also asked the military authorities to consider laying the minefield which had been hinted at in a note to Great Britain early in February. Neither side was convinced. Quisling's agents told the Germans that Koht's statements were part of an elaborate deception. The British had decided to lay the mines themselves and were not interested in the Norwegian suggestion.

A small expeditionary force codenamed *R4* was added to the minelaying operation in order to be sent to Narvik, Stavanger, Bergen and Trondheim 'the moment the Germans set foot on Norwegian soil, or there is clear evidence that they intend to do so.'[34] There was still no idea that the Germans might act independently rather than in response to the British minelaying. Hence the inability to interpret correctly the mass of intelligence pointing to large-scale German action, with Scandinavia as the most likely target. Hence too the misreading of German naval movements off the coast of Norway as an attempt to break out into the North Atlantic – an eventuality with which the Admiralty had been 'obsessed' (in the words of Admiral Pound, the First Sea Lord) since the beginning of the war. On this assumption, a few hours after *Wilfred* had been carried out, the troops embarked for Norway were disembarked to allow the navy to chase the German ships. Plan *R4* was abandoned, and with it the last chance of gaining a foothold in Norway.

Conclusion

The British government apparently gave little thought to the way in which the Norwegians might react to the laying of mines in their waters. It was assumed that they would not sweep the mines themselves except under German pressure. British destroyers would have stood guard for 48 hours, but thereafter the minefields would have been unsupervised. So far from expecting the Norwegians to sweep the mines, Chamberlain actually declared that the departing destroyers should tell them that 'the responsibility for safeguarding shipping against the danger of mines thereby passed into Norwegian hands.'[35] In fact the Norwegian government decided on 8 April to ask the British to remove the mines. And they had resolved to clear the mines themselves – once the 48 hours had expired – if the British did not do so.

The episode was symptomatic of the casual nature of British decision making during the Phoney War, as well as of the negligent British treatment of Norway. At the beginning of the war too much was expected of the Norwegians. The Foreign Office told the Chiefs of Staff in August 1939 that 'The sympathies both of the Government and of the people would be likely to favour the British cause, to a greater extent perhaps than in any other neutral country'.[36] Excessive reliance was placed on the conspicuously pro-British inclinations of King Haakon VII, the armed forces and some business circles. Disappointment with the conduct of the Norwegian government after the outbreak of war was thus all the greater and was compounded by the ostensibly more forthcoming attitude of the Swedes. No doubt Koht's conduct of relations with Great Britain was frequently ill-judged, and it was understandable that the leaders of the Norwegian government in exile should have made a conscious break with his approach. Yet it was also natural that a country so dependent on Britain should seek to emphasise its independence – much as General de Gaulle was to do in wartime London. And it is not clear that a more accommodating attitude would have been more advantageous to Norway. Once British policy had become focused on Scandinavia, Norway was bound to be entangled one way or another.

References

1   Minute of 29 March 1939, Public Record Office, London (PRO), FO 371/23652, N1674/31/63. All documents cited are in the PRO unless otherwise stated.
2   Dormer to Collier, 3 October 1938, FO 371/22283, N4973/4973/30.
3   Vansittart to Backhouse (First Sea Lord), 14 April 1939, ADM 1/9956.
4   Halifax minute, 18 August 1939, FO 371/23654, N1764/64/63.
5   Lascelles (FO) to Secretary of Committee of Imperial Defence (CID), 24 August 1939, ibid.
6   'Norwegian neutrality. Report by Chiefs of Staff Committee', CAB 66/1.
7   Dormer to FO, 16 September 1939, FO 371/23049, C14318/454/18.
8   Minute of 8 September 1939, FO 371/23658, N4218/64/63.
9   Patrick Salmon, 'Churchill, the Admiralty and the Narvik traffic, September – November 1939', *Scandinavian Journal of History* 4 (1979), pp. 305–26; quotation from Donald Cameron Watt, *How War Came: the immediate origins of the Second World War, 1938–1939* (London, 1989), p. 165.
10 OPC 4, 2 February 1939, Drax Papers, Churchill College, Cambridge, DRAX 2/10.
11 'Summary of W.P. Papers' dated 'Sept 1939', ibid.
12 CAB 66/3.
13 Meeting of Chiefs of Staff, CAB 79/2.
14 'Assistance to the Scandinavian countries in the event of Russian and/or German aggression', 21 November 1939, CAB 66/3.
15 R. Macleod and D. Kelly (eds.), *The Ironside Diaries 1937–1940* (London, 1962), pp. 186–7 (entry for 21 December 1939).
16 Montagu-Pollock to FO, 7 January 1940, FO 371/24820, N295/19/63.
17 Conversation between Lascelles and Jens Bull (Secretary-General of Norwegian Foreign Ministry), 11 January 1940, Utenriksdepartementets arkiv, Oslo, 38 D 2/40; Wollebæk (Stockholm) to UD, 12 January 1940, ibid.
18 Collier minute, 16 December 1939, FO 371/23660, N7522/64/63.
19 See Colban's despatch of 30 January 1940, quoted in Arne Bergsgård, 'Utrikspolitikk', in *Innstilling fra Undersøkelsekommisjonen av 1945*, Bilag, vol I. (Oslo, 1947), p. 237.
20 *Ironside Diaries*, pp. 219, 221 (entries for 19 and 20 February 1940).
21 War Cabinet meeting, 18 February 1940, CAB 65/11.
22 Winston S. Churchill, *The Second World War*, vol. I, *The Gathering Storm* (2nd. edn., London, 1949), pp. 679–80.
23 Dormer to FO, 12 February 1940, FO 371/24826, N2106/22/30; War Cabinet meeting, 29 February 1940, CAB 65/5.
24 Letter to Ida Chamberlain, 2 March 1940, Neville Chamberlain Papers, Birmingham University Library.
25 Memorandum of 28 February 1940, CAB 66/6.
26 Magne Skodvin, 'Norwegian neutrality and the question of credibility', *Scandinavian Journal of History* 2 (1977), p. 139.
27 The minutes of the meeting were subsequently captured and published by the Germans. English-language edition of German White Book No. 4: *Britain's designs on Norway: Documents concerning the Anglo-French policy of extending the war* (New York, 1940), pp. 61–4.
28 *Ironside Diaries*, p. 226 (entry for 11 March 1940).
29 War Cabinet meeting, 11 March 1940, CAB 65/12.
30 *Ironside Diaries*, p. 226 (entry for 11 March 1940).

31   Memorandum of 5 April 1940, FO 371/24819, N4064/7/63.
32   War Cabinet meeting, 1 April 1940, CAB 65/6.
33   War Cabinet meeting, 3 April 1940, CAB 65/12.
34   Memorandum by Chiefs of Staff, 31 March 1940, CAB 66/6.
35   War Cabinet meeting, 5 April 1940, CAB 65/12.
36   Note 5 above.

2 Norwegian neutrality and the challenge of war

MAGNE SKODVIN

DR Salmon has delivered another valuable contribution to an area of study that continues to be of great interest to Norwegian historians. His research is all the more meritorious since, with some outstanding exceptions, British historians have shown comparatively little interest in studies in depth of the problems he deals with. Strategic planning and subsequent warfare by the United Kingdom and Allied powers in the Scandinavian area, however dramatic, remain among the trials and errors of the beginning of the beginning, easily overshadowed by the tremendous events and efforts that were to follow. Most Norwegians, on the contrary, are likely to feel that the developments of 1939 and 1940, for the first time, revealed to what extent the country had now become part of the world where world wars originated and were fought, or perhaps: to what extent it had become possible to stay aloof. In the history of Norway the 'phoney' war became a moment of truth.

I propose to offer a few remarks on points where Dr Salmon's paper adds substantially to the knowledge of Norwegian historians, and similarly on matters where, from Norwegian points of view, it may seem possible to bring additional information, or at least food for thought.

Almost inevitably, we return to Winston Churchill, his initiatives, his bold strokes, his personal influence. In most Norwegian minds, it is Churchill the victorious who looms on the horizon, and his image as a winner is frequently projected backwards so as to include the first half-year of the war. He becomes the architect and the prime mover and, *eo ipso*, also the man who manoeuvred Norway into the war. His relationship with the men of Munich in the War Cabinet, however, his periods as an *enfant terrible* in British politics, and his reluctance to go all out in a Scandinavian expedition are less known. Today's paper adds another nuance to the picture, inasmuch as Dr Salmon points to pre-war studies in the Admiralty, led by Admiral Drax. It may take more such reminders to modify the picture of Churchill pushing and dragging his somewhat hesitating naval strategists, assisted chiefly by an ageing and submissive Pound.

Dr Salmon gently reminds us that from a strategic point of view, Norway was for a long time only part and parcel of considerations concerning Sweden, and that the main advantage of gaining a foothold in Narvik might well be an increased ability to exert pressure on the Swedes. The same applies to German strategic thinking. The war in Poland, the Hitler-Stalin pact and the Finno-Russian war had changed the role of the German navy in the Baltic, leaving Sweden alone as a power to be reckoned with, and Narvik as a controlling position. With German domination of the Baltic entrances and the Narvik railroad, Sweden would be bottled up.

And now to another controversial public figure: Norwegian minister of foreign affairs, Halvdan Koht. There is possibly no other person in recent Norwegian history of whom writers have held such strong, and frequently conflicting opinions. Was he an obstinate, a dogmatic mind, a naive believer in the virtues of neutrality, 'a politician for the 1920s' as has been said recently – the twenties then probably to be understood as the Locarno honeymoon – was he biased against England and correspondingly unrealistic as regards Hitler's Germany? I submit that all of these descriptions are oversimplifications, and that Koht suffered the fate of politicians who are victims of circumstances beyond their control, and pay the price for it according to the rules of the game. It was his policy to observe the principles and practices of international law, in this case the conventions and precedents concerning the rights and duties of neutrals, and who could blame him for that? He did not believe in formally correct neutrality as a guarantee of peace, but as one of the few areas where a small and powerless state could justify its policy against arguments of power politics. We must behave strictly in accordance with the rules of international law, he stated, but immediately added, significantly; 'then nobody could *rightly* blame us". He knew perfectly well that Norway was best served by an allied victory – and that is a deliberate understatement – but he also knew perfectly well that such views, if publicly expressed, would jeopardise his policy of neutrality. He was convinced that if a situation materialised where Norway was forced to abandon neutrality, there was no question of which would be the right side to choose, and equally convinced that this must never be said aloud, and particularly not to the British, so as not to end up on the slippery slope of gradual submission. In this he was successful: witness the numerous British speculations as to what the Norwegians might or might not do, in case of an allied landing. It is, on the whole, surprising that British planners could seriously engage in such far-reaching projects with so little elementary knowledge of things Norwegian. Koht suspected British attempts to drag Norway into the war – and he was right. This does not mean that he neglected, or overlooked, the possibility of similar German initiatives. In closed sessions of the Storting, he repeatedly warned against the German intervention that must inevitably be expected if Norway allowed a transit of Allied troops, ostensibly to assist Finland. On this count he was far more realistic and explicit than such experienced politicians as Hambro and Mowinckel. Dr Salmon's brief summing up of the reasoning behind Koht's much-quoted utterance about not being drawn in 'on the wrong side' stands head and shoulders above what has so far been written by scholars abroad.

With more time and pages to his disposal, I presume that the Dr Salmon would have dealt more extensively with the intricate problems of French-British relations, and more specifically with the permanent French pressure beginning in mid-December 1939, in favour of an all-out operation, even including a possible new theatre of war along a front across the Swedish lakes toward the Oslo Fjord. From this point of view, the period between the

Finno-Soviet armistice on 13 March 1940 and the Supreme War Council on the 28th seems to have been less thoroughly analysed, so far, than the subsequent haggling and quarrelling about Operation *Royal Marine*.

Dr Salmon's paper deals with complicated and intricate problems in the masterly way which is the rare quality of those scholars who dominate their area of studies to the extent that they are able to offer, in summaries like this one, what others fail to achieve in volumes. His insight into the Norwegian side of the story places him in the leading field of international historians attracted by the developments that, so suddenly, made Norway the target of the belligerents – and their victim.

3 The balance sheet of the Norwegian campaign

MAURICE HARVEY

A T 0515 on Tuesday 9 April 1940 the German invasion of Norway, Operation *Weserübung*, heralded five years of unrelenting occupation. The plan was bold in concept, meticulously organised and impressively implemented. It took both the Norwegians and the Allies by surprise, in consequence of their failure to recognise or heed the many signs which were available in the preceding weeks. All the major ports were in German hands by the end of the first day, but despite their military successes, they had not achieved one of their main aims which was to secure the immediate and total capitulation of the Norwegian government. The Allied response was hesitant, ill prepared and inadequately executed, and the German divisions moved relentlessly through southern and central Norway forcing the evacuation by the end of April of the four brigades that the Allies managed to get ashore at Namsos and Åndalsnes.[1] The situation in the north at Narvik was hardly more encouraging. Though isolated and woefully short of supplies, the German commander General Dietl was nevertheless able to hang on to Narvik for over two months before being forced to withdraw in the face of overwhelming odds. Even so he was able to re-occupy the town within little more than a week as the British, French and Polish troops made an undignified if inevitable evacuation following the German invasion of France.

After this catalogue of disasters it is somewhat intimidating to try to embark upon a balance sheet. A balance implies some sort of equilibrium – assets offsetting liabilities, accrued benefits weighed in the scales against perceived debits. At first sight the Germans would appear to have won this contest by a wide margin, achieving most of their objectives with minimal losses except at sea, a risk which had been fully recognised, at least by Admiral Raeder, before they embarked upon the enterprise. However, I shall look at the balance, as it subsequently materialised, from the viewpoint of each country involved. I shall touch upon the naval aspects only where they impinge on the wider strategic implications of the aftermath of the campaign in Norway. It may be sufficient, however, to remark at this point that, in my view, whereas the land and air campaign was an almost unrelieved sequence of disasters, the Royal Navy at least earned a draw.

Before assessing the balance, we need to enquire a little more deeply into the German objectives in seeking to impose their hegemony upon Norway and Denmark.[2] I think we can dispose of Denmark fairly quickly. It was regarded by the Luftwaffe as an essential stepping stone for their role in the subjection and resupply of Norway and it provided added security in the approaches to the Baltic. Whether this was really necessary if the northern littoral was occupied is debatable, but in any case, the occupation of Denmark was not considered difficult, and so it proved.

One consideration behind the German invasion was the preservation of Swedish iron ore supplies through Narvik. Germany needed two key products from abroad – oil and iron ore. It was calculated by MEW that Germany required nine million tons of iron ore from Sweden during the first year of the war to avert a major industrial breakdown. Of this amount, some two million tons came through Narvik during the winter months when other outlets were closed by ice; the balance was exported mainly through Luleå which the Allies would have had great difficulty in disrupting. Although the closure of the Narvik outlet would have been unwelcome to Germany, its loss would by no means have been catastrophic. In fact the supply of ore from Narvik had fallen considerably during the winter of 1939–40 as the merchant ship captains were unwilling to face the risks posed by the Royal Navy. In the event, it was the Germans themselves who largely destroyed the ore processing plant in Narvik before they abandoned the port. And it was a shortage of oil rather than iron ore which became Germany's main source of economic misfortune later in the war. Thus I think we may conclude that safeguarding the iron ore supplies via Narvik was not the most important factor in the German invasion of Norway, nor did the loss of those supplies significantly affect the subsequent balance. It would, however, have been a different matter if the Allies had been able to stem completely the flow of iron ore from Sweden. The Germans had a strong interest in not allowing Scandinavia to fall within the British sphere of direct influence. Even after the end of the Russo-Finnish war in March, they had reason to worry about British interest in Scandinavia, as the minelaying operation in Norwegian waters showed. Hitler may also have been worried that, following Russia's success against Finland, albeit achieved at very high cost, she might try to assert her influence in the wider Scandinavian area.

Although the economic advantages to Germany of occupying Denmark and Norway were less great than many German experts might have hoped, Germany did gain something from their incorporation in the Nazi New Order, not least because it became much easier to exert pressure on Sweden.[3] Ideologically too, some Nazi leaders, notably Alfred Rosenberg, were attracted by the possibility of forging links with 'nordic' Norway under the leadership of the Norwegian National Socialist leader Vidkun Quisling.[4] However, the economic and political balance did not shift significantly in favour of Germany as a consequence of the invasion. The same cannot be claimed for the strategic military balance. It is not surprising that German interest in occupying Norway arose first within the Kriegsmarine. The advantages of Norway's one thousand miles of coastline open to the wide reaches of the Atlantic had been apparent during the First World War, but on that occasion Norway's fragile hold on neutrality had just been maintained.[5] It was not that Germany herself was short of good ports; Wilhelmshaven, Bremerhaven and Cuxhaven were all defensively very strong, screened by offshore islands, their estuaries protected by sandbanks and treacherous channels. The Baltic Sea was almost as secure, safeguarded by the narrow channels through the Danish islands. But they all suffered from the same weakness, the bulk of the UK landmass – described by Admiral Jackie Fisher as 'a vast breakwater' – and the Norwegian peninsula to the north narrowed the only exit to the wider oceans of the world. A defensive barrier between the Orkneys and southern Norway could prevent surface raiders and to a lesser extent submarines departing for the lucrative hunting grounds of the North Atlantic. Such a mine barrier had ben constructed by the Allies in 1918, and the Admiralty was planning to do so again in 1939–40. Furthermore, this narrow passage was a serious impediment to Germany's vital imports even when contained in neutral shipping. A naval blockade had been maintained throughout the First World War and in 1939 blockade again became one of the main planks of British strategy.

Germany's strategic dilemma had been comprehensively expressed in a book by Vice-Admiral Wegener in 1929.[6] As early as 3 October 1939 the Naval War Staff were directed to study the feasibility of gaining bases in Norway either by political or military means. Although Admiral Raeder initially expressed doubts about the scheme, he was always in the van in bringing it to Hitler's attention. Hitler was also sceptical but the scuttling of the *Graf Spee* in December 1939 had reopened his mind to the weakness of his navy, and the *Altmark* incident in February 1940 was instrumental in convincing Hitler that the British would step into Norway ahead of him if he did not himself make a decisive move. Likewise, the use of Norwegian airfields would pose an entirely new threat to the air defence of Great Britain.

I think we may conclude, therefore, that apart from the need to secure his exposed northern flank against Allied interference before the launching of the long-delayed German offensive in the West, it was naval and air strategy, particularly the former, which impelled Hitler along this path and it is in this respect that we need to assess the balance.

In the event, many of the strategic advantages which were expected to result from the occupation of Norwegian ports and airfields were overtaken by the unexpectedly rapid collapse of France. The acquisition of airfields in France, much closer to Britain, reduced the value of those in Norway although it did force the RAF to retain fighter squadrons in Scotland which were badly needed in southern England in the summer of 1940. However, the greater benefit for Germany arose from gaining control of ports in the Brest peninsula and the Bay of Biscay which gave even better access to the Atlantic and became secure havens for U-boats which were almost impervious to the RAF until the advent of the 'Grand Slam' bomb towards the end of the war. The value of Norway was further reduced by the British occupation of Iceland in May 1940. Nevertheless, the Norwegian northern ports were a useful base for ships attacking the convoys to Murmansk, and it was only with extreme difficulty and heavy losses that this vital link to Russia was kept open. The Norwegian fjords also proved a relatively safe haven for the German capital ships although this advantage was imperfectly exploited. Even so, it forced the Royal Navy to intensify their surveillance of the much wider Iceland-Faeroes gap and allowed them to enter only the Shetland-Bergen gap in strength. It is noteworthy that even in 1944 Bomber Command had to deploy two squadrons to the Kola Peninsula to carry a sufficient weight of bombs to sink the *Tirpitz* in the

Tromsø Fjord. The command of both littorals of the Baltic Sea also gave the Germans a greater degree of security to their northern flank.

One further aspect of the strategic balance should be mentioned briefly. Admiral Raeder had warned that the conquest of Norway might cost Germany her navy: hence his initial doubts regarding the viability of the project. In a broad sense he was right: the surface fleet never again posed a decisive threat and the emphasis swung towards submarine warfare. But the damage sustained in the Norwegian adventure precluded the Kriegsmarine from providing the necessary support for Hitler's planned invasion of Britain. It is perhaps doubtful whether Hitler ever expected to accomplish an invasion of Britain unless the circumstances were particularly propitious, but the lack of a naval covering force would in any event have been a major deterrent.

On the debit side of the balance, Germany had to maintain a garrison in Norway which eventually grew to 300,000 men. This inevitably became an increasingly onerous burden when they had to maintain three main fronts: in France against the prospect of re-invasion, in Russia, and in Churchill's 'soft underbelly of Europe' in Italy and the Balkans. However, once again this undoubted strain on manpower cannot be seen as a decisive factor in the longer-term balance as the overwhelming numerical superiority of Russia and the United States was mobilised in the last three years of the war.

Overall, I think we may conclude that Germany improved her strategic and tactical situation by the invasion of Norway although the potential benefits were not exploited to the full after the acquisition of ports in France and the sinking of the *Bismarck* in May 1941. She also marginally improved her relative economic advantage by controlling the Scandinavian peninsula, although the loss of the resources previously obtained from this area by the Allies was not serious. Far more significantly, the Allies gained a very substantial benefit from the support of the Norwegian mercantile fleet, which was subsequently profitably employed in the Atlantic convoys and elsewhere.

*   *   *   *   *

So much for the German side of the balance. At first sight there would appear to be little counterweight on the other side apart from those benefits I have mentioned above. Let us, however try to be positive. In terms of casualties the campaign in Norway was far less expensive than it might have been – about 2,000 military and civilian personnel plus those lost at sea. Nor was it costly in logistical terms even though much of the equipment sent to Norway had to be abandoned. Although both RAF squadrons based in Norway were totally lost (263 Squadron lost all its aircraft twice), the majority of the planes were obsolete Gladiators which had no future role. In fact one of the reasons why the military campaign was so unsuccessful was the drastic shortage of almost every type of operational and support equipment – artillery, anti-tank weapons, signals and transport. Only the French employed a handful of tanks, although the British lost a few on the *Effingham* which never saw operational service.

The fighting troops, the area in which Britain most needed to conserve its resources, were all recovered thanks to the sterling efforts of the Royal Navy. Furthermore, virtually all the soldiers and middle ranking officers sent to Norway had never previously seen combat, and although the action in Norway was very different from that which they were likely to meet elsewhere, no amount of training can replace real battle experience. In material terms, therefore, the Norwegian campaign was to have little direct influence on the future conduct of the war and some useful battle experience was acquired. I think we may confidently say that the troops employed in Norway – French, British or Polish – would not have altered the course of events in France over the same period; indeed they might well have been lost in the subsequent evacuation from Dunkirk!

Still on the subject of experience, there were many lessons which might have been learned from the brief campaign in Norway, but perhaps the most fundamental is that a nation, or for that matter an alliance, should not become embroiled in exploits in areas in which it is not likely to succeed. The British and French governments spent the whole of the winter of 1939–40 agonizing over what they could do in Scandinavia from mining the Leads to direct action in support of Finland, but little or no thought seems to have been given to how they would react if the initiative was seized by Germany. Almost nobody in Britain seems to have regarded that as a likely consequence of all the probing in which Britain and France were involved in the area, much of which was known to Hitler and which in the end resolved his doubts on invasion. France, of course, had a still more cogent reason for wishing to become embroiled in Scandinavia; she was desperate to deflect German interest away from action on the central front. The Allies were thus largely unprepared for the invasion, even at the last minute still believing that the German fleet was making a break for the open sea rather than actually mounting an expeditionary force. Nevertheless, ill prepared, inadequately equipped and with little thought given to on-going supply, the Allies leapt into the breach. The outcome might well have been predicted. Indeed, with the experience of Gallipoli and Antwerp of the First World War behind him, one might have expected that Churchill would have been more cautious. In fact, he did not learn the lesson even from Norway, for a year later he was bounding into Greece in much the same ill-thought out and unprepared way that had characterised the Norwegian expedition.

There were other lessons which might have been learned on the Allied side. The Norwegian campaign was the first occasion that land, sea and air forces fought a combined action. The inevitable difficulties of command and control should have been foreseen and worked out in advance. Although there was a Joint Planning Staff, each Service issued its own directions and these were frequently contradictory. This was perhaps most blatant in the differing orders given to Lord Cork and General Mackesy, the naval and military commanders, before their hurried departure for Norway. For a brief period supreme command was given to Lord Cork, but this was intended more to overcome what was perceived as Mackesy's dilatory approach than as an essential component of combined operations. It required the greater realism of the Americans to introduce effectively the concept of a joint command structure much later in the war. The dangers of deploying troops in penny packets against all the principles of concentration of force was another lesson which was only tardily absorbed. It was perhaps understandable, given the events unwinding on the other side of the Channel, that no proper post-mortem was ever carried out on the Norwegian campaign, but it is nevertheless surprising that the lessons to be learned, so obvious in retrospect, were not heeded more at the time.

Whilst this may be a somewhat negative aspect of the balance sheet, war is inevitably a learning process, particularly when few of the combatants have previous operational experience, and the general failure to learn the lessons of this campaign should be held in the balance sheet as a lost opportunity for the Allies.

One direct consequence of the Norwegian campaign for Britain was the emergence of Churchill as prime minister. This is ironic as there can be little doubt that it was Churchill who was the driving force behind the disastrous intervention in Norway. It was his insatiable urge for action which led him constantly to promote Allied involvement in affairs in Scandinavia, ignoring the practical difficulties and the likely consequences. However, it was Neville Chamberlain who had to bear the odium for the conduct of the war (and the policies which preceded it). Although the Conservative Party achieved a majority in the historic debate in the House of Commons of 8 May 1940, he was unable to command cross-party support and after much internecine manoeuvring, Chamberlain was replaced by Churchill on the 10th – the day the Germans invaded the West. As Churchill's accession arose directly out of the Norwegian debacle, I think this must be taken into the balance. Of course, Churchill might have risen to the top without the stimulus of the Norwegian campaign, but it was by no means an inevitable outcome. It was perhaps the single most significant event for Britain in the course of the war; for who would claim, whatever his faults, that any other leader could have sustained the nation so successfully in the dark days ahead? There was another factor. Germany had clearly been seen in the neutral world, particularly in the United States, as a brutal aggressor. This contributed to the forming of public opinion in favour of America's active intervention in the war. It must be remembered that at this stage President Roosevelt was well ahead of the thinking of the vast majority of Americans.

In conclusion, therefore, the overall outcome for the Allies (except for Norway, to which I shall come in a moment) was not quite so disastrous as might appear at first sight. There was of course little in it for the French, who were soon to depart the scene more dramatically; but there was some satisfaction perhaps for the Poles who had participated in the capture of Narvik, and who were determined to strike back at their oppressor in any possible way. Britain, however, had escaped in material terms more lightly than could reasonably have been hoped; and even the losses at sea had not been catastrophic. She had also gained from the support which Norway provided for the rest of the war, particularly in maritime terms, both commercial and naval, but also in a valuable contribution in the air. It was a pity that the British generally failed to make good use of the strategic and tactical lessons which might have been learned from the action, but on the other hand they gained Churchill as a far more effective war leader than Chamberlain could ever have been.

*   *   *   *   *

Whatever may have been the eventual balance for the Allies as a whole, I am sure my Norwegian colleagues would claim that the balance was overwhelmingly tilted in Germany's favour as far as they were concerned. Condemned to foreign occupation for over five years, it was very difficult indeed to see a silver lining. However, it could have been worse. Hitler been assured by Quisling that he would secure the complete collapse of Norway without a fight: this he did not achieve. Although eventual defeat was inevitable given the far from adequate support received from the Allies, the Norwegian armed forces had their moments of glory, among which stand out the sinking of the *Blücher* and the recapture of Narvik. Perhaps above all, the Germans failed to capture the King, who was able to provide a focal point, spiritual as well as material, for future resistance against the tyranny.

There is, however, one more important point which had little direct influence on the balance at the time, but has been vitally important in the history of the last fifty years. Norway, along with the other Scandinavian countries had clung resolutely to neutrality throughout the first four decades of the century. The country had neglected its defences in the hope of remaining aloof from any future conflict in Europe. How nearly this had failed in 1918 was soon forgotten and the attempts to remain neutral in 1939–40 – for example in the *Altmark* incident – cannot have been good for the self-esteem of a proud and independent nation. The war swept away this equivocal attitude and Norway has been among the most stalwart supporters of NATO since it was formed to face another tyrant in 1949. Would this have happened without the traumatic events of 1940 and the subsequent years of occupation? Sweden was not subjected to the same dreadful experience and has to this day remained neutral. It could be argued of course that Sweden has somewhat cynically accepted that her territorial integrity would *de facto* be included under the NATO umbrella, but the psychological uplift provided by Norway's unequivocal support of a new sense of order in Europe has been totally vindicated by the collapse of the Soviet empire. Furthermore, Norway has adopted a far more realistic approach to its defence posture and capability since the humiliation of 1940. In summary, therefore, the balance which looked so irrevocably one-sided in July 1940 was not, perhaps, weighted quite so heavily in favour of Germany as it seemed.

References

1   The most authoritative account of the campaign remains that of the official historian, T.K. Derry, *The Campaign in Norway* (London, 1952).

2   For summaries of recent research on the subject, see Hans-Martin Ottmer, 'Skandinavien in der marinestrategischen Planungen der Reichs- bzw. Kriegsmarine', in Robert Bohn, Jürgen Elvert, Hain Rebas and Michael Salewski (eds.), *Neutralität und totalitäre Aggression. Nordeuropa und die Grossmächte im Zweiten Weltkrieg* (Stuttgart, 1991), pp. 49–72, and Michael Salewski, 'Das Wesentliche von "Weserübung"', ibid, pp. 117–26.

3   For Norway's economic role in German-occupied Europe, see Alan Milward, *The Fascist Economy in Norway* (Oxford, 1972).

4   Hans-Dietrich Loock, *Quisling, Rosenberg und Terboven. Zur Vorgeschichte und Geschichte der nationalsozialistische Revolution in Norwegen* (Stuttgart, 1970).

5   Olav Riste, *The Neutral Ally: Norway's relations with belligerent powers in the First World War* (Oslo, 1965).

6   Wolfgang Wegener, *Die Seestrategie des Weltkrieges* (Berlin, 1929). For a discussion of the influence of Wegener's ideas on Operation *Weserübung*, see Carl-Axel Gemzell, *Raeder, Hitler und Skandinavien. Der Kampf für einen Maritimen Operationsplan* (Lund, 1965).

4 Norway 1940: the balance of interference

DAVID BROWN

THERE is a current fashion for drawing 'lessons learned' from recent conflict. Military planners and armchair strategists alike, deprived by long years of relative peace, seize the moment to portray as new theories and practices which were understood by Napoleon and Nelson and crystallised by Clausewitz. The acronym C^3I is today very much in vogue: it stands for Command, Control, Communications and Intelligence and refers to all levels of strategic and tactical direction. Only the expression is new – all the better commanders of history understood and employed the principles; they also well knew that a fifth element can be added to the formula which then becomes C^3I^2, which can then become a recipe for disaster. The magic ingredient is Interference and the higher the level of interference, the greater the potential for such disaster.

The first violation of Norwegian neutrality occurred before dawn on 8 April 1940, 24 hours before the historically accepted start-time of the campaign, and the Royal Navy was the agent. Winston Churchill's plan to mine the Leads, advocated since September 1939 and opposed until mid-February 1940 by the Foreign Office, was executed by four destroyers which laid 234 mines close inshore in the southern approaches to Vestfjord. Another, larger minefield was to have been laid simultaneously off Stadlandet, but this operation had been cancelled on the previous evening following the receipt by the Admiralty of a series of signals reporting sightings of units of the German Fleet in the North Sea. Simultaneously, intelligence was obtained of a German expedition to land in Jutland and at Narvik. Although the latter was passed to the Home Fleet with the unfortunate caveat 'All these reports are of doubtful value and may well be only a further move in the war of nerves,'[1] the Commander-in-Chief brought the Fleet to one hour's notice for steam and was thus ready for sea when a further signal was received reporting the sighting of a second, more powerful German squadron.[2] By midnight on 7 April, three capital ships, seven cruisers and 21 destroyers were at sea looking for the German units and a fourth capital ship, a cruiser and 14 destroyers were far to the north, involved in the Vestfjord minelaying operation.

Left behind in the Firth of Forth were four more cruisers, each of which had embarked an infantry battalion; these were to have sailed on the evening of 7th, ready to land two battalions at Stavanger and two at Bergen as soon as the Germans, prompted by the minelaying, violated Norwegian territorial neutrality. There was evidence that such violation was imminent but the Admiralty delayed their departure until the situation at sea clarified.

Frequently disregarded in the published orders of battle were the eight submarines which the Vice-Admiral, Submarines – Sir Max Horton – had deployed in the Kattegat and Skagerrak; convinced that a German invasion of Norway was imminent, he had despatched six more boats to the area during the afternoon of the 7th.[3] During the following morning, one of the original patrols provided confirmation that a German invasion was under way, sinking a merchant ship (the *Rio de Janeiro*) carrying uniformed troops, just outside Norwegian territorial waters off Kristiansand South. An impressive feature of this incident, and of subsequent activity, was the speed of communications between the submarines and their admiral, who was able to correlate these reports with those he was receiving from the Admiralty and, in his shore operations room, formulate an accurate picture on which to make his dispositions. The Home Fleet admirals (Forbes and Whitworth) at sea in their flagships, were not so fortunate. They were more subject to 'noise' – raw information coming in from their own ships and detached units and from co-operating aircraft, processed information signalled by the Admiralty and, particularly, instructions from Whitehall, not only to themselves, but also directly to their subordinates, and which, they had to assume, were based on better information than they had available on the spot. The Home Fleet was subject to all of these on 8 April and they had a lasting effect on the campaign.

Four hours before the interception of the *Rio de Janeiro*, and some 400 miles to the north, the destroyer *Glowworm* encountered and reported two German destroyers; an hour later, she sank after ramming (and damaging severely) the heavy cruiser *Hipper*. This first contact rivetted the Admiralty's attention on the threat to Narvik and fresh dispositions, to forestall the invasion and to catch the German heavy squadron believed to be at sea, were made without reference to the Commander-in-Chief. Not until all the instructions had been despatched did the Admiralty draft a signal informing the surface commanders of the sinking of the troopship off southern Norway. On the eve of the expected invasion of Norway, virtually all naval forces were steaming, or at least looking, the wrong way. The one exception was the submarine command: Vice Admiral Horton remained convinced of the real purpose of the German movements and made only minor adjustments to intercept the heavy ships instead of the major realignment directed by the Admiralty. That evening, a naval tanker en route for Oslo, the *Stedingen*, was torpedoed and sunk, while a transport bound for Bergen had a narrow escape.

It is timely to summarise German intentions and worries. No fewer than six assault groups, comprising 38 warships and 22 coastal craft, were at sea, besides a heavy covering (or diversionary) group. These ships, representing the entire German Fleet, would land a first wave of nearly 9,000 troops, to be followed into the southern ports (Bergen, Egersund, Kristiansand, Arendal and Oslo) by 3,500 troops, 670 horses, 1,300 vehicles and 5,000 tons of stores embarked in a dozen merchant 'Trojan Horses', which were to loiter off their destinations until the appropriate moment. Six more 'innocent' merchantmen would be waiting off the two northern destinations (Trondheim and Narvik) with military stores. Raeder, in presenting his final plan to Hitler, had not underestimated the risks, but considered that despite the undeniable superiority of the Home Fleet, 'provided that surprise is complete, our troops can and will successfully be transported to Norway'.[4] With regard to the landings at Trondheim and Narvik, this confidence extended only as far as the landings and initial stage of consolidation ashore. The outward passage could be accomplished safely. The German Naval Staff, the Seekriegsleitung, considered that if the warships were sighted, then the activity would be assessed as a raid in force into the Atlantic, to which the Admiralty was likely to react by moving the Home Fleet into the Shetlands-Iceland gap, where it would be no threat to the southern landings, as well as being wrong-footed to intercept the northern operations. There was more concern about the return passage, which could expect superior and fully alert opposition, and despite the pleas and protests of the Army the ships were ordered to withdraw as soon as the targeted bases and their defences had been seized.[5] As the destroyers which were to ferry the assault troops would have insufficient fuel for the return voyage, orders were given to preposition two oil tankers at Narvik and one at Trondheim.

With hindsight, and even in the light of conventional staff wisdom of the day, it would be difficult to conceive of a more hare-brained scheme. The overall plan was incredibly convoluted, with piecemeal forces to be landed on schedule in defended localities over 1,000 miles of coastline, the troops critically dependent on independently-sailed unescorted merchant ships for reinforcement and sustenance and the entire operational destroyer force of the German Navy on the arrival of three tankers. Surprise was the essential key to the success of the landings and if that was lost then reliance was placed in the hope that the Admiralty would misread the information.

As we have seen, both tactical and strategic surprise *were* lost. The ships sailed on 6 April, were sighted on the following morning and were thereafter intermittently reported by aircraft. Accurate intelligence of the intention to seize Narvik was available to the Admiralty and though insufficient weight was attached to this information at first, the approaches to Narvik were dominated on 7 and 8 April by the fortuitous presence of the minelaying force and its supporting battlecruiser, and the main body of the Home Fleet sailed, not to the north-west but to the north. To add to the German Navy's difficulties, heavy weather delayed and scattered the forces bound for Trondheim and Narvik and led to the unwanted encounter with the *Glowworm*. That southern Norway was also targeted was betrayed by the sinking of the 'Trojan Horse' transport off Kristiansand. If probability does indicate the outcome of campaigns, as the war-gamers claim, the Germans had lost this one, before a single soldier was landed.

But interference causes more damaging random effects than dice and a series of Admiralty signals altered the probabilities. Of the four important orders transmitted on 8 April, the first was clearly wrong at the time, the second provides one of the great 'might-have-beens' of the war, the third (to Vice-Admiral, Submarines) was, as we have seen, virtually ignored and the fourth was unrealistic.

The first instructions, issued after the *Glowworm's* action but before the *Rio de Janeiro* was sunk, ordered the destroyers patrolling the Vestfjord minefield to join Admiral Whitworth in the battlecruiser *Renown*, then over

100 miles to the south-west, thereby removing the only force covering the direct approach to Narvik.[6] Whitworth, on the other hand, was not ordered to block this approach, but was merely informed that the intelligence about landings at Narvik 'might' be true.[7] He was more influenced by an aircraft report of a battlecruiser, two cruisers and two destroyers heading west on the latitude of Trondheim and, as soon as the destroyers from Vestfjord joined him he made for a position to the west of the Lofotens, to cover any attempt to break out into the Atlantic. It is doubtful whether Admiral Whitworth would have reacted as he did had he known that the force to the west of Trondheim actually comprised a heavy cruiser and four destroyers, heading away from the coast as it loitered while waiting for the appointed hour to land its embarked troops. The Admiralty's lack of clear direction and the aircrew's poor ship recognition contributed to the poor position in which Whitworth now found himself and a 'Most Immediate' order from the Admiralty, to prevent German forces from reaching Narvik, came too late.[8] The ten destroyers bound for Narvik had a clear run into and through Vestfjord, well to the west of the mines and to the east of Whitworth's squadron.

The Admiralty's main obsession was, throughout, with the German heavy units. In order to give the Home Fleet additional cruisers for scouting and striking, a surprising decision was taken to disembark the soldiers from the four ships in the Forth, despite all the indications that the circumstances for which they had originally been embarked were imminent.[9] Had the ships sailed with their troops for their intended destinations, at the same time as they left to join Admiral Forbes (who had not asked for them), two battalions would have been landed at Stavanger before the arrival before the arrival of the 120 German paratroops who were dropped to secure the airfield. While the cruisers carrying the other two battalions would have arrived at Bergen after the German force, their superior firepower and the assurance of early reinforcement should have tipped the balance against the invaders. The airfield at Stavanger proved, in German hands, to be a vital feature in the campaign and its loss, by sheer default, provides an intriguing 'might have been'.

The importance of Stavanger and Bergen was recognised by the Admiralty's signal to the Home Fleet.[10] While Admiral Forbes' main task was to prevent the return of the German forces from the north, he was also to 'deal with possible German forces reported passing Great Belt at 1400/8, if they are going to Stavanger or Bergen'. At the time of receipt, Forbes' flagship was 250 miles north of Bergen, with less than ten hours left before the scheduled time of the German landings, and, although neither the Admiralty nor the Fleet could know it, the forces reported were in fact bound for Oslo. The Home Fleet was thus in a position to deal only with the cruiser and four destroyers of the Trondheim force, which had been sighted but whose mission was quite unknown to the British, who believed it to be a much more powerful squadron heading away from Norway and, in any case, had no indication that this important port and town was under threat.

The Admiralty was not alone in its misreading. A Norwegian torpedo boat and fishing boats rescued some hundreds of German uniformed troops from the transport sunk off Kristiansand and reported that these men had been

en route to Bergen, 'to protect it against the Allies'. This report does not appear
to have unduly alarmed the Chief of the Norwegian Naval Staff, who at 1600
informed the British Naval Attaché that the German battlecruisers, cruisers
and small craft were still in the Kattegat, intentions unknown.[11] When the
Navy's report of the rescues off Kristiansand reached the Storting that evening
it was still not fully believed – no steps were taken to warn the Royal
Norwegian Navy or coast defence artillery, or to take any other precautionary
measures.[12] Only Reuter's news agency reacted, reporting the sinking at 2030;
this announcement led to the German Naval Staff to conclude that 'Operation
'Weserübung' has left the stage of secrecy and camouflage . . . Our enemies
have been warned. Since the element of surprise is lost we must now expect
engagements at all points.'[13]

For most practical purposes, the Royal Navy's surface ships were off the
board for the first day of the campaign. The *Renown*, hopelessly out of position
to defend Narvik, met the battlecruisers *Scharnhorst* and *Gneisenau* to the
south-west of the Lofotens and got the best of the first duel of the war between
capital ships, while the Home Fleet, holding a position between the Shetlands
and Bergen came under repeated air attack, in the course of which a destroyer
was damaged and had to be scuttled. Inshore, the only effective resistance to
the seaborne landings came from heroic individual actions by the Norwegian
Navy and coastal defences which in themselves resulted in the sinking of three
ships (*Blücher*, *Albatros* and the transport *Roda*) and contributed to the later
destruction of a third (*Königsberg*), although at heavy cost to the defenders.
The Royal Navy's submarines scored a further success off Kristiansand on the
9th, sinking the cruiser *Karlsruhe* as it withdrew from the port behind
schedule. In the north, the German logistics timetable had gone badly awry for
of the six transports and three tankers expected at Trondheim and Narvik,
only one tanker had arrived at the latter and the only transport to get through,
to Trondheim, was delayed until 12 April.

Such British successes as there were owed little to the Admiralty's
direction. Faced with its first test in a theatre close to home, the highest level of
command failed in all its objectives, even though coincidence had given the
Royal Navy all the advantages. Advance warning of the invasion, though
admittedly not of all the objectives, came to hand in time for the Home Fleet to
sail on its own initiative, but Whitehall played down its importance; confirmation, provided by the sinking of the Kristiansand troopship, was passed on too
late to the forces at sea. A blocking force was across the approaches to Narvik,
but it was moved away at just the wrong moment and for several critical hours
no clear directions were given to the senior commander, while the Admiralty
muddled its priorities, attracted by the prospect of inflicting a defeat on the
German Fleet. The Home Fleet was given contradictory directions which took
little account of time, distance and the weather and sent it to a position where,
on 9 April, its only useful function was as a 'honey pot' for the Luftwaffe. Out
in overwhelming strength, the Fleet was reinforced by four cruisers which
were neither requested nor required, at the expense of the one effective land
intervention which could have been undertaken at short notice.

The contrast with the German higher direction was marked. Once the ships had sailed, there was no interference from on high. The Seekriegsleitung had reason to be nervous, as it received successive accurate reports of British naval movements, all of which appeared to threaten the risky Trondheim and Narvik expeditions, and the presence of British submarines off southern Norway was confirmed. Whatever temptation there may have been to interfere was resisted, and the commanders at sea were left to themselves to carry out the intricate plan.

There can be little doubt as to whose hand was stirring the Admiralty pot. Winston Churchill, the First Lord of the Admiralty, had not learned the lessons of his First World War tenure of the same office, during which his interference in purely military matters had led directly to his own fall and that of his First Sea Lord. The Admiralty's handling of the situation on 7 and 8 April 1940 bore all the Churchillian hallmarks of impatience, unchallengeable self-confidence and near-complete lack of comprehension of detail. He himself subsequently admitted to interference in the campaign: 'Looking back on this affair, I consider that the Admiralty kept too close a control upon the Commander-in-Chief . . . we should have confined ourselves to sending him information.'[14] This, however, related to the events of the day of the invasion, not to what went before. He could hardly have been expected to confess that his hand might have tipped the balance, by overloading his own side, or that it was he, and not Hitler, who had missed the bus.

References

1 Admiralty Telegram 1259/7th; ADM 199/2159 (Admiralty War Diary, 7 April 1940) p. 85. All documents cited are in the PRO unless otherwise stated.
2 Admiralty Telegram 1720/7th (ibid).
3 ADM 234/52(1), p. 28.
4 Führer Conferences on Naval Affairs 1939–1945, published in *Brassey's Naval Annual* 1948, 9 March 1940. Neither this, nor any other contemporary source, suggests that Raeder anticipated serious losses, let alone 'the loss of the German Navy'.
5 Führer Naval Conference, 29 March 1940.
6 Admiralty Telegram 1045/8th (cited in ADM 234/17, p. 13).
7 Admiralty Telegram 1114/8th (ibid, p. 14).
8 Admiralty Telegram 1850/8th, received at 1915 (ADM 199/2159 – Admiralty War Diary, p. 97).
9 Admiralty Telegram 1216/8th (cited in ADM 234/17, p. 15 & fn); it is worth noting that the decision to embark the troops had been taken by the War Cabinet, as part of the preparations for Operation *R.4*, but the decision to land them was taken in the Admiralty.
10 Admiralty Telegram 1842/8th, received at 2000 (ibid, p. 16).
11 ADM 199/2159 (Admiralty War Diary) p. 93A.
12 ADM 234/17, p. 13.
13 German Naval Staff War Diary, 8 April 1940 (MSS translation held by Naval Historical Branch).
14 Winston S. Churchill, *The Second World War*, vol. I, *The Gathering Storm* (2nd. edn., London, 1949), p. 470.

5 Postscript on the campaign in Norway

H.F. ZEINER GUNDERSEN

I T is a pleasure and an honour to be asked to comment on the papers by Maurice Harvey and David Brown. They are both excellent papers and, for what it is worth, I agree with much of what they say. But it is exactly for that reason that commenting is a difficult task. Balance sheets also usually deal with quantifiable matters like figures. Here we base our evaluations on judgements. I have chosen to discuss the 'balance' at least partly as seen from slightly different angles. Some of these angles may also be fairly controversial.

We are all subject to our background. Maurice Harvey perhaps takes a rather British-slanted point of view. I, on the other hand, admit openly that I am a rather biased native of my country and this probably colours my words and viewpoints. The facts are that the Norwegian Campaign lasted for about *two months*. The war went on for about *five years* after its close. I think we must see that campaign in that perspective. And, what is more, we attempt to discuss the 'balance sheet' nearly *half a century* after the end of the war. My impression, rightly or wrongly, is that the 'balance sheet' discussed in the papers is the overall wartime 'balance sheet' – but as it appears fifty years later. Could there be two 'balance sheets', namely the *immediate* 'balance sheet' on the campaign and the 'balance sheet' as it appears long after the war? In part this is touched upon. I would, however, have liked some more reflections on it. This may admittedly be nationally slanted. But I do think the campaign as such, although it was lost – or maybe even for that reason – has had considerable long-term effects as well as immediate effects. I shall come back to this point.

But first I would like to comment on the 'balance sheet' as it *now* appears it could have looked during the five years of the war following this campaign. It is, of course, an open question whether those responsible at that time saw it the same way, *could* see it that way, and could do something about it. There was – and is – of course a stratego-political, a psychological and a strictly military part of these 'balance sheets'. Some of them may overlap and I shall therefore repeat myself. They may furthermore have looked different to the Allies as a whole, to Norway and to Germany.

First the *stratego-political* aspect. As seen both from the overall Allied and the more limited Norwegian wartime point of view, the campaign as such was a disaster. But what of the consequences? What of the *German* point of view? They started it. They conquered Norway and stayed there with huge garrisons and fortifications until the end of the war.

They obviously earned naval and air bases, something I will revert to. But they lost a large part of their navy. Was it worth it in the long run? They were in a position to put pressure on Sweden in 1940 and for a long time afterwards. But Sweden was, at least in 1940–1, rather favourably disposed to Germany anyway. Looking at it from a rather longer wartime point of view they did not really obtain much benefit for their overall war effort, particularly after the fall of France as Maurice Harvey points out. Some benefit there was. Keywords *Banak* and convoys. Considering Hitler's obsession with the iron ore and the so-called Aryan race, could this have been foreseen and influenced matters? I do not know and we shall possibly never know. The possession of Norway during the war cost the Germans dearly in the long run. Was the campaign therefore, as seen from their point of view, in reality a Pyrrhic victory?

Turning to the *Allies*, initially, as the two papers say and as I agree, the 'balance sheet' showed disaster. But did it in the long run? I am not altogether certain. Is it not a fact that Winston Churchill was rather preoccupied with Scandinavian undertakings, although his military advisers, led by Sir Alan Brooke, opposed him and successfully? Could it be that Churchill, who, according to Lord Ismay, was head and shoulders above anybody else regarding grand strategy, clearly saw the disadvantages of Germany having to sit in Norway and having to garrison and fortify it strongly? Could it be that he nurtured their fear of invasion in Norway, thereby helping to tie their hands? Besides, planning for an invasion in Norway did take place on the Allied side during the war. The huge German garrison could not easily be moved to other areas where it might have been of better use. By and large, for the Allied side as a whole, the initial disaster of the Norwegian campaign turned into something of an advantage – though admittedly this may be a rather cynical view.

Let me then look at *Norway*. The campaign was, as previously stated, a disaster. So was the occupation. We were bound to lose when it started, and we lost. Economically, both the campaign and the occupation cost us a great deal, although we may have fared better than some other nations. On the credit side of the sheet comes the increased status of our Royal family due to the King's personality and moral courage. He became *the* focal point of our resistance. The nation was closely knit together irrespective of pre-war political differences. This continued for some years after the war too. We learned our lesson. It lasted for a long time. One might also say that the war as such, with that lost campaign, contributed to the nation's outlook and awareness of not being in a remote corner of Europe any more. This was a significant political matter. It is therefore an interesting question to ponder whether this campaign and its results and effects in all spheres, when we look at it today, should be characterised as a disaster for Norway, a temporary setback, or a good thing in the long run. I defer giving a view. But the question remains.

A few words on the *psychological* side of the 'balance sheet'. It is touched upon in Maurice Harvey's paper and I have already made some remarks about Norway. How about the war as a whole? I think Maurice Harvey is quite right when he points out that the campaign helped to fulfil the intentions of President Roosevelt. We probably all remember his 'Look to Norway' speeches. But I am also certain that had not that small country, ill-prepared and badly armed as it was, *decided to fight*, the psychological impressions around the world might have been rather different. I would say that seen from the psychological point of view the campaign, or rather the fact that Norway fought, served the overall Allied cause well. This is irrespective of whatever military shambles, Allied or Norwegian, there might have been during the campaign. And there were some. Some of the shambles made a not too favourable impression on parts of our population. I, for one, am grateful the Germans did not utilise this as much in their propaganda as they might have done.

Turning now to the wartime *military* 'balance sheet'. As this overlaps the stratego-political aspect, you must kindly bear with my repeating myself in parts. It is furthermore not easy to speak on this without touching on 'lessons learned'. These are, however, discussed in the paper by Clive Archer. I believe Harvey and Brown are right in stressing the German naval interest in bringing about the campaign. Admiral Raeder obviously had considerable influence. But I also believe, possibly more so than the two authors, there was a rather important air aspect in the interest in Norway. In retrospect the fact that France fell rather diminished this. This must have been difficult to foresee when the planning of the German campaign began. In this respect, the fall of France was a bonus effect for the war in the air. But it also meant that, from the German point of view, the possession of Norway was rather reduced in value. But they were still there and with Hitler and his obsessions at the helm, they had to stay there. Another important part of the *German* military 'balance sheet' was the demonstration of the success of strategic surprise, even recklessness. This lesson was applied successfully by them later in the war and in other areas. They probably then became overconfident.

On the *Allied* military side, I agree with the papers stressing the lesson of 'combined command structure', slowly realised in many circles, conservative as most of us military men usually are. But I think there is another point, not mentioned too clearly, that of the value of regular, well-trained units, compared to the Territorial Army units with scant training. This was by no means surprising. That lesson *was* learned, for application in other areas and later in the war.

Speaking more particularly of *Norway*, the 'balance sheet' showed us that military units cannot be improvised and need solid training. This, I think, may have been a long-term post-war bonus effect of the immediate 'balance sheet'. This has been realised and acted upon by Norway's political masters – at least up to the present day.

In sum, the military part of the 'balance sheet' was that the immediate result was a somewhat better German strategic situation. In the long run their military hands became too tied and the immediate success may have led to their being overconfident. The short-term Allied military 'balance sheet' was rather gloomy. A longer-term view may, however, show a different picture. The Allies knew where they had about 300,000 German troops that could only be moved with difficulty. The overall wartime Norwegian military picture was by and large a fairly black one.

Summing up my views on the overall wartime 'balance sheet', both immediate and later, I would say that Germany came out best in the short run. In the long run their wartime 'balance sheet' shows failure. The Allies on the other hand began disastrously, but in the long run they had the advantage because of this short campaign.

We have an old Norwegian proverb saying: 'High mountains cast long shadows'. Comparing the Campaign of 1940 now to such a mountain, it might well be said there have been consequences long after the war. This leads me to my point about a longer-term 'balance sheet'. I believe the campaign contributed to Allied and maybe world policy towards dictatorships, long after the war and up to the present time. The result is that small countries on the whole have a much safer existence today than before 1940 (though there are obviously a number of other reasons for this).

As for my own country, I am convinced that the longer-term 'balance sheet' up until now has been that we have taken a much more realistic view of world politics and its consequences for defence and security. In other words, I am asking the question whether the 'balance sheet', as seen in the long-term perspective, possibly shows a positive dividend for Norway and the whole West, maybe even further afield. However, the campaign and its wartime aftermath were a thoroughly bad experience – or cure? Did we need it?

Discussion

The main themes were intelligence and secret operations in Scandinavia before the German invasion of Denmark and Norway. There was some discussion of the 'Rickman affair', an abortive British attempt to sabotage the iron ore loading facilities at the Swedish Baltic port of Oxelösund.[1] *Sir Brooks Richards* remarked on Winston Churchill's involvement, pointing out that Churchill's first contact with Stewart Menzies, the head of SIS, late in 1939, was to discuss precisely how Section D of SIS could attack the iron ore traffic. He also noted that one of those involved in the affair was Gerald Holdsworth, who was taken prisoner in Sweden while reconnoitring for possible attack on Oxelösund. The story goes that he was carrying in his pocket a letter from Charles Hambro (then of the Ministry of Economic Warfare, later of SOE) to the Norwegian prime minister accrediting him as a member of an organisation for aid to Norway. The Swedes probably hesitated to put on trial the bearer of this document because of possible embarrassment. He was allowed to escape to Finland and from there reached Great Britain. *Colonel Andrew Croft* recalled his own involvement, first with arms supplies to Finland during the Winter War, and later as one of three British officers detailed to go to Norwegian ports early in April 1940 to meet the British forces due to land there if Operation *R4* had gone according to plan. He went to Bergen but met the Germans instead. A similar fate befell Malcolm Munthe at Stavanger. Here, according to *Sir Peter Tennant*, 'he put his secret documents in his squeeze-box, played "Deutschland über Alles" to the Germans, and was evacuated to Sweden'. Croft meanwhile escaped and eventually reached Ålesund, where he boarded a British destroyer. On reaching the War Office in London, he was sent back to

Norway without delay under Brigadier Gubbins and his Independent Companies (forerunners of the Commandos) and took part in the Norwegian campaign from Mosjøen to Bodø. After over four weeks of fighting, the force was evacuated by destroyers, during four concentrated and frightening nights, to Harstad. Here Croft lunched with General Auchinleck and learned that we had to evacuate Norway, since events in Holland, Belgium and France were moving too fast and our troops were needed for the defence of Britain.[2]

Edward Thomas commented on the state of British intelligence in the pre-Enigma period. There was no machinery for assessing intelligence as a whole. MI3 estimated that Germans would need 25 to 30 divisions to invade Norway and Sweden, but could only locate six: on these grounds they rated an invasion unlikely. It later turned out that six was, in fact, the number used by Germany in April 1940. Whitehall's preconceptions about the deterrent effect of British naval power added to the general disinclination to think an invasion likely. In the days immediately preceding the Germans' move numerous clues as to their intentions were received by Whitehall departments. Its failure to coordinate this wealth of evidence and to interpret it correctly is a disgrace to British intelligence. *Professor Skodvin* and *Professor Riste* elaborated on Dr Salmon's suggestion that the British found it easier to talk to the Swedes than to the Norwegians. Norway had a very small foreign office at the time and Norwegian politicians and officials had relatively little experience of the outside world: 'Before 1940 the average Norwegian cabinet minister was less familiar with Whitehall than today's average Norwegian housewife is with Oxford Street.' The British legation in Oslo talked to pro-British people in Norway; they did not talk to the government because it was Labour. Professor Riste interviewed Sir Cecil Dormer after the war and found that 'all he could remember was dinners at the palace'. *Sir Alexander Glen* commented that this changed dramatically with the appointment of Laurence Collier, a remarkably able personality, as minister to the Norwegian government in exile (and subsequently as ambassador in Oslo), while Erik Colban, Norway's minister in London, was a great representative of his country.

References

1   For details see Thomas Munch-Petersen, 'Confessions of a British agent: Section
    D in Sweden, 1938–1940', in *Utrikespolitik och historia. Studier tillägnade Wilhelm
    M. Carlgren den 6 maj 1987* (Stockholm, 1987), pp. 175–88.
2   For further details see Andrew Croft, *A Talent for Adventure* (Hanley Swan, 1991).

PART II

The Anglo-Norwegian alliance

6 Relations between the Norwegian government in exile and the British government

OLAV RISTE

Introduction

I should like to begin by presenting two contrasting pictures: The first, from June 1940, shows a Norwegian government in profound despair: driven into exile as refugees from the enemy-occupied homeland; alienated from a people which seemed to be turning their backs on them; weighed down by the burden of a failed foreign and defence policy; and linked in destiny to weak allies retreating before a seemingly invincible enemy. Contrast this with the picture five years later: a government returning to the home country as a worthy and recognised partner in a mighty and victorious alliance; unchallenged leaders of a nation united; at the helm of a functioning government apparatus, armed forces of all three services numbering about 27,000 men, and a severely decimated but still powerful merchant navy.

How was it possible? The first answer is the obvious one: the victory of Norway's great power partners in the Grand Alliance made it possible. And in that victory Norway played but a minor part. However, a minor power in a great power alliance may also suffer defeat in victory. So, since the Allied victory was also Norway's victory, additional answers must be sought.

In a farewell message to their people the government had expressed the purpose of their continued struggle in words that were modest in tone but far-reaching in their ambition: They saw their task 'to be the free spokesmen for the national aspirations of the Norwegian people', with the aim 'that our fatherland in the hour of victory can stand forth with pride and assert its national freedom'.[1]

The Norwegian government in exile thus faced two major, separate but interdependent, challenges that were implicit in our picture from June 1940: first, they had to establish and assert their authority and leadership towards their own people; second was the necessity to establish a relationship with the allies that would enable them to safeguard Norway's national interests. Failure in either endeavour would have dire consequences also for their chances to succeed in the other one. But it is to the latter challenge this paper will be addressed.

The groundwork

In a previous conference at St Antony's College a well-placed observer characterised Anglo-Norwegian relations during the summer of 1940 as 'profoundly unhappy'.[2] Experiences both before and during the campaign in Norway had left both parties with feelings of having been let down by the other. The arrival in London of the Norwegian government as a *de facto* ally changed nothing in itself. The material resources which Norway could contribute to the war effort were either insignificant or – in the case of the merchant navy – not immediately visible. The image of Britain 'standing alone' in that period thus remained, and still does today.

However, Norway's place and role in the alliance would not only be determined by her material contribution. They would also depend on how the Norwegian government organised that contribution – in other words, on how Norway shaped her posture in the alliance. Five prominent Norwegian intellectuals, who had followed the government into exile, fastened on this point in a letter to the government dated 5 July 1940. Stressing that the war was an ideological struggle of democracy against fascist dictatorship, whose final outcome could be decided by the peoples of Europe rising against their oppressors, they saw the exiled governments of the European democracies as a vital moral resource for the alliance. By keeping alive the spirit of resistance in their home countries they could make a contribution out of all proportion to their limited material resources. Norway should therefore cooperate to the fullest possible extent with her British ally, thereby also serving Norway's own interests:

> Only by effectively supporting our British ally will the government be able to assert Norwegian sovereignty as well as their own authority towards the British government during the war. If the British government is convinced that the Norwegian government does its utmost, then its authority will be respected and it will, at least to some extent, be consulted. If the British government sees the Norwegian government as a co-belligerent that is half-hearted, unreliable, or which goes its own separate ways, then this will sooner or later lead to the British authorities pushing aside our own military and administrative authorities.[3]

This call for the fullest possible cooperation with a great power ally, based on mutual trust, required a considerable mental *volte-face* from traditional neutralist and isolationist Norwegian attitudes. Opinions in the Cabinet were divided, with some advocating a cautious approach in which cooperation should be based on carefully worked out contractual obligations with precise safeguards for Norwegian special interests. An intermediate position was represented by the foreign minister, Halvdan Koht. He favoured all kinds of practical cooperation with the British, but cautioned against commitments that would limit Norway's stance as an independent, sovereign co-belligerent. He was not entirely convinced of a British victory, and thought that a Norway which avoided formal ties to Britain would stand a better chance of obtaining

Soviet support for Norwegian independence in case of a compromise peace.

The ensuing debate lasted until late in the autumn of 1940.[4] A clear indcation of its likely outcome came when Dr Koht took leave from the post of foreign minister at the end of November, and was replaced by Trygve Lie whose closest adviser was Dr Arne Ording, author of the July letter to the government. Publicly, Norway's alliance policy was first announced in a radio speech by Trygve Lie on 15 December, which stressed Norway's determination to establish the closest possible cooperation with the western powers, her natural allies, both during and after the war. An editorial in *The Times* on the following day hailed the speech as a brave and encouraging sign that Norway, as the first of the minor powers in Europe, had abandoned her pre-war neutralism and stretched out her hand to Britain, not just in friendship but in a long-term commitment to close political and economic cooperation.

By the end of 1940 it still remained for the Norwegian government to formalise the new basis for her alliance with Great Britain. Negotiations about a formal military agreement had begun in August, based on a Norwegian memorandum of 10 July which outlined the terms on which Norway intended to continue the armed struggle 'together with our allies and as far as our resources allow' until the final victory. The intention was to form units that were identifiably Norwegian, even while operating under British operational control. When the agreement was finally signed on 28 May 1941, after various delays mostly due to complex jurisdictional issues, it also contained a political clause as proposed by the Norwegian government. Here the contracting parties expressed their mutual determination to prosecute the war to a successful conclusion, and declared as their common war aim 'the re-establishment of the freedom and independence of Norway through its complete liberation from German domination'.[5]

1940–2: Trial and Error

By the time the Anglo-Norwegian military agreement was signed cooperation in practical terms, both military and otherwise, had been going on for almost a year. The forms that this practical cooperation took are the subject of several of the other contributions to this book. My purpose in this essay is to attempt to relate that practical cooperation to the overarching principles of alliance policy established by the Norwegian government, and to assess the result of Norway's particular alliance policy in relation to its professed aim. In other words, did Norway in exile practice what she preached? And did her alliance policy produce the desired results, in terms of benefits to Norwegian national interests? Or if not, why not?

For the purpose of seeking answers to those questions it seems useful to divide the war years into two periods, with the first one, up to the end of 1941, as essentially one of trial and error. No wonder: alliance cooperation was an entirely novel experience for Norwegians. Also, British war policy as it affected Norwegians or Norwegian interests was often haphazard and inconsistent, marked as it was by Britain fighting with her 'back against the wall', feeling her way with improvisations and short-term expedients. The consequent *ad hoc* character of Anglo-Norwegian cooperation in this period meant that the Norwegians had their hands full with reacting to a variety of British initiatives – a situation in which neither British challenges nor Norwegian responses bore the mark of consistency.

In general, however, Norway's policy translated into practice as a far-reaching willingness to cooperate. At the level of 'high politics', concerning matters deemed to be of vital national interest and dealt with by the whole cabinet, a line had to be drawn. An early and clear example was the refusal, in October 1940, to give in to Sir Kingsley Wood's demand that the government relinquish control over Norway's gold and hard currency reserves. There was also determined resistance to pressures to put most or all of the Norwegian merchant navy at the disposal of the British – pressures that provoked a remark by prime minister Nygaardsvold that 'they could at least allow us influence to the extent that we may administer our own losses'.[6] The successive compromise agreements concerning shipping did, as Dr Thowsen's chapter explains, severely curtail the Norwegian government's control over the fleet. But the terms of the agreements, both financially and otherwise, were seen as generally satisfactory to Norwegian interests. Hence the Norwegian government saw no need to insist when prime minister Nygaardsvold's oral request for Norwegian representation in the highest Allied shipping boards, at a luncheon with Churchill in February 1942, was deflected with a disarming caution against 'too many voices in the choir'.[7]

On the other hand individual Norwegians, including one or two cabinet ministers, sometimes carried cooperation to excess, particularly in relation to 'upstart' British organisations such as SOE or the Directorate of Combined Operations. Playing on the requirement for secrecy and a wish to exclude the full Norwegian cabinet from those who 'needed to know', these agencies were able to enlist cooperation from individual Norwegians in plans and activities with actual or potential severe repercussions for people in the occupied country. Resistance leaders in Norway were the first to feel the brunt of such activities, and relations between them, SOE, and the Norwegian government at one stage in the summer of 1941 were strained almost to breaking point. Blame for allowing the situation to develop that far should probably be fairly evenly distributed among all the parties involved.

Initiatives to remedy this state of affairs would have to come from the Norwegian government, if for no other reason than that the Norwegian government had one fairly straightforward war aim: the liberation of Norway, whereas British war policy had to satisfy a plethora of different and often conflicting concerns. This helps to explain why it was the Norwegian authorities which, at the end of 1941, took the first steps towards working out a war policy in regard to Norway that would be both consistent and long-term.

1943–5: Target – the Liberation of Norway

The process of shaping a unified and consistent Allied war policy concerning

Norway turned out to be a 'paper war' of some duration. Its character was one of Norwegian pressure to persuade the British to subordinate all their plans and activities concerning Norway to the perspective of the complete and final liberation of Norway. At issue was not only paramilitary activities related to the resistance, but also more overarching questions concerning sovereignty, administration, and jurisdiction, as well as operational planning, for the liberation.

Norway's efforts to those ends were undoubtedly helped by the distinctly cooperative profile of her general alliance policy, stressing the common war effort first, and Norwegian self-interest second. The balancing act that such an alliance policy required was once expressed in concentrated form by Oscar Torp, who as finance minister and then from late 1941 defence minister was one of the most influential members of the government. In a conversation in June 1941 with Arthur Greenwood, a Labour member of the British War Cabinet, Torp took his cue from renewed British pressure to gain control of the Norwegian merchant navy in order to state the following dilemma:

> To what extent can the practical concentration of power and decision in the hands of the British government – itself a proper and necessary consequence of the war – be said to lead to a limitation of the independence of the smaller allied countries and a reduction of their war effort, in such a way that the ideals of democracy and cooperation of equals that we are fighting for may be endangered?

The reasoned tone of Torp's question, devoid of strident or bombastic declarations about the superior values of national sovereignty, was in itself symbolic of Norway's pragmatic alliance policy. And it fell to Torp to reform the command structure of the Norwegian armed forces in exile in preparation for better and more orderly cooperation with their British counterparts. The three armed services were subordinated to a unified High Command, whose main task would be planning for the liberation. A separate section within that command dealt with plans and operations in occupied Norway, and it formed the Norwegian leg for cooperation with SOE and DCO through an Anglo-Norwegian Collaboration Committee (ANCC) which was constituted in the spring of 1942.

On that basis, through 1942, there gradually emerged a joint Allied policy towards the military resistance movement in Norway in line with Norwegian desires to keep it in reserve for the final liberation. Raids or sabotage actions before that time would in the main be carried out by specially trained agents from the Norwegian forces in the United Kingdom, against targets agreed in the ANCC. As regards bombing of military or industrial targets of value to the German war effort, cooperation was less complete. Norwegian authorities supplied the British Air Ministry with up to date information and recommendations about targets, but the Allied bomber commands reserved their right to make their own decisions. In practice, however, Allied bombing in Norway was on a very restricted scale, with only two or three cases resulting in official Norwegian protests.

Turning to the level of long-term planning for the liberation, Norway's 'lobbying' met with varying degrees of success. Most successful were efforts to achieve an agreement on 'civil affairs' during the liberation which would protect Norwegian interests against excessive interference from Allied military authorities. By taking the initiative at an early stage, the Norwegian government negotiated an agreement with the British authorities which met Norway's desires in all essentials, and which became the pattern for similar agreements between the allied great powers and allied governments of occupied countries.

Least successful were the Norwegian efforts to take an active part in the military planning for the reconquest of Norway. Several reasons account for this. First, operational planning at this grand strategic level was for obvious reasons the jealously guarded preserve of the great powers which provided the bulk of the armed forces to be employed. Second, the need for secrecy called for a very restrictive interpretation of the hallowed principle of 'need to know'. Third, it was becoming increasingly clear as the war went on that the liberation of Norway would be a side-show and a dead end in terms of the decisive battle to defeat Germany. Forces nominally earmarked for Norway would therefore be subject to recall at the last minute if required in other and more important theatres of operations.

While the Norwegian military authorities no doubt understood the reasons why they were kept at arm's length from the higher councils of war planning, it would be too much to expect the government to acquiesce in the apparent lack of British or Allied interest in the liberation of their home country. Hence no stone was left unturned in their efforts to push Norway higher up on the priority list. Crown Prince Olav, Commander-in-Chief of the Norwegian forces since July 1944, who had personal access to President Roosevelt, went to Washington in February 1945 to work on the Combined Chiefs of Staff, and in April King Haakon lunched with Churchill to press the Norwegian case.

All this was in vain, as were the – somewhat reluctant – Norwegian efforts in the final stages of the war to transfer to Sweden the centre of gravity for preparations for the liberation. Neither Swedish nor Allied authorities were willing to contemplate the employment of the 15,000 Norwegian so-called 'police troops' as first line liberation forces. And Norway's attempt to persuade Sweden to mobilise her army, as a deterrent against German attempts to hold on to Norway after a general armistice, resulted only in an acrimonious diplomatic exchange. It was doubly fortunate therefore that the 'best case' scenario happened in the end: the over 300,000 Germans in Norway effected an orderly surrender to General Sir Andrew Thorne's skeleton 'Allied Land Forces Norway' assisted by some 40,000 men of the Norwegian military resistance.

The Theory and Practice of Alliance Cooperation

It will be apparent from the other contributions to this book that Norwegian-British relations during the war, while generally remarkably free from the dire problems which plagued British relations with some of the other European exiles – notably the Free French – varied from time to time and from sector to sector. Least problematic were the easy working relationships established between the armed forces of the two countries, firmly based on the Anglo-Norwegian Military Agreement of 28 May 1941 and cemented by the mutual trust and respect which seems to have developed between the men directly involved. Between the two countries' intelligence organisations cooperation was also, on the whole, satisfactory. Without belittling the importance of the Military Agreement, or the many personal contributions towards a smooth relationship, it needs to be said that the very smallness of Norway's military contribution helps to explain the absence of major controversies at the operational level. As the obviously junior partner in those respects, Norway harboured no pretence towards equality of status or influence.

In matters relating to the Norwegian military resistance, and to military or paramilitary action against targets in the occupied country, relations were rather more difficult during the first two years of the war, but caused few difficulties after the end of 1942. Some of the more tangible reasons for the problems in the earlier period have already been touched upon. But there is another aspect which concerns the relationship between the government and the people in occupied Norway: the government was – and in fact remained throughout the war – conscious of the residual mistrust felt towards them by the people at home after the 1940 *débâcle*, and only slowly overcame their reluctance to authorise activities demanding sacrifices of life and property at home.

Turning to matters of 'high politics', we have already explained why Norway's efforts to influence Allied priorities for the liberation of Europe failed: the Allied road to the defeat of Germany, *pace* Churchill's colourful phrase about 'unrolling the Nazi map of Europe from the top', did not go by way of Norway. And as long as 350,000 Germans stayed quietly tied up in Norway there was no reason to disturb them. The 'scorched earth' policy instituted by the Germans when withdrawing from Finnmark at the end of 1944 changed that situation somewhat. But Allied resources were scarce, especially as regards operations in Arctic conditions, and the risk of collision with the Russians was another reason for the British not to get involved there. However, the bitterness of the people of North Norway, having felt abandoned and seemingly forgotten by both their own government and the Western allies during that winter, lives to this day.

Perhaps the clearest test case for the success of the Norwegian government's particular brand of alliance policy was that of the Norwegian merchant navy. Here was a case in which Norway was very much a senior partner, and therefore justified, if she had been so inclined, to demand her proper share in Allied decision-making. That Norway did not do so, and still succeeded in having vital Norwegian interests well cared for, is a strong indication that the flexible and pragmatic approach was not only practised, but that it also served its purpose.

As suggested at the outset of this paper, the adoption by the Norwegian government of their particular pragmatic approach to alliance policy was by no means a foregone conclusion. If tradition had been allowed to set the tune,

Norway would have approached the alliance with a great power with extreme caution, carefully assessing her own interests as a basis for erecting jealously guarded protective barriers before embarking on any cooperative ventures. We cannot of course know what the end result of such a policy would have been. But it seems reasonable to assume that in a strictly contractual, business-like relationship of that kind Norway would have had to negotiate from a position of marked weakness. In particular, she would have lacked the reserves of mutual trust which enabled Norway and Britain to achieve workable and satisfactory compromises in cases where interests conflicted – in the shipping agreements, in the military agreement of 1941, in the policy towards military or paramilitary activities in occupied Norway, or in the 'civil affairs' agreement.

The philosophy behind Norway's particular brand of alliance policy was not based on any disregard for the truism that relations between a minor and a major power in an alliance will always to a large extent be determined by considerations of power politics. But it also took into full account the assumption that relations between states and governments are never governed solely by quantitative or objective factors. Psychological and moral factors also play their part, perhaps particularly in wartime, and may be decisive in determining the general atmosphere of policy-making.

The earliest and clearest manifestation of Norway's alliance policy line came in the field of foreign policy, through what *The Times* hailed as the breach with isolationism and neutralism. This policy change struck sympathetic chords in the British Foreign Office. In his valedictory despatch as minister to the Norwegian government, Sir Cecil Dormer drew particular attention to Trygve Lie's further elaboration of his broadcast ideas about a post-war Atlantic security system: 'I refer to the question of Great Britain and the United States being invited after the war to keep naval and air bases in Norway'. The 'exceptional importance' of such a scheme was such that

> His Majesty's Government should bear it steadily in mind in all their
> dealings with the Norwegian Government, and be careful that the latter
> retain their present enthusiasm for it. It will also be almost equally
> important to help the Norwegian Government in any way possible to
> regain and retain their popularity in Norway, so that at the end of the
> war, or whenever they can return to Norway, they may be strong enough
> to carry their plans through.[8]

The minutes on Sir Cecil's despatch amounted to strong support for his suggestions in the higher echelons of the Foreign Office. And, while the 'foreign bases' aspect of Norway's new 'Atlantic policy' gradually faded away, the evidence suggests that the Norwegian government throughout the war was able to draw on a special reserve of goodwill and support in the Foreign Office.

Concluding Remarks

'Why do you think the émigré governments play such a melancholy role in history? It is because in the long run they adopt the attitudes of their hosts and become an object of contempt for their own people.'[9] That statement, made by General de Gaulle in London in 1942, serves by implication to illustrate the stark contrast between the alliance policy of the Free French, which went from one crisis to another fuelled by demonstrations of French independence, and that of Norway. To outsiders, indeed, Norway's policy of whole-hearted cooperation, and the general absence of flag-waving demands for sovereign equality within the alliance, ran the risk of appearing as acceptance of the role of a docile protégé of Great Britain. And enemy propaganda in Norway at every opportunity sought to sell the image of the 'émigré' government as having 'sold' Norway to the Allied great powers. But the alliance policy of the Norwegian government was the result of a deliberate choice, and the extent of Britain's willingness to take the Norwegians into their counsels convinced the government that its choice had been right. Whether it would have been the right choice under materially different circumstances is another matter. Such a policy may well have been a luxury only to be afforded by a government which stood on firm ground. Starting from a secure constitutional position, in firm alliance with a popular King, and enjoying financial independence, the Norwegian government gradually achieved also a remarkable degree of political acceptance on the home front. On that basis they could, without resorting to demonstrative gestures, successfully assert their claim to be the undisputed wartime guardians of Norwegian sovereignty and national interests in the Grand Alliance.

References

1   Quoted from the Cabinet proclamation issued from Tromsø on 8 June 1940 (my translation).

2   Dr T. Kingston Derry, in *Proceedings of a Conference on Britain and European Resistance 1939–1945* (St. Antony's College, Oxford, 1962. Mimeogr.) p. Nor.11. Dr Derry worked in British Political Intelligence during the war, with particular reference to Scandinavia.

3   UD (Norwegian Foreign Ministry) archives, file 34.1/19, letter from Dr Arne Ording and others to the Norwegian government 10 July 1940.

4   The debate is extensively reviewed in chapters 3 and 4, vol. I, of my two-volume work *'London-regjeringa': Norge i krigsalliansen 1940–1945* (Oslo, 1973–79). (Hereafter cited as *'London-regjeringa'*)

5   See *'London-regjeringa'*, vol. I, Appendixes 1 and 2.

6   Letter from Prime Minister Nygaardsvold to the senior Norwegian Labour leader Martin Tranmæl, then in Stockholm, in May 1941 (Archives of the Parliamentary Commission of Investigation, box 30, file 17).

7   London archives of the Norwegian Ministry of Defence, dossier 630, Nygaardsvold/Lie memorandum of conversation at a luncheon in No. 10 Downing Street, 9 February 1942.

8   PRO, FO 371/29421: Sir Cecil Dormer to Mr Eden 1 April 1941, with minutes by L. Collier, O.G. Sargent, A. Cadogan, and R.C. Butler.

9   Translated from the French version cited by D.W. Johnson in an unpublished paper on 'Le Gaullisme à Londres' for the 1977 London conference on 'Governments in Exile in London during the Second World War', p. 20.

7 Business goes to war: The Norwegian merchant navy in Allied war transport

ATLE THOWSEN

Introduction

IN 1986 the Norwegian government commissioned a history of the Norwegian Shipping and Trade Mission (Nortraship), and the war experiences of the merchant marine. Four historians were engaged to write the five-volume history, and my own contribution was published in 1992.[1] It may well be asked why such an important part of Norwegian history has not previously been dealt with by historians. There are several reasons for this. I think that the main one has been a lack of interest on the part of the government and in particular of the Norwegian shipowners who manned the leading positions in Nortraship, the organisation which managed the Norwegian merchant navy during World War II.

The history of Nortraship is not only the history of thousands of people joining hands in harmony in a fight with a common goal, namely to win the war against the Axis. It is also a story of strong conflicts with the British and the Americans, of fights inside Nortraship between leaders with strong and uncompromising attitudes – leaders who were more accustomed to giving orders than to obeying them. Their motives were sometimes a strange mixture of profit and patriotism. Clashes between these leaders and members of the Norwegian government in exile in London occurred throughout the war. In the post-war period there has until recently been a common fear among the parties involved that if the history of Nortraship was written it would mean that a lot of dirty linen would have to be washed in public.

The intention of this paper is not to perform such a public laundering. It must be looked upon merely as an attempt to examine some of the problems involved when a business, in this case the Norwegian shipping industry, goes to war. I shall concentrate on three major subjects:

1 The problems of neutrality – Norwegian shipping policy during the 'Phoney War'.
2 Norway's transition from neutral to ally and its consequences for Norwegian shipping and Allied war transport.
3 The relationship between the American, British and Norwegian maritime authorities.

The problems of neutrality: Norwegian shipping policy during the 'Phoney War'

The main priority of Norwegian policy between September 1939 and 9 April 1940 was to keep the country out of the war.[2] The means to achieve this goal was neutrality and the guardian of that policy was the Ministry of Foreign Affairs. Two factors complicated and endangered the success of this policy: the large Norwegian merchant marine and the country's dependence upon supplies from abroad. The Norwegian merchant fleet was far greater than the country's own demand for tonnage. Consequently the largest proportion of the tonnage was chartered by other nations. After the outbreak of war chartering of too large a portion of the Norwegian tonnage to one of the belligerent parties could be interpreted as a breach of Norwegian neutrality by the other party. Therefore, in order to control chartering of tonnage, the Norwegian government made chartering dependent upon the approval of an official body (Fraktkontrollen) set up with governmental consent by the Norwegian Shipowners' Association.[3]

The main difficulty facing neutral Norway at this early stage of the war was the double role played by Britain in relation to Norway. Due to the war Great Britain's demand for tonnage had increased considerably and the British looked to Norway in their efforts to have their demand met. Because of Britain's role as major supplier of goods to Norway it seemed almost impossible for the Norwegians to prevent the British government from chartering Norwegian tonnage on a large scale. But Norwegian shipping was a free enterprise and not likely to be easily dictated to by governmental wishes and orders. Due to the great risks involved and the steep rise in war insurance premiums, Norwegian ships stopped calling at British ports immediately after the outbreak of war. The consequences could have been fatal for Britain and, as in World War I, the British pressed hard for an Anglo-Norwegian Tonnage Agreement. Both the Norwegian government and the Norwegian Shipowners' Association tried to bargain for time as they knew that there was more money to be earned on a steadily rising freight market. After a short time, however, they had to give in because of the pressure exerted by the British. Britain refused to supply Norwegian ships with bunker coal and hinted that British exports to Norway might have to be curtailed.

An ally in disguise – Memorandum of Arrangement 11 November 1939

The first Anglo-Norwegian shipping negotiations in September 1939 failed, mainly due to the fact that the Norwegians tried to get a war trade agreement with Britain in exchange for a tonnage agreement.[4] The British attitude towards the Norwegian negotiators did not help to ease the atmosphere. The British delegation had been instructed by their government 'to deal somewhat stiffly with the Norwegian representatives', especially with regard to the question of chartering Norwegian tankers, and to 'avoid being what is called blackmailed'.[5] Both the rates and the conditions offered by the British were considered totally unacceptable by the Norwegian delegation.[6] One of the Norwegian delegates, a representative from the Norwegian Shipowners' Association, stated that no laws prevented Norwegian ships from sailing to Britain, but the 'decisive factors were simply rates and conditions offered'. Other countries offered a better price and it was only 'just and right that these offers were accepted'. Clearly the intention of the Norwegian shipowners at this stage of the war was to let their policy be governed by the laws of supply and demand. The British, on the other hand, wanted by all means to avoid conditions similar to those of World War I when the freight levels were more or less decided by what the British considered to be war-profiteers.

The Norwegians were, however, soon forced back to the negotiating table. The basis for the new negotiations was the British desiderata presented to the Norwegians during the first negotiations.[7] In principle Britain wanted all the tonnage she could get, but the chartering of 150 large Norwegian tankers was considered the primary objective. In the period 8–18 October 1939, negotiations were held in London between representatives of the British government and the Norwegian Shipowners' Association. Officially the Norwegian government took no part in these negotiations. Instead they tried to nourish the impression of the talks being conducted strictly on a business footing. The representatives of the Norwegian delegation acted, however, in full accordance with instructions from the Norwegian government and the final agreement had to receive governmental approval before the chief negotiator could put his initials on the document called *Memorandum of Arrangement* on 11 November 1939. The agreement was later to be referred to as the *Scheme* and the vessels chartered as *Scheme-vessels*. Also acting on instructions from their government, the Norwegian negotiators tried in vain once more to use the tonnage agreement as a lever to reach a trade agreement with the British in order to secure supplies to Norway. But in the first round they failed to secure such an agreement and an Anglo-Norwegian trade agreement was not signed until 11 March 1940.

The negotiations had been tough. The British delegation had to a large extent followed the advice of the First Lord of the Admiralty, Winston Churchill, to use 'both the bait of any price under twenty shillings, combined with the maximum threat of all retaliatory measures, to force prompt agreement'.[8] The Anglo-Norwegian Shipping Agreement implied that before February 1940 Britain could charter almost half the Norwegian tonnage. From a British point of view it was perhaps even more important that they were being offered 150 large and modern tankers for charter. This was of vital importance to Britain and her allies, as the experts in the Mercantile Marine Department in the Board of Trade as late as in 1938 had grossly underestimated Britain's need for tanker tonnage in the event of war.[9] If the tanker situation for some reason or another should deteriorate, the experts had sought comfort in the assumption that at least 150 neutral tankers would be available and that this would give Britain a surplus of tanker tonnage.[10]

At first the shipping agreement seemed, from an economic point of view, favourable to the Norwegian shipowners. But as freight rates on the open market rose, the economic advantages of the agreement diminished and finally the Norwegian shipowners complained of having to 'subsidise British warfare'. Britain feared that Norway might in certain circumstances be tempted to break the agreement.

Such a situation came at the beginning of April 1940 when the British War Cabinet decided to put into effect operation *Wilfred* and mine Norwegian territorial waters. The plan would be an obvious breach of Norwegian neutrality. The British assumed that the operation would be met by Norwegian counter-measures, of which the most likely would be the termination of the Anglo-Norwegian Shipping Agreement. In order to meet this eventuality the Admiralty, with the consent of the War Cabinet on 4 April 1940, started to make plans for a 'forcible possession of Norwegian shipping . . . in the event of the Norwegian Shipping Agreement being denounced.'[11] The British requisitioning of the Norwegian merchant fleet would be enforced in accordance with a much disputed principle in international law, the right of angary.[12]

From neutral to ally: 9 April 1940

The German invasion of Denmark and Norway 9 April 1940, however, changed the situation fundamentally. Neither Norwegian nor Danish tonnage could any longer be requisitioned by the British with reference to the right of angary. In the case of the Danish fleet the problem was relatively simple. The Danish government had capitulated on the same day as the invasion had started. Danish ships were thus defined as enemy property by the War Cabinet and were 'put into Prize Court and requisitioned for the duration of the war.'[13] The situation of the Norwegian tonnage was much more obscure. The Norwegian government had avoided falling into the hands of the Germans and had instead managed to put up a fight against the invaders. But the British doubted that the Norwegians could hold out for very long against a superior enemy. If the Norwegian government capitulated the War Cabinet decided that 'the decision taken in regard to Danish Shipping should apply *mutatis mutandis* to Norwegian vessels.'[14] In the meantime all Norwegian ships should be sent into an Allied port 'on some pretext or other. All Norwegian ships in British ports or arriving, or sent in, subsequently (were) to be detained until further orders.'

After 9 April 1940 four parties were fighting to gain control over the Norwegian merchant fleet:

1   The Norwegian government on the run from the Germans.
2   The British government.
3   The German invaders and Quisling.
4   Representatives of the Norwegian government and Norwegian shipping interests abroad, first and foremost in London and New York.

During the first days the struggle was fought over the radio, the different parties trying to get in contact with the Norwegian ships and giving them orders. From broadcasting stations in Norway and in other German-controlled areas the vessels were, in the name of the Norwegian Shipowners' Association, ordered to go to Norwegian or neutral ports.[15] The British on the other hand warned the Norwegian ships that these messages were dictated by the Germans and should not be followed.[16] Instead the vessels should proceed to the nearest British or Allied port. After a few days the 'radio-fight' was won by the British when they, in full agreement with Ingolf Hysing Olsen, representative of the Norwegian Shipowners' Association in London and Erik Colban, the Norwegian minister in London, transmitted a message to all Norwegian ships on 13 April stating that: 'Your ship is held covered by the British Government against War and Marine risks on the values and conditions under which she is at present insured.'[17] The condition was that the ships at once proceeded to the nearest British or Allied port. Given the choice between sailing with or without insurance of vessel and cargo, the decision seemed to have been an easy one for the Norwegian masters. All of them chose to follow the directives from London. The question was, however, what to do with the Norwegian ships after they had reached their destination? Their owners were in occupied territory and could consequently give them no directives or orders, but what about the Norwegian government?

The establishment of Nortraship

As they had no radio contact with the surrounding world, the Norwegian government could not at first take part in the struggle to gain control over the Norwegian tonnage. This communications failure also complicated the efforts to reach a more permanent solution with regard to the administration of the Norwegian merchant marine. British proposals to put the whole Norwegian merchant fleet under the British flag for the duration of the war were turned down both by Colban and Hysing Olsen.[18] Instead the two started, in cooperation with Norwegian shipping people in Britain, to set up a body to administer the Norwegian merchant marine from London. A few days later a similar body was established in New York as a result of the combined efforts of the Norwegian consul-general in New York and representatives of Norwegian shipping interests in the USA.

Britain now gave up the idea of hoisting the British flag on Norwegian vessels and instead proposed that the Norwegian government itself should requisition the merchant fleet.[19] When they finally managed to get in contact with the Norwegian government, via the Norwegian legation in Stockholm, the Norwegians consented to the proposal.

By the Provisional Order in Council of 22 April 1940, the Norwegian merchant marine was brought under government control for the duration of the war.[20] At the same time, Øivind Lorentzen, who had been appointed director of Norwegian Shipping at the outbreak of the war, was given the power of attorney stating that he should 'act as Director of the Norwegian Shipping Directorate to be established in London.' Lorentzen set off for London at once, but when he arrived there on 25 April he found to his great surprise that an organisation under the leadership of Hysing Olsen, had already been established, under the auspices of the British Ministry of Shipping, to administer the Norwegian merchant marine. The organisation, called the Norwegian Shipping and Trade Mission, with the telegraphic address Nortraship, had opened its offices at 144 Leadenhall Street only a few hours before Lorentzen's arrival.[21] In accordance with his power of attorney Lorentzen took over the whole organisation and for a short period Hysing Olsen was relegated to the background. In June 1940, however, it was decided, much to the dismay of the British, that Nortraship should establish a new main office in New York in addition to the one in London. Lorentzen became manager of the new office, whereas Hysing Olsen took over in London. Lorentzen was still to be the formal leader of the whole organisation, but as the Norwegian government had their offices in London, Nortraship's London office, at least at this stage of the war, became the most important one. Consequently Hysing Olsen was in many ways looked upon as the real leader of the organisation.

How important was the Nortraship fleet to the Allied cause and how was this large fleet managed? Let us begin by looking at the number and types of ships and the total tonnage of the Nortraship fleet.

The Nortraship fleet

At the time of the German invasion the Norwegian merchant marine (ships above 500 gross tons) consisted of 1172 ships totalling more than 4.4 million gross tons. Of the Norwegian merchant fleet 252 vessels totalling almost 2 million gross tons were tankers. In addition there were 13 whale factory ships and more than a hundred whalers.

In accordance with the Anglo-Norwegian tonnage agreement, with later addendums, the British Ministry of Shipping had already chartered or obtained an option to charter 1.8 million gross tons, or almost 40 per cent of the total Norwegian tonnage. One hundred and sixty tankers totalling about 1.2 million gross tons, i.e. about 60 per cent of the total Norwegian tanker fleet, were sailing on time-charter for Britain.

Nortraship controlled more than a thousand vessels with a total tonnage of over four million gross tons, of which 241 vessels, totalling 1.9 million gross tons, were tankers. It employed 25,000 seamen. Nortraship was thus the largest shipowning firm in the world, even though it did not control the 13 per cent of total Norwegian tonnage which was in Norwegian or German-controlled waters at the time of the German invasion. Both from an economic and a political perspective, Nortraship proved to be the most valuable asset possessed by the Norwegian government during the war. The profits generated made the government in exile economically independent, while the assistance to the Allies brought much political good will.

Division of management and Anglo-Norwegian controversies

As previously mentioned, in the summer of 1940 Nortraship established a branch in New York. In November the management of the Nortraship fleet was divided between London and New York. Under the management of London came, roughly speaking, all ships sailing on Scheme for Britain and most of the tramps engaged in the Far East. The New York office was left with most of the liners and the so-called 'free' tankers and tramps. Thus the majority of the Nortraship fleet was run by the London office, but the dollar-earning part of the fleet was managed from New York. This division between pound- and dollar-earning ships gave rise to conflicts within Nortraship itself, between Nortraship and the Norwegian government in exile, but first and foremost between the Norwegians and the British.

Table 1: **Management of the Nortraship-fleet divided between London and New York** (as at 21 November 1940)

	London	New York
Liners	27	88
Free tramps	80	126
Tankers on neutral charter	–	54
Tankers on British charter (Scheme)	151	10
Dry-cargo ships on British charter (Scheme)	241	–
Ships in the service of the Norwegian or British government	5	1
Ships detained in French ports	23	3
Ships in Sweden and Finland	43	–
Total	**570**	**282**

Before Pearl Harbor British demands for additional tonnage for the 'war effort' were met with reluctance by the Norwegians. Their argument was that the transfer of 'free' tonnage to Britain would lead to a reduction of Norwegian dollar-income, an income needed for the payment of interests on Norwegian debts in the USA and to build up a reserve for rebuilding the country and the shipping industry after the war. The Norwegians had little or no confidence in the value of the pound after the war and preferred to stick to convertible currencies.

Late in 1940 and in early spring 1941 the first serious crisis occurred. Britain demanded more Norwegian tonnage and complained of Norwegian unwillingness to contribute to the war effort.[22] Meeting the British demand would mean giving them dollar-earning liners managed by Nortraship in New York. Nortraship in London was partly willing to meet the demands, but Lorentzen in New York put his foot down.[23] Lorentzen had earlier rejected British accusations that Norway was not contributing enough to the war effort.[24] According to the Director of Norwegian Shipping, Norway's real economic contribution to the war effort was 'concealed by the policy of Nortraship in London and by accepting Scheme-rates far below actual market-rates'. In order to give the correct picture of the Norwegian contribution, Lorentzen suggested that in the future Nortraship should demand 'full market-freights in dollars' from Britain. The difference between Scheme- and market-rates could then be put at the disposal of Britain, either as a gift or a loan. Lorentzen could not have picked a worse moment to put forward such a proposal: Britain's dollar reserves were at their lowest. In spite of all the difficulties, however, Britain and Norway concluded a new tonnage agreement in March 1941.[25]

The controversies led William Weston of the Ministry of Shipping to analyse Britain's shipping relations with Norway.[26] In March 1941 he concluded that the Norwegian Director of Shipping had no idea whatsoever about the shipping situation of the Allies. Neither was the attitude of the Norwegian government totally satisfactory to Britain. In the Ministry of Shipping the feeling was that only the Norwegian foreign minister, Trygve Lie, stood for a 'whole-hearted co-operation with us'.

The gist of the problem, however, was the two different attitudes that Hysing Olsen and Lorentzen represented. The Director of Nortraship in London, Hysing Olsen, stood for whole-hearted, but not unconditional co-operation, whereas Lorentzen in New York was more interested in dollars and in protecting the post-war interests of the Norwegian shipowners. In Weston's opinion it would be for the good of the British cause if the prime minister found time to meet members of the Norwegian government and make clear to them 'the gravity of the present shipping situation and how greatly we depend upon their full co-operation at whatever sacrifice of immediate shipping interests'.

Britain demands the rest of the Norwegian merchant navy

At the end of April 1941 Sir Kingsley Wood, the Chancellor of the Exchequer, demanded that the rest of the Nortraship fleet be put at the disposal of Britain for the benefit of the war effort.[27] The demand must be seen in relation to the Battle of the Atlantic which had been declared the month before, and Britain's desperate need for tonnage.[28] The Norwegians could no longer reject the demand on the grounds that the transfer of New York-managed tonnage would lead to a loss of dollar-income. The Lend-Lease Act, passed the month before, made it possible for Britain to meet the Norwegian demand for dollars.

Politically, it was impossible for the Norwegian government and Nortraship to refuse to negotiate with the British. The Norwegians were, however, still reluctant to place more tonnage, especially American-chartered tonnage, at the disposal of the Ministry of War Transport. Both they and the British knew that this would mean 'sacrificing their liner interests in America and other trades'.[29] This meant that years of hard labour could go down the drain. It would also create an opening for American and British competitors to take the place of the Norwegian operators. A withdrawal of the liners from American trades could also lead to maritime transport problems for the USA and thus create problems for the relations between Britain and the USA.

In discussions with the Ministry of War Transport in May 1941 the

Norwegian government pointed out that two-thirds of the Norwegian merchant navy had already been chartered to the British.[30] The merchant navy was their only source of income and a further chartering to the British would weaken the political and economic situation of the Norwegian government in exile. The Norwegians recognised, however, Britain's desperate supply situation and were prepared to contribute 'for the benefit of the common war effort'. The Norwegian government declared its willingness to discuss any proposal put forward by the British. They also supported the British proposal to establish an Anglo-Norwegian Shipping Committee. The ships Britain wanted most were mainly navigating in American waters. It was thus necessary to bring the Americans, i.e. the US Maritime Commission, into the discussions.

The news that the Norwegian government and Nortraship in London had given in and agreed to negotiate with Britain about further transfers of ships was received with shock by Nortraship in New York.[31] The British demands, they believed, would ruin the future of Norwegian shipping. Britain consented to tripartite negotiations. From May to October 1941 talks were held in Washington between the newly established British Merchant Shipping Mission, the US Maritime Commission and Nortraship.

The Norwegians had pressed for American participation, hoping for American support in their efforts to limit the transfer of their American-chartered tankers and liners to an absolute minimum. This hope proved to be futile. After the re-election of President Roosevelt in December 1940 it became more and more clear that the USA was willing to support Britain by all means short of war. The British Merchant Shipping Mission in Washington had, under the leadership of Sir Arthur Salter, been successful in its efforts to create a pro-British atmosphere in the American capital. The first thing Sir Arthur had asked for and had been promised after his arrival in March was massive and immediate tanker assistance. During the summer and autumn of 1941 the British negotiators could report home with satisfaction that nearly all the British demands had been met. The prediction of a Treasury spokesman in May that the Norwegians 'are going to be tough nuts to crack' did not come true. The combination of Sir Arthur Salter's Shipping Mission and the US Maritime Commission proved too strong for the Norwegians, even when some of the charterers of Norwegian vessels tried to come to their assistance. In the summer of 1941 the power of the US Maritime Commission was greatly increased with the passing of the Ship Warrant Act and Ships Requisitioning Act.[32] In reality it became impossible to navigate in American waters without a warrant from the US Maritime Commission. If Nortraship or the charterers did not give up the ships in question voluntarily , then the Commission had the powers to force them.

The October agreement and the establishment of the Anglo-Norwegian Shipping Committee

On 10 October 1941, the British Minister of War Transport, Lord Leathers, and the Norwegian Minister of Shipping Arne Sunde signed the October agreement, an agreement the British hoped would be 'an agreement to end all agreements'.[33] They proved to be wrong.

In the October agreement the Norwegians committed themselves in their future employment of Norwegian tonnage to give 'absolute priority to the transport of vital war supplies'.[34] An Anglo-Norwegian Shipping Committee was established to function in an advisory capacity in questions dealing with the allocation of Norwegian vessels. Ships coming under the new agreement were called Plan-ships to distinguish them from the Scheme-ships.

In accordance with the so-called Tripartite Agreement, 80 per cent of the hire for the Plan-ships was paid in dollars and the rest in pounds. The dollars were supplied by the Lend-Lease administration. Lend-Lease could not simply hand over the money to Britain. The Plan-ships were therefore chartered by the US Maritime Commission who in turn let the British have them. Most of the tankers that Britain had demanded were sailing on long-time charters for American oil companies. The companies were brought into the negotiations with Nortraship, the British Merchant Shipping Mission and the US Maritime Commission, and a so-called Quadruple Agreement was signed. Under this agreement the oil companies transferred their charters to the Ministry of War Transport and the Norwegians received a 100 per cent dollar payment.

The British could look back on the Anglo-Norwegian tonnage agreements concluded in 1941 with satisfaction. At the end of the year almost three-quarters of the Norwegian tonnage was sailing for the British. The Norwegians, however, could also claim to have been partly successful. Britain had accepted that the Norwegian demand for payment in dollars was a just one and should not be mistaken for greed and war profiteering.

The Squeeze: Nortraship between the British Ministry of War Transport and the American War Shipping Administration

Before Pearl Harbor the Norwegian government and Nortraship negotiated with Britain on tonnage matters. After the USA had entered the war American interest in the Norwegian merchant navy increased considerably. At the same time American control over foreign shipping in American waters was strengthened. At the beginning of February 1942 The War Shipping Administration was established under the leadership of Admiral Emory Land, a man whose chief ambition was to make the USA the world's greatest maritime nation.

The British and the Americans had different views on the utilisation of Norwegian vessels. From time to time the Norwegians were able to take advantage of the conflicting views to promote their own interests. After Churchill and Roosevelt had agreed to the establishment of the Combined Shipping Adjustment Board the co-operations between the British and the Americans on shipping matters improved.[35] The Board had one division in London led by Lord Leathers and Averill Harriman, and one in Washington headed by Sir Arthur Salter and Admiral Emory Land.

The Norwegians tried in vain to get a seat on the Board. They only received assurances that Norway would be represented when the Board discussed matters concerning Norwegian interests. The only time the Norwegians were called in was 6 August 1942. Then they were confronted by an Anglo-American demand that the rest of the Norwegian merchant navy should be chartered to the Ministry of War Transport. The Norwegians protested and demanded negotiations.

In January 1942 Nortraship in New York had proposed that the Norwegian government should enter into tonnage negotiations with the USA. The Norwegians hoped to benefit from the increased American tonnage demand and to strengthen Norwegian-American maritime relations, thus diminishing the British pressure for more tonnage. The Norwegian plan was, however, frustrated by the British, who rightly feared that bilateral negotiations would result in their losing control over Norwegian shipping in American waters. Instead Britain suggested, and in November 1942 the Americans agreed, that tripartite negotiations should take place in Washington. The basis of the negotiations was the disposal of the remaining part of the Norwegian merchant navy.

The result of the negotiations was that a group of 53 ships of the remaining Norwegian tonnage was time-chartered to the British Ministry of War Transport, who in turn re-let them to the War Shipping Administration. Freights were paid in dollars. Another group of 63 ships was allowed to sail in American waters, but under the control of the War Shipping Administration. As a result of the negotiations an American-British-Norwegian Shipping Committee was established in Washington.

The agreement was concluded on New Year's Eve 1942 and was called by the Norwegians and Americans the *Hogmanay Agreement*. The British reaction to the christening can best be illustrated by a telegram from one of the British negotiators: 'attempt agree official name deplorable failure. Other two parents only exerted brains utmost destructively or worse. Nortraship suggested Washington . . . but WSA considered inappropriate. Hogmanay now being freely used not only by US and believing squatter's rights well established suggest you consider adopted.'[36] The Hogmanay Agreement was the last agreement to be concluded involving Norwegian tonnage. The atmosphere of the negotiations may best be described by the eyewitnesses' reports of two of the chief negotiators, Erling Dekke Næss from Nortraship and William Weston from the British Merchant Shipping Mission.

First Næss:[37]

> The men I had to negotiate with on behalf of Nortraship were William
> Weston, of the British Ministry of War Shipping, and David Scoll of the
> US Maritime Commission. Bill Weston was a lean, red haired British
> civil servant. Dave Scoll was a lawyer with little or no shipping
> experience. They were a strange pair. Bill Weston, diabolically clever
> and astute in international shipping and finance, was determined at all
> cost to advance the British interests. In spite of the United States

controlling everything from money bags to military hardware, the British member dominated the team.

My obvious strategy was to appeal to Dave Scoll's basically kind feelings. Were we not both confronted by this wily and cunning Englishman? If we did not oppose his Machiavellian plots would not Dave himself be his next target? It worked.

Secondly Weston:[38]

Our discussions with the Norwegian Shipping Delegations have proceeded in two hectic bursts lasting for about seventy-two hours almost without a break in each case. The battle has been fast and furious and not without vituperation. I caused a diplomatic incident by a personal remark to Næss . . . , on a private occasion after our second lengthy bout of negotiations. It was late and Næss was arguing that the ships we wished to charter are already completely serving the war effort. This is an affirmation which has been made by every Norwegian I have met in this country, both diplomatic and commercial, until I am tired of hearing it. I replied to Næss, 'Yes, provided the cargo is going in the right direction and the dollar freight is enough'. The Norwegian Embassy, to whom Næss reported this remark, displayed great irritation and it took me a lunch and two visits to the Embassy to calm them down. This incident illustrates the touchiness of the Norwegians here and their great distance from the reality of this war.

The costs

The heavy contribution of the Norwegian Merchant Marine to the Allied cause was achieved at a terrible cost. During the war nearly two million tons of the Nortraship fleet were sunk, and more than 3,200 sailors and passengers on board Norwegian ships lost their lives. In addition came the losses in the period from September 1939 to 9 April 1940: 120,000 tons were sunk and nearly 400 people lost their lives.

Concluding Remarks

This paper has focused on some of the economic aspects of a particular business, namely the Norwegian shipping industry, in World War II. There has been a lot of reference to dollars and pounds, to chartering conditions and hard bargaining, and this may have left the impression that Nortraship and the Norwegian government in exile were filled with money grubbers. To talk about business in connection with war sometimes leaves a bad taste in the mouth. The concept of business seems inconsistent with war. When business tries to keep the wheels turning in times when the nation has been occupied by the enemy, it is sometimes referred to as collaboration. When business takes an active part in warfare and demands to be paid for it, it runs the risk of being characterised as war profiteering.

To give a precise distinction between economic resistance and collaboration in an occupied territory is a task full of pitfalls. The same goes for the distinction between profit and patriotism when we try to describe the part of the Norwegian shipping industry in World War II. The shipping industry of neutral Norway was forced into the war in 1939 and in return they demanded what they considered a fair economic compensation for risks and wear and tear. The shipping industry of belligerent Norway went to war in 1940 with two goals to be achieved: to win the war together with Norway's allies and to survive as a business. The second goal could only be reached with the help of money, preferably convertible currency which could be used for the contracting of new tonnage to replace what was lost. It was also important that the Norwegians managed to keep up the established international shipping system and their part of it, i.e. the liner trades, the long-term charters with the international oil companies etc., that they had managed to build up through years of hard labour and heavy investments.

When judging the behaviour of the Norwegians where shipping is concerned, we must also keep in mind that there were mixed motives on the British and American sides as well. It was not only the Norwegians who had to man their wartime shipping administration with people from the shipping industry itself. To a large degree the American War Shipping Administration had to depend on the services of the so-called 'dollar-a-year-men', executives put at the disposal of the WSA by the shipping division of oil companies and firms like United Fruit. One influential group in the War Shipping Administration was referred to as the 'banana-boys' because of their background. The real professional bureaucrats were to be found on the British side. Based on the experiences from World War I, the British were able to establish a smooth-running shipping machinery, based on a highly developed shipping expertise.

To keep the shipping industry alive was also an important goal for the Norwegian government in exile during World War II. The Norwegian economy was highly dependent upon the currency-earning ability of their shipping industry. That is why the Norwegian government after the war resolved that a large proportion of the nation's scanty stocks of foreign currency should be reserved for the rebuilding of the merchant fleet to its pre-war capacity. Thus the merchant fleet would be able to resume its position as the nation's principal earner of foreign currency and would in turn be able to finance the reconstruction of other sectors of the Norwegian economy. The British and American economies were not as dependent on their shipping industries. Britain and the USA had much more diversified economies to rely on when peace was restored.

In World War II it became a national goal for Norway to fight for the continued existence of her shipping industry. Let me draw a parallel of a more recent date. We all remember the so-called 'Cod War' between Britain and Iceland. To Britain this war only involved the interests of a rather small and local sector of British economy; to Iceland it concerned the future existence of the only national industry earning enough currency to keep the country going.

What fishing is to Iceland, shipping was to Norway. I say *was* because, as we all, know this has been changed by the new oil and gas industry, but that is a different story.

References

1   Atle Thowsen, *Handelsflåten i krig 1939–1945. Nortraship*, Vol. I, *Profitt og patriotisme* (Oslo, 1992).

2   Nils Ørvik, *Norge i brennpunktet. Fra forhistorien til 9. april 1940*, vol. I, *Handelskrigen 1939–1940* (Oslo, 1953).

3   Ibid, p. 76f.

4   Minutes of departmental meeting held on 26th September 1939 to consider the plan for Norwegian negotiations for a war trade agreement, MT 59/1405, PRO.

5   'The urgency of chartering neutral tonnage', Memorandum by the First Lord of the Admiralty, 16 October 1939, MT 59/1541, PRO.

6   Norwegian tonnage negotiations, 29 September and 2 October 1939, MT 59/1405, PRO.

7   General paper No. 2, from Board of Trade to the Norwegian delegation, 4 October 1939, ibid.

8   Memorandum by the First Lord of the Admiralty, 16 October 1939 (note 5 above).

9   W. K. Hancock and M. M. Gowing, *British War Economy*, History of the Second World War (London, 1949), p. 122ff.

10   J. D. Payton-Smith, *Oil: A Study of War-time Policy and Administration*, History of the Second World War (London, 1971), p. 57f.

11   Notes from a meeting at the Admiralty, 7 April 1940, ADM 116/4251, PRO, and extract from Conclusions of a meeting of the War Cabinet, 8 April 1940, ibid.

12   In international law the *right of angary* is defined as a belligerent nation's right to requisition neutral material such as railway-material and ships, which may be utilized in the warfare.

13   Present position with regard to Danish and Norwegian Merchant Shipping, 12 April 1940, FO 371/25180, fol. 18, PRO.

14   Extract from War Cabinet Conclusions 87 (40), 10 April 1940, ibid, fol. 440, PRO.

15   Per Huseklepp, *Kapteinane og 9. april*, unpublished MA thesis in history, Oslo University, 1970, p. 23.

16   Hans Fredrik Dahl, *'Dette er London'. NRK i krig 1940–1945* (Oslo, 1978), p. 117.

17   ADM 199/495, fol. 23, PRO.

18   Note on the proceedings of the first meeting of the Interdepartmental Co-ordination Committee to deal with Scandinavian and Danish shipping, 12 April 1940, MT 59/1661, PRO.

19   Telegram from Colban, Norwegian minister in London, to the Norwegian legation in Stockholm, 13 April 1940, Archives of the Norwegian legation in London, box 317, K1B3 (I) 1940, Riksarkiv (Norwegian National Archives).

20   Provisional Order in Council 22 April 1940, published in *Samling av provisoriske anordninger, kgl. res. m. v. 1940–1945*, published by the Kgl. Justis- og Politidepartement, London.

21   Benjamin Vogt, *Vår ære og vår avmakt* (Oslo, 1967), p. 23.

22   Memorandum of 3 December 1940, concerning Hysing Olsen's discussions with W. G. Weston, Ministry of Shipping, 26 and 29 November and 2 December 1940, HD, Skipsfartsavd. 1940–1960, box 548, 22.03/2, Riksarkiv.

23   Telegram from Nortraship, New York to Nortraship, London, ibid.

24   Telegram from Lorentzen to Sunde, 20 December 1940, copy in ibid.

25   Second Memorandum of Agreement regarding chartering of additional Norwegian tonnage, ibid.

26   Minute Sheet with notes on Norwegian Shipping, W. G. Weston, 22 March 1941, MT 59/1736, PRO.

27 Letter from Sir Kingsley Wood to Torp, 29 April 1941, ibid.
28 The Battle of the Atlantic. Directive by the Minister of Defence, 6 March 1941.
29 28. Note on the Norwegian dollar earnings from their ships, 20 March 1941, MT 59/1736, PRO.
30 4th Anglo-Norwegian Shipping Negotiations, Summary of Discussions on the 21st May, 1941, 22 May 1941, HD, Skipsfartsavd. 1940–1960, box 548, 22.03/3, Riksarkiv. See also Weston's note on Norwegian Negotiations, Minute Sheet, 23. 5. 1941, MT 59/1736, and UK Documents No. 5, 'Flag discrimination', No. 6, 'Norwegian Contribution to the War Effort' and No. 7, 'Proposed Anglo-Norwegian Shipping Committee', all dated 20 May 1941, MT 59/1879, PRO.
31 Telegram from Gogstad to Lorentzen, 25 May 1941, HD, Skipsfartsavd. 1940–1960, box 548, 22.03/3, Riksarkiv.
32 US Maritime Commission, Report 1941, p. 6, and Payton-Smith, *Oil*, p. 201.
33 F. C. Hampden's memorandum on Norwegian Shipping Agreements, 31 March 1942, MT 59/1529, PRO.
34 Order in Council of 7 October 1941, HD, Skipsfartsavd. 1940–1960, box 548, 22.03/5, Riksarkiv.
35 On the Combined Boards see S. McKee Rosen, *The Combined Boards of the Second World War: An Experiment in International Administration* (New York, 1951).
36 Telegram from Anderson to Weston, 2 April 1943, MT 59/596, PRO.
37 Erling Dekke Næss, *Autobiography of a Shipping Man* (London, 1977), p. 98f.
38 Letter from Weston to Hampden, 17 December 1942, MT 59/1436, PRO.

8 Anglo-Norwegian naval cooperation

ØIVIND SCHAU

Introduction

I shall deal first with the Norwegian navy during the period of Norwegian neutrality, as certain incidents at that time had a marked influence on the attitude of the British and Norwegian governments to Anglo-Norwegian cooperation in the early phases of the war after the invasion of Norway. Secondly I want to deal with the early efforts of the Norwegian navy in contributing towards the war in the UK. Thirdly I will briefly touch upon the arming of the Norwegian Merchant Navy. This required a large amount of resources from the already strained Naval Staff in London, and indeed worldwide.

The period of neutrality

Norway declared its neutrality in the war that broke out in September 1939. Bearing in mind the experience of the 1914–18 war, the naval authorities assumed that the navy should be set on a wartime footing from the outset. However, this was not possible in 1939 because of a catastrophic lack of trained personnel resulting from drastic reductions in the interwar budgets. As far as material was concerned, most of the combatant ships had been built around 1900 and were consequently hopelessly obsolete. The situation was particularly serious in the field of communications: the captains of some ships had to go to the nearest port and use the public telephone to contact their crews. One other serious drawback was that before the war all training had been carried out in tactical units. Now the ships were spread out along the long coastline without any possibility of training.

Such then was the naval status at the outbreak of war and indeed during the whole period of Norwegian neutrality. The situation put a great strain on the commanding officers of the ships, often lieutenants or sub-lieutenants in their twenties. It was only to be expected that various incidents occurred involving one or both belligerents. By far the greatest number of violations were carried out by British forces, presumably to test the efficiency of the Norwegian neutrality. On the other hand it should not be forgotten that the Germans in the period from 3 September 1939 to 8 April 1940, before Norway entered the war, had sunk 55 Norwegian merchant ships with a loss of 393 lives.

On 30 November 1939 the war between Finland and the Soviet Union broke out. It lasted until 12 March 1940. Although no dangerous incidents occurred, the navy's responsibilities were considerably increased. Climatic and other conditions also made it necessary to deploy the most modern and efficient units to the area. A further complication arose when the Germans introduced a new category of ships flying what they termed the *Reichsdienst-flagge*. They further claimed that those ships should have all the privileges of the naval ensign and those of the merchant navy flag as well. This caused some confusion over the two German ships the *Westerwald* and the *Altmark*. The *Altmark* incident was particularly embarrassing as the ship had several hundred Allied prisoners from captured merchant vessels on board. The naval authorities wanted the ship to be stopped and searched, but were overruled by their political superiors in Oslo. Consequently the British navy entered Norwegian waters, forced the *Altmark* into a Norwegian fjord and freed the prisoners.

In the same period three British merchant ships were sunk, probably in Norwegian territorial waters: the *Thomas Walton*, *Garoufalia* and *Deptford*. The German authorities strongly denied that the three ships had been sunk by a submarine as they claimed 'no German submarines had been in these waters at the time'. After the war it was asserted at the Nuremberg Trials that the ships had been sunk by the German submarine *TH 38*. The fact that the Norwegians seemed unable or unwilling to fulfil their duty as a neutral nation made the British naval authorities as well as the general public react unfavourably. A typical reaction is contained in the *Economist* of 24 February 1940:

> Norwegian territorial waters almost compensate Germany for her lack of a navy. They are the safe channel of return of German ships of every description, submarines fresh from attacks on merchant men, cargo-boats laden with Swedish ore, warships conveying British prisoners to prison camps in Germany. It is difficult to imagine what Germany would do without Norway's territorial waters.

This was obviously not a good start to negotiations for cooperation btween the two navies.

On the evening of 5 April 1940 there occurred an incident that might have been considered the end of Norwegian neutrality. The British and French ministers to Norway handed to the Norwegian Ministry of Foreign Affairs a note which stated that 'The time has come to notify the Norwegian government frankly of certain vital interests and requirements which the Allies intend to assert and defend by whatever measures they may think necessary.' The British minelaying operation presaged by this note took place on 8 April, shortly before the German invasion.

The beginning of Anglo-Norwegian naval cooperation

At the conclusion of hostilities in Norway in June 1940, a few units of the

Norwegian navy were evacuated to the UK. With the exception of one small modern destroyer the ships were of insignificant value, if any, to the war effort. The Norwegian naval authorities in the UK consequently concentrated their efforts on acquiring ships that could contribute to the war at sea. From May 1940 onwards the Norwegians had the impression that there were doubts about their reliability in the prosecution of the war. This was undoubtedly partly inspired by certain newspaper articles reporting from the days of the invasion which gave the impression that Quisling's party was more influential than was in fact the case. However, it must be emphasised that this was not the case in the attitude of the British Admiralty towards the Norwegian naval authorities in London.

In 1939 the Norwegian navy had ordered eight motor torpedo boats from two British yards. These boats were nearing completion when the Norwegians first attempted to establish a navy in the UK. In fact two of the boats were already undergoing trials when the Admiralty, despite Norwegian protests, confiscated the remaining six. There then occurred a most regrettable incident. The local admiral in Portsmouth asked the Norwegian officers on the spot whether they were willing to take their boats and participate in the evacuation of the British Army from Dunkirk. The answer from the crews was, of course, positive, but the matter had naturally to be referred to London, where the Norwegian reply was negative. Thus it came about that those two boats were lying idle while one of the most dramatic operations of the war took place. However, the two boats were based in Dover from 2 July and took part in all operations from that port. There developed a close and positive relationship between the two crews and Vice-Admiral Dover where the Admiral himself, later Admiral Sir Bertram Ramsay, personally took great interest in their activities.

As the Norwegian navy became established, it became apparent to the British that the Norwegian officers and crews were loyal to their senior staffs on shore and at sea. Their qualifications were proved to be of a high standard that compared favourably with their British opposite numbers. The Norwegian plans for the rebuilding of the navy outside Norway had, of course, as first priority the prosecution of the war at sea, but certain consideration was also given to operations in Norwegian waters. Here, however, the manning situation caused a serious bottleneck.

The relationship between the two navies was regulated through various bilateral agreements. Units of the Norwegian navy were to operate under the Norwegian naval ensign and the manning was to be the responsibility of the Norwegians. The crews would be subject to Norwegian administration, but operationally under British command. The question of jurisdiction and discipline was to be a Norwegian responsibility. There was never any question of command as far as the staffs on shore were concerned: they obviously had to be British.

As it was impossible for the Norwegian navy to build or buy ships during the war, it became necessary to take over the ships that the Admiralty found it most acceptable to transfer. The ships were to be subject to the same alterations and modernisations as comparable British ships. This was to be paid for by the Admiralty. However, as the Norwegian navy acquired larger units such as corvettes and destroyers the question of command within a force at sea arose. The Admiralty considered that the British officers were more conversant than the Norwegians with the relevant tactics and use of the modern British equipment, and therefore, regardless of seniority, should be in command. In the negotiations the final decision was postponed and the problem was to be taken into consideration when commanding officers were to be appointed. Quite soon, though, the problem solved itself. Various British admirals expressed the opinion that British and Norwegian units worked so well together that there was no longer any difference between them. There was no longer any national separation and integration became complete. After that there were various instances of Norwegian officers in command of units which included British forces. This was the case in the Channel, in the Western approaches, in the minesweeping forces in Scotland and in the MTB forces in the Shetlands. Another result of this development was that brand new ships were transferred to the Norwegian navy straight from the builders' yards. The crowning example must have been when the British navy's newest and most modern destroyer was given over to a Norwegian crew in which none of the officers was more than 30 years old.[1]

The question of basic and advanced training of officers was another problem which was quickly and satisfactorily solved. Staff training was made available to Norwegian officers at Liverpool and Greenwich. Furthermore, young officers were able to become cadets at the Royal Naval College at Dartmouth and at the Engineering College at Keyham. As part of their training these young officers also served as midshipmen on British ships of all descriptions on an equal footing with their British contemporaries.

The arming of the Merchant Navy

This subject is a very much neglected aspect of the activities of the Norwegian navy. It is not as colourful as battles between warships. It is what may be called an 'endless story' in which the Atlantic was the main battlefield. As Churchill put it, 'The battle of the Atlantic was the dominating factor all through the war. Never for one moment could we forget that everything that happened elsewhere, on land, at sea or in the air depended ultimately on its outcome'.[2] The defence of the merchant navy comprised several elements: de-gaussing, barrage balloons, rockets and so on. I have chosen the gunnery element because this presents the biggest problems involving international law, personnel, technical and economic and even psychological aspects.

After the outbreak of war in 1939, following British experiences from the First World War, Norwegian shipping circles and the shipbuilding industry approached the Director of Naval Ordnance on the subject of arming merchant ships. Various alternatives for strengthening ships were worked out. The economic consequences were also considered. Representatives of the shipping industry approached the political authorities in Oslo where there was no interest in the matter. Consequently no preparations that involved the spending of money were possible. Such then was the situation that faced the Norwegian authorities when Norway became a co-belligerent based in London.

The principal problem in this difficult period was the availability of weapons. It was only natural that British ships were given priority in the allocation of British resources. To begin with the British DEMS (Defensively Equipped Merchant Ships) equipped some Norwegian ships with guns and equipment that could be spared from British resources. This work was carried out by Norwegian naval authorities in cooperation with Nortraship.

During the course of 1941 new agreements were established whereby Norwegian ships were to be equipped on a similar scale to British ships. However, the implementation would take time. The status by the end of 1941 – after the loss of 198 ships – was that 80 of the remaining 690 ships were reasonably well armed against submarines and aircraft, 345 were inadequately armed, and 265 were entirely without armament. Not unreasonably a certain amount of resentment was felt among the Norwegian crews, particularly when sailing in convoys where British ships were armed on a much more adequate scale. The Norwegian Director of Naval Ordnance in the UK was given the task of coordinating the efforts to equip the rest of the ships adequately. An organisation was consequently established in New York termed Royal Norwegian Merchant Marine Defence. This organisation was similar to the British and American organisations and had subordinate establishments several places in North America. During the first 18 months armament was installed in 325 ships and quite soon the scales were met 100 per cent. This was of course only possible as a result of the enormous expansion in the American armament industry.

One condition connected with the delivery of equipment was that adequate personnel should be made available to use and maintain the armament. This task fell naturally on the Norwegian navy which established its headquarters at Dumbarton in Scotland to meet this requirement. Dumbarton also became the administrative and training centre. In addition personnel were trained in Lunenburg, Canada and Travers Island in New York and to a limited extent in Australia. As the equipment got increasingly complicated it became necessary to train officers to supervise the activities on board, particularly on the bigger ships. To give an idea of the extent of this work it should be stated that altogether 365 gunnery officers and 1,900 gunners were trained. In addition 800 British gunners were recruited and administered. The civilian crew members were also given some training, and by the end of the war there was hardly a Norwegian sailor who had not been given a course of varying duration.

It is obvious that exceptional efforts were called for from an already strained naval organisation to operate these activities. By the end of the war the organisation was installed and active in 13 different ports in the UK, as well as in New York, San Pedro, New Orleans, Baltimore and Norfolk; in Sydney and Melbourne; in Bombay, Cape Town, Alexandria, Port Said, Port Tewfic and Algiers; and after the invasion of Italy also in Naples and Taranto.

Because of the nature of the organisation's activities, it was important to establish efficient contact and cooperation with the local authorities not only on the naval side but also on the civilian. Communications with central authorities in London were not always easy, and the local officers on the spot had to act independently. This seems to have worked well and the following quotation from Australia may be typical of their success:

> I am directed by the Australian Commonwealth Naval Board to express their appreciation of the work performed by Commander W. Oscar Thoresen, Royal Norwegian Navy, during his service in Australia since February, 1942. The excellent record of the NORWEGIAN Merchant Navy in Australian waters during this period has been an important factor in the conduct of the war. . . The efficiency of that Service and the absence of industrial trouble has been in large measure due to the personal efforts and ability of Commander Thoresen.

References

1   At the Oxford colloquium, Sir Robin Maxwell-Hyslop pointed out that many other
    nationalities, apart from the Norwegians, were integrated in the Royal Navy. Six
    nations were under the command of his father, Captain A.H. Maxwell-Hyslop, at
    Devonport. The Norwegian had two particular advantages: they were used to
    rough seas (unlike the Poles), and a much higher proportion spoke English.
2   Winston S. Churchill, *The Second World War*, vol. V, *Closing the Ring* (London,
    1952), p. 6

9 The build-up and operations of the Royal Norwegian Navy in the period 1940–5

BAARD HELLE

Background

ON 17 May each year Norway celebrates its national holiday. At this time in 1940 the southern half of Norway was occupied by the advancing German military forces. The northern half of the country was still in Norwegian hands. Allied forces including quite a considerable force from the Royal Navy took part in the defence of Northern Norway. On that day, 17 May, the King of Norway delivered a speech to his nation from the only free broadcasting station left in Norway – the station in the town of Tromsø. The King, himself a naval officer, thanked all those who had done their utmost during the past weeks to detain and stop the intruding enemy. To the Norwegian navy he said: 'I want to convey a special thanks to our navy for its war efforts. Its operations have been fully equal to its best traditions and are highly appreciated by our allies.' Thus the cooperation between the two navies started, albeit on a small scale, during the Norwegian campaign. However, hardly anyone at that time could have foreseen that the cooperation would be developed much further and would last throughout the five years of war.

The close links between the two countries were of course founded on the overall political and military agreements of the two governments. However, the very close cooperation that developed between the two navies was first and foremost based on mutual professional respect and confidence. This made it possible to achieve practical arrangements within the operational, administrative, educational and logistical sectors of the two navies in a short time. What was most important in this connection was the fact that the combatant units of the Royal Norwegian Navy soon proved their operational efficiency and trustworthiness in war. The following extract from a message to its Commander-in-Chief, sent by the Admiralty after the end of the war in Europe, illustrates the good standing of the Norwegian navy:

> Now when the end of organized resistance in Europe has marked the triumph of the allied forces, the Board of Admiralty wish to express their deeply felt admiration for the heroic services that the Royal Norwegian

Navy have rendered the allied cause in the war at sea. The results achieved are paid for with hard work, grievance, set backs and losses. On behalf of all ranks in the Royal Navy and the Royal Marines, the Board of Admiralty wish to express its sympathy towards officers and men of the Royal Norwegian Navy over the loss of their courageous comrades.

The rebuilding of a combatant navy

The war in Norway, which lasted for two months, came to an end. The King and his government left Norway on board HMS *Devonshire* on 7 June 1940. The fight for freedom was to continue from Great Britain. A nation of fewer than three million people could of course not afford to have a large navy. In addition there was the fact that Norway, like many other nations in Europe, had neglected its defence forces for years. Thirteen naval ships, most of them very old, together with about 400 officers, petty officers and men left for Britain with the King and his government. This was the beginning of a new Norwegian navy capable of making its fair contribution to the struggle for freedom. Of the thirteen ships only one, a small destroyer, was fairly modern (launched in 1936). The other destroyer was hopelessly old, having been launched in 1908! The other ships were patrol vessels and fishery protection vessels.

The Norwegian naval headquarters was established in London in June 1940. Priority was given to the task of rebuilding and manning a new combatant navy capable of taking an effective part in the war at sea against Germany. The work towards this goal was started in close cooperation with British naval authorities, first and foremost the Admiralty who always gave positive and wholehearted support, particularly as time passed and the different Norwegian naval units proved their operational capacity in the war at sea.

Most of the previously mentioned thirteen ships were partly re-equipped and put into useful service in British waters during the summer and autumn of 1940. For example the small but relatively modern destroyer HNMS *Sleipner* was incorporated into the Rosyth Escort Forces, whose mission was to protect the coastal convoys. The operational area stretched from Greenock to the Thames around the north coast of Scotland. This was *Sleipner*'s main task until 1944–5. During these years she escorted 156 convoys and was involved many times in actions against enemy attacks. During the critical years of 1940–1 even the very old destroyer mentioned earlier became useful in the strained defence of Britain. First she served as depot ship in Portsmouth for the two newly commissioned Norwegian torpedo boats. Then she was deployed to Lowestoft and served as guard destroyer and coastal convoy escort in the English Channel. When the threat of invasion was over, she returned to Port Edgar and served for the rest of the war mainly as depot ship for Norwegian naval personnel.

The two Norwegian MTBs ('5' and '6') were, as Commodore Schau's paper points out, actually the first combatant ships commissioned for the

Royal Norwegian Navy in Britain. They operated in the Channel from early summer 1940 as part of the British 11th MTB Flotilla. Enemy activity, which at this time was very intensive, kept the MTBs busy in operations of different kinds: fighting off E-boat attacks, torpedo attacks on enemy ships, protecting own convoys, rescue operations etc. Towards the end of 1940 the MTB '6' sprang a leak in heavy weather and had to be abandoned. In July 1941 the other Norwegian MTB was destroyed by an explosion while in Dover harbour. These were the first losses the new Norwegian navy suffered. More were to come as time went on and the navy acquired more ships and took part in operations on a much wider scale than hitherto. These losses came in addition to the rather heavy losses our navy suffered during the war in Norway.

By this time, however, five new and bigger MTBs formed the Norwegian MTB Flotilla Portsmouth. These boats were not very seaworthy and were therefore taken out of offensive service by midsummer 1942. They were replaced with bigger and better boats (Fairmale 'D' class). Eight boats formed the 30th MTB Flotilla which was deployed in November 1942 to Lerwick in the Shetland Islands. From this base very daring, but successful, offensive operations started against German shipping along the western coast of Norway. These are discussed under 'Northern Atlantic and the North Sea' operations below (pp. 79–80).

The remaining eleven naval ships which were evacuated from Norway were, as indicated earlier, re-equipped and put into useful service again during the years 1940–1. A Minesweeping Flotilla was established, trained and thereafter deployed to Dundee in Scotland. This flotilla was later reinforced by other Norwegian minesweepers and did a very good job throughout the war in clearing the coastal convoy routes of mines. The Norwegian naval authorities wanted more modern and bigger combatant ships transferred to our navy. However, at this critical period of the war (1940–1) the Royal Navy itself suffered from material shortage and naturally had no modern ships to transfer.

On the other hand, the British naval authorities requested the Norwegian navy to help fill 'gaps' as there was a general shortage of minesweepers, patrol vessels and auxiliaries for different types of naval service. Norway could actually make a contribution from the large Norwegian whaling fleet which was in the Antarctic at the time of Germany's invasion of Norway. These numerous whalers were sturdy and seaworthy ships of 300–500 tons. They were well suited for conversion to minesweepers, patrol vessels, escort vessels and different types of naval auxiliaries. A large number of these ships was requisitioned by the Norwegian government. To begin with, sixteen were converted to minesweepers and patrol vessels manned by the Norwegian navy. Forty-nine were transferred to the Royal Navy; some of these were later reinstated in the Norwegian navy.

A training camp for the crews to man the ships was established in Lunenburg, Canada. Later on more whaling vessels were commissioned for the Royal Norwegian Navy and served throughout the war in different waters: minesweeping in the Persian Gulf, the Suez Canal, the inner Mediterranean and along the southern and eastern coast of Great Britain. Whalers converted to patrol and escort vessels could be seen at work from Gibraltar in the south to

Iceland in the north and the Irish Sea in the west. These naval ships also carried out missions involving special expeditions to Spitsbergen, Jan Mayen and Greenland as well as a few clandestine operations to Norway.

Status and operations from the turn of the year 1942–3

The regular combatant navy had grown steadily. By the turn of the year 1942–3 the Royal Norwegian Navy consisted of more than 5,000 officers, petty officers and men. The total number of units under the Norwegian naval ensign had increased to 58. The fleet then consisted of destroyers, corvettes, submarines, subchasers, patrol and escort vessels, minesweepers, motor launches and auxiliary vessels. The following is a short review at this stage of the war of some of the operational activities in which different categories of Norwegian naval ships played a role.

The Atlantic

At the turn of the year 1942–3, two destroyers, four corvettes and three patrol/escort vessels were engaged in the Battle of the Atlantic. The ships, with the exception of one of the destroyers, were part of the Liverpool Escort Forces under command of the C-in-C Western Approaches. One destroyer was part of the Western Local Escort Force, Halifax. Of the 50 ex-US 'Town' class destroyers transferred to the Royal Navy in 1940, five were taken over by the Norwegian navy. For a certain period the Norwegian part of the Liverpool Escort Forces consisted of five destroyers, four corvettes and three patrol/escort vessels. However, by the turn of the year 1942–3 only two destroyers were left in our navy. One had been sunk in August 1941 by German torpedoes when escorting a convoy to Gibraltar; 89 of her crew were killed. Two had been returned to the Royal Navy and were decommissioned. In the period from August 1941 to January 1942 the Royal Norwegian Navy commissioned five new corvettes of the 'Flower' class. By the turn of the year 1942–3 they were veterans in the fierce Battle of the Atlantic. One was torpedoed in the Atlantic in November 1942 with the loss of 47 of her crew. One sank in the Atlantic in 1944 after a collision with a destroyer, and one struck a mine off the coast of Finnmark (Northern Norway) and sank shortly afterwards in December 1944. However, the heavy losses were compensated for. The Norwegian corvettes either damaged or were directly credited with sinking several German U-boats.

The spirit and operational efficiency of the Norwegian corvettes were honourably mentioned many times. In a message sent in November 1942, for example, the C-in-C Western Approaches stated: 'The senior officer of the escort, the commanding officer of the *Potentilla*, is to be warmly congratulated on his successful handling of the escort.' The convoy in question was ONS 144 consisting of 33 ships. It was escorted by four Norwegian and one British corvette. The commanding officer of the escort was the captain of HNMS

Potentilla. After four days the corvettes were reinforced by the Norwegian destroyer *St. Albans*. This westbound convoy was attacked again and again over a period of five days. It was later estimated that the attackers consisted of a pack of six U-boats. During this convoy battle the Norwegian corvette *Montbretia* was sunk after two torpedo hits. C-in-C Western Approaches reported to the Admiralty: 'The loss of this gallant ship which had played such a distinguished part in recent convoy battles, will be greatly felt in both navies.'

The English Channel

Two modern 'Hunt' class destroyers, HNMS *Glaisdale* and HNMS *Eskdale*, entered service in mid-1942. Both were deployed to Portsmouth where they joined four British 'Hunt' class destroyers to form the 1st Destroyer Flotilla. The tasks of this flotilla were offensive operations against enemy shipping and enemy naval activity along the coast of France, escorting convoys, protecting minesweeping and minelaying operations, and in general patrolling the Channel waters to prevent enemy E-boats attacking own shipping. The Norwegian destroyers operated as part of 1st Destroyer Flotilla for a rather long period. They participated in a number of battles against enemy forces and had their share of destroying and damaging German ships, as well as suffering damage and loss themselves. The *Eskdale* was hit by two torpedoes and sunk as a result of several German E-boat attacks on a convoy on 14 April 1943. Twenty-five of her complement of 180 perished. However, months before this, in connection with the Allied landings in North Africa in November 1942, the two Norwegian destroyers were busy escorting convoys to and from the landing areas. It was an extra satisfaction to escort Norwegian merchant ships as about 30 of them were part of the first convoys to supply the landing forces.

The lost destroyer *Eskdale* was not replaced by another 'Hunt' class destroyer until December 1944. HNMS *Arendal* was, however, deployed to Harwich as part of the 16th Destroyer Flotilla. HNMS *Glaisdale* continued her war efforts as part of the 1st Destroyer Flotilla, Portsmouth to be described later. She participated successfully in the Normandy landings on D-day. Unfortunately she struck a mine and was badly damaged some time later off the coast of Normandy.

The 2nd Minesweeping Division, consisting of five Norwegian minesweepers, had been deployed to Plymouth and Falmouth in 1941. Its mission was to keep the convoy routes free of mines and also to sweep channels in enemy minefields when necessary to help secure safe passage for own forces on offensive operations along the French coast. The units were also frequently used as additional escort vessels for coastal convoys in the Channel area. In February 1943 the number of vessels in the 2nd Minesweeping Division was reduced to four. One of the vessels was torpedoed by a German E-boat, and 22 of the complement of 24 were killed.

Another separate Norwegian naval unit, the 4th Motorlaunch Flotilla, was operating in the Channel at the turn of the year 1942–3. The flotilla was originally formed in 1940. Later, in April 1941, the number of boats was increased from four to eight. For a short period, from July to September 1941, the flotilla was transferred to Iceland (Reykjavik) to cover the need for air/sea rescue duties there. The rough weather in this area proved unsuitable for these craft and they returned to Channel duties. In May 1942 the number of boats in the flotilla was again reduced to four. All of them were now equipped for minelaying and renamed the 52nd ML Flotilla. Together with the British 50th ML Flotilla they successfully carried out offensive minelaying along the coast of Northern France, Belgium and the Netherlands. The flotillas suffered the loss of ships and men. However, replacements were received, and on D-day 6 June 1944 the two flotillas were busy laying smokescreens and artificial fog to protect the invasion fleet.

East Coast of Great Britain

As previously mentioned, a small but relatively modern Norwegian destroyer, HNMS *Sleipner*, continued to carry out her convoy escort duties along the coast. Now, at the turn of 1942–3, the Norwegian minesweepers deployed to Dundee, Scotland consisted of seven ships forming the 1st Minesweeping Division. This division carried out most of the minesweeping duties off the eastern coast of Scotland. They continued thus until the end of the war. The division lost a ship in March 1945 when a U-boat torpedoed one of the minesweepers on duty off Dundee. Five of the crew were killed and five wounded.

Northern Atlantic and the North Sea

As mentioned earlier, the Norwegian Naval Independent Unit based in the Shetland Islands carried out their clandestine operations on the coast of Norway. Their naval colleagues manning the ships of the 30th MTB Flotilla (later renamed 54th MTB Flotilla) had their base not far away at Lerwick. The MTBs' offensive operations against German shipping along the western coast of Norway developed very satisfactorily. Their main enemies were the German escorts and the stormy and rough weather encountered in the North Sea at that time of year. However, the success of these operations depended on using the dark season of the year. This period offered the best chances of slipping unnoticed into the inner sailing leads along the coast. Very often the MTBs would lie for days in camouflaged positions in the inner leads waiting for a suitable target to attack.

The number of operational boats in the flotilla varied from eight to eleven. Wear and tear as well as battle and storm damage meant that boats had to be withdrawn from time to time and replaced by new boats. A total of 21 Fairmale 'D' class boats saw wartime service on the coast of Norway. From the start of these operations in November 1942 until the end of the war, a total of 161 operations on the coast of Norway were carried out, resulting in the sinking of

20 merchant ships and the destruction of seven enemy naval ships. The flotilla had of course its painful losses. However, they were relatively small compared with the enemy's loss of ships and men.

By the turn of the year 1942–3 the Norwegian navy had two submarines in commission. One was very old (launched in 1922) and was only useful for training purposes with the Asdic school of the 7th British Submarine Flotilla. The other, a British-built U-class was transferred to the Royal Norwegian Navy in December 1941. She was part of the 9th Submarine Flotilla and was fully operational in March 1942. Her operational area, and that of the two succeeding submarines, was to be the North Sea and the coastal waters of Norway. In addition to reporting and attacking German ships, the submarines also carried out a number of clandestine operations to and from Norway. The first submarine, *Uredd*, carried out seven missions successfully, but never returned from her eighth mission (February 1943). Long after the war the wreck was found in the waters south of the town of Bodø. She had sailed into a German minefield and had sunk with her crew of 33 as well as six agents who were to be landed in Norway.

At this time a second submarine had been commissioned for the Norwegian navy. She successfully carried out 14 operations before the end of the war. Our third submarine was operational in November 1944. She completed three missions before the war ended. In all, the three Norwegian submarines carried out 22 attacks on German ships, which resulted in the sinking of seven merchant ships, one naval escort and one German U-boat. In addition a 6,000-ton tanker was damaged. The results of attacks on two other U-boats and one merchant ship are unknown.

The Norwegian naval unit on Iceland consisted of seven patrol vessels. They were stationed there throughout the five years of war. In addition to their patrol and guard duties they carried out local escort and transportation duties of different kinds. Also special expeditions to Arctic areas were often the responsibility of this unit.

The sinking of the German battleship *Scharnhorst*

A modern 'S' class destroyer, HNMS *Stord*, was transferred to the Norwegian navy in August 1943. She was deployed to Scapa Flow and joined the Royal Naval Home Fleet's 51st Destroyer Flotilla (later the 23rd Destroyer Flotilla). The *Stord*, commanded by Lt.Cdr. Skule Storheil, played a gallant part in the pursuit and sinking of the German battleship *Scharnhorst* on 26 December 1943. In winter darkness and stormy weather the *Scharnhorst* met her destiny 60 nautical miles off the North Cape. *Stord* was one of the four 'S' class destroyers ordered to obtain an advantageous position for firing torpedoes. After more than two hours using maximum speed, she and the RN destroyer *Scorpion* fired their torpedoes from an easterly direction. When *Stord* fired her eight torpedoes she was about 1,500 yards from the *Scharnhorst*. Her artillery also engaged the *Scharnhorst* and hits were observed. After the sea battle Admiral Fraser sent the following message to the Admiralty: 'Please convey to the C-in-C Norwegian navy. *Stord* played a very daring role in the fight and I am very proud of her.' In an interview in the *Evening News* on 5 January 1944 the statement of the commanding officer of H.M.S. *Duke of York* was: 'the Norwegian destroyer *Stord* carried out the most daring attack of the whole action.' Both before and after the sinking of the *Scharnhorst*, the *Stord*, as part of the Home Fleet, participated in the escort of many of the important convoys to Murmansk.

The invasion of Normandy

Early in the morning on 6 June 1944 amidst the great armada of ships were eleven Norwegian naval ships. The two 'S' class destroyers, one of them HNMS *Svenner* commissioned three months previously and one 'Hunt' class destroyer (the veteran *Glaisdale*) sailed to obtain their bombardment positions according to the pre-planned bombardment programme. However, shortly before arriving at her position *Svenner* was hit by a German torpedo. She broke in two and sank rapidly taking 34 of her crew down with her. She was the first casualty of the great D-Day armada. The other Norwegian ships like the rest of the invasion fleet carried out their duties successfully according to the operation orders. In the first wave of merchant ships carrying troops and supplies six were flying Norwegian flags. On the days following the landing, 43 more Norwegian ships helped to bring in more troops and supplies to the advancing Allied troops.

Another loss for the Norwegian navy was to come. On 26 June off the coast of Normandy *Glaisdale* struck a mine and was badly damaged. After having been towed back to base, she was later decommissioned and taken out of service for the remainder of the war. The *Glaisdale* up to this time had served with the 1st Destroyer Flotilla for two years. The captain of the flotilla very much wanted the complement to take over a new destroyer as soon as possible, reporting to C-in-C Portsmouth that they were 'a fine and efficient crew who have worked together so well in the past.'

The end of the war

In March 1945 the Royal Norwegian Navy commissioned the last four ships of the war. They were brand new, modern minesweepers which formed the 3rd Minesweeping Division operating from Cherbourg in France. On 7 May 1945 the division was sailing through the English Channel bound for Norway. In the evening one of the ships was torpedoed by the U-boat U-1023. This was the last ship lost by the Royal Norwegian Navy during the war. Twenty-two of a complement of 33 were killed. The very last torpedo to hit a Norwegian ship, however, did so some hours later just outside the Firth of Forth. A Norwegian and a Canadian merchant ship were sunk by U-boat U-2336. However, it could very well have been the Norwegian destroyer *Stord* instead, because minutes earlier she had passed that same area. The *Stord* was on her way from Scapa

Flow to Rosyth doing 30 knots in fine weather. Because of *Stord*'s high speed the U-boat was unable to manoeuvre into firing position. Instead, it attacked the outbound convoy from Methil. HNMS *Stord* searched the waters for U-boats that evening and night with negative results. Next morning she was ordered to Rosyth just in time for the complement to participate in the Victory Europe celebrations in Edinburgh on 8 May 1945.

One can grieve over the loss of life due to U-boat attacks in the evening of 7 May 1945 – even more so knowing that Admiral Doenitz had sent a signal to his U-boats as early as 4 May ordering them to stop all hostilities and sail for harbour. In addition it was already officially broadcast that unconditional surrender had been signed in General Eisenhower's HQ at 0241 7 May, even though the armistice should formally be in force as from 0001 9 May. Obviously some of the commanding officers of German submarines had either not received these orders and information, or had simply ignored them!

Conclusions

In spite of heavy losses, at the end of the war the Royal Norwegian Naval Fleet consisted of 51 combatant ships and about 7,500 officers, petty officers and men of whom about half were manning the combatant fleet. The others were manning staffs, training centres, depots and other types of support centres in Britain as well as other places in the world. During the war the navy lost 27 ships, excluding the losses in Norway in 1940. About 25 per cent of the men manning the Norwegian naval ships lost their lives during the war.

Cooperation with the Royal Navy had developed extremely well. As stressed before, this positive development was due to a mutual professional respect and trust in each other's efficiency, spirit and will to fight the common enemy. The following message from the C-in-C Home Fleet to the Norwegian Admiral Danielsen dated 13 May 1945 expresses very well the feelings between the two navies that had fought side by side throughout the war:

> On your return to Norway in H Nor MS *Stord* I should be grateful if you
> will convey to Lieutenant Commander Øi and to the officers and ships
> company my keen appreciation of the honour I feel in having had them
> under my command in the Home Fleet. Their efficiency and fine fighting
> spirit have been the admiration of us all and although we are glad that
> they now should be reaping the reward of their great contribution to the
> liberation of Europe we shall miss them in the Home Fleet. We hope that
> some of us may soon have the pleasure to renew our friendship in
> Norwegian port. To you personally I send my warm regards and sincere
> thanks for your helpful co-operation with me at the Admiralty. Good
> luck and happiness to you all.

10 The contribution of the Norwegian air forces

WILHELM MOHR

Introduction

FROM a small nucleus of servicemen who arrived in the UK after the campaign in Norway, the Navy and Army elements were soon enabled to establish a recruitment and training centre in Canada. Through this organisation flowed an increasing stream of aircrew and technicians to man newly-created Norwegian fighting units under the control of the Royal Air Force. In addition individual aircrew served in RAF squadrons of all commands, as well as in training elements and even on staff assignments. A special unit alongside the British Overseas Airways Corporation (BOAC) provided transport for Norwegian personnel to and from Sweden.

In May 1945 the numbers totalled 505 officers and 2,133 NCOs OR. In addition there were 63 Norwegian WAAFs. The Norwegian Air Forces represented, after Poland, the second largest of the Allied Air Forces established outside their own occupied country. Only after North Africa had been liberated did the French Air Force exceed that of Norway.

This paper deals with three phases in the development of the Norwegian air contribution to the Allied war effort:

1 The arrival of Norwegian air elements in Britain following the capitulation of Norway in 1940, and the early endeavours to establish identifiable Norwegian air units.
2 The deliberations in London between the Norwegian Armed Services, the Norwegian government and the British authorities; this phase includes the training centre established in Canada for the Norwegian Air Forces.
3 Operational aspects of the Norwegian Air Force Units and personnel serving with the Royal Air Force, and other Norwegian contributions to the air war.

1 The early endeavours

Before the war the Norwegian Army and Navy each had their own air forces. The remnants from both these forces arrived in the UK during and after the campaign in Norway. At the outset the naval side numbered 17 pilots, navigators and technical personnel who brought with them four Heinkel 115 reconnaissance/torpedo seaplanes, one of which was captured, and a captured German Arado Ar 196. From the Army some 60 trained pilots were available, including four with civil engineering background, plus some 25 mechanics, radio and armament specialists.

Prior to the war the Norwegian government had placed orders in the USA for a large number of modern, high-quality aircraft for both the Navy and the Army Air Forces, as well as a smaller number from Italy. The delivery of fighter aircraft from America had partly begun, though none was ready for use when the Germans attacked Norway and five *en route* were in crates in Britain. The contingent of personnel in Britain in the early summer of 1940 and the equipment that was under way formed the nucleus of a Norwegian air force that could continue the war outside the country. Meanwhile in Norway the war was still going on. It could no longer be sustained in South Norway, but the Norwegian Commander in Chief, General Otto Ruge, instructed Captain Bjarne Øen (the senior Army Air Force officer) to encourage trained personnel to go to the UK and seek whatever assistance might be available to re-establish fighter units for the Northern theatre.

I must insert a personal note here, because it actually fell to me at the time to obtain and carry these instructions to Captain Øen. I recollect from the conversation with General Ruge that he expressed doubts whether North Norway could be held at all for the length of time required, but emphasised for reasons of future national interest the importance that any national contribution to the war, whatever it achieved, be clearly identifiable.

At the beginning of the war the Norwegian legation in London had no military representation. In mid-April 1940 a post of military and naval attaché was created, and a month later a Military and Naval Mission was established. This mission became the intermediary between the British authorities and the very meagre Norwegian military headquarters of that time. The British first offered to have Norwegian pilots trained by the RAF in the same manner as their own 'Volunteer Reserves'. These pilots were then to be deployed into units already serving in North Norway, or earmarked for that theatre. Five pilots commenced such training.

Meanwhile the members of the Norwegian Naval Air service who had arrived in the UK with their aircraft had established themselves as a unit. Efforts were made to have this unit carry out operations with or within the British Fleet Air Arm. This was soon deemed impractical, mainly because of the type of aircraft involved. The element was therefore assigned to the RAF Experimental Establishment at Helensburgh in Scotland, but was later disbanded. (The aircraft were taken over by the RAF, and were flown by Norwegian crews in clandestine operations in North Africa, until destroyed by enemy air attacks on Malta.)

Captain Øen and his small staff now addressed themselves to the possible establishment of identifiable Norwegian air units that would either cooperate with the RAF, or be contained within it. It was soon made clear by the British that this was not feasible for a number of reasons: Norwegian equipment was not compatible with that of the RAF and furthermore depended on a cross-ocean supply line; no training facilities could be made available in the UK; and the looming invasion threat to the UK set limits to such efforts. An alternative solution was then sought vis-à-vis the French. They possessed

Curtiss P 36 fighters in their inventory and were interested in the other types of Norwegian aircraft as well. However, developments in France made this solution impossible and by this time the campaign in Norway had come to an end. The British enquired whether Norway would now let available pilots join British air units at the discretion of the British authorities. Pending a decision, the training that had already begun for the five pilots in the RAF was terminated.

The basis for these endeavours was set out in a memorandum dated 17 June 1940 by Captain Bjarne Øen. In this Captain Øen, following closely the view expressed by General Ruge, said:

> The arrangement now proposed by the British authorities must presumably be based on a voluntary acceptance by each pilot, but this may not be deemed a recommended solution to the Norwegian authorities. For the latter it must be considered of overriding importance to manifest towards the world and not least towards the people of Norway now under occupation, that the struggle be continued within a national framework. It is only in such perspective that our existence outside Norway can be justified. Seen from outside, nothing much will be gained by letting our people join individually within the Allied forces. It must be Norwegian units that can show our colours, and that will stand identifiable when victory comes and settlement takes place. The importance of this cannot be exaggerated and is deemed a necessity if we are to hope that the will of resistance shall be upheld by the people at home.

Naturally – and Captain Øen made the same point – the group of inactive pilots in London at the time were becoming frustrated and impatient. Their main wish was to get into the RAF and take their share in the war as soon as possible. Captain Øen concluded that, as France had now capitulated, Canada offered the only opportunity for Norway to establish a training base in order to raise identifiable Norwegian air units. The government of Norway was by this time established in London. Captain Øen's proposal, supported by the Army Command, was approved on 19 June. A similar arrangement for the training and furnishing of naval air units was also approved. An aide-mémoire reflecting this view was submitted to the British government on 10 July 1940.

It is fair to assume that the Norwegian proposal was not accepted by the British without reluctance. At the time the British wanted as many pilots as they could muster. Poles, Czechs, Belgians and Dutch were already in service. They did, however, acquiesce, whereupon the British Air Ministry gave the plan its full support.

All efforts were now focused on setting up a joint training establishment in Canada. This became known as 'Little Norway'. Rapid progress was made. The camp was erected adjacent to the Island Airport in the harbour area of Toronto. Elementary training aircraft were acquired and the operational aircraft on order, mentioned earlier, were delivered. The camp was inaugurated on 10 November 1940. Personnel at that time numbered about 300. Most of the student pilots had escaped from Norway via the UK or via Sweden and Russia (Siberia and the Pacific). Many of the technical trainees were selected from the Merchant Marine and they were indeed to become the backbone of the future Royal Norwegian Air Force. The clear objective was undoubtedly to bring fighting units forward at the earliest possible time.

2 Deliberations on further goals

In the meantime a joint HQ of the Army and Naval Air Force elements was formed in London, presenting itself as the 'Royal Norwegian Air Forces HQ' within the Norwegian Armed Forces structure. This was a practical measure for the benefit of its single Royal Air Force counterpart, the Air Ministry. It functioned as an amalgamation of the two elements into one single Service authority, although the organisational ratification of this change was not carried out until much later. This development did not signify that the RNAF HQ was independently free to deal with its corresponding British authority. (The same applies to the Navy and Army.)

There is little doubt that the British regarded Norway as an Allied nation. Our merchant fleet had already made an essential contribution to the war effort. Yet we provided no fighting elements. The Norwegian government on foreign soil must undoubtedly have felt its position of uncertainty and weakness, not least in regard to the occupied population left behind. Thus its first stumbling efforts might well have left the British uncertain whether a lingering attitude of ingrained Norwegian neutralism still prevailed. While these matters were deliberated on a political level, the established Norwegian Defence Staff increasingly asserted its position as a joint military planning authority. In accordance with government ambitions this pertained to acquiring national influence and participation in allied operations directed towards Norway, and in particular to the coordinating of forces outside Norway with resistance movements within the country. The overriding aim was to have maximum influence in the process that could bring about the liberation of Norway.

Although the practical issues of establishing Norwegian Armed Forces in Britain had already been set in motion, the formal Governmental Agreement to regulate the relationship was not drawn up until 28 May 1941. The gist of the Agreement lies in the formulation of Article 1 which reflects the unified policy mentioned above:

> The Norwegian Armed Forces in the United Kingdom shall be used
> either for the defence of the United Kingdom or for the purpose of
> regaining Norway. They shall be organised and employed under British
> Command as the Armed Forces of the Kingdom of Norway allied with
> the United Kingdom.

Thus the policy prevailed, though by their nature the Air Forces (and the Navy) came to acquire more freedom in its exercise than the Army. The question of command and control represented no specific problem, at least not for units of the Air Forces.

Norwegian recruits continued to flock to the training centre in Canada from all over the world. Even some Danes joined. The elementary training was followed up by practice on the available Curtiss, Douglas and Northrop aircraft. Soon arrangements were made through the RCAF to participate in the Empire Air Training Scheme, which then opened for Service Flying Training at Moose Jaw in Saskatchewan and Medicine Hat in Alberta. Norwegian instructors were provided in both places. The General Reconnaissance Course was made available for pilots and navigators, as well as courses for other aircrew categories as required. Basic technical training was done by ourselves while specialist application on type or function as required was to follow in the UK. As a finishing touch Norwegian pilots were given advanced flying training on the Curtiss and Douglas before they went overseas.

As the volume of flying training increased, it became practical in May 1942 to move the camp to Muskoka, about 100 miles north of Toronto. Recruitment of volunteer Norwegians and basic air force training continued here until the 'Farewell to Canada' ceremony took place on 16 February 1945. Training was then transferred to the UK. The reason for the transfer was the cost of the establishment, which on average had a strength of 700 personnel; and latterly most of the recruits were refugee Norwegians brought across to the UK from Sweden. At that time facilities for training were made available at RAF Station Winkleigh in North Devon.

3   Operational aspects

330 SQUADRON, COASTAL COMMAND

Because of the occupation of Norway, the strategic importance of the Northern waters and regions to the Battle of the Atlantic was highly accentuated. Even before North Norway fell, British forces had occupied Iceland and placed army and air forces there for its protection and to carry out sea and air operations. The last six months of 1940 had seen very large losses inflicted by the German submarines on merchant shipping and the threat seemed ever-increasing. In addition the cruiser *Scheer* was active, shortly after followed by the *Hipper*. Soon the battleships *Scharnhorst* and *Gneisenau* were expected to play their part.

In late 1940 discussions between the Commander of the joint Norwegian Air Forces HQ in London and the Air Ministry highlighted the value of using our 18 available Northrop seaplanes in support of the Coastal Command activities in Icelandic waters. The tasks were to be maritime reconnaissance, control and search, anti-submarine operations, convoy escort, transport and any other defence support needed for Iceland proper that might arise.

The first contingent of the squadron arrived in Iceland from the UK on 12 April 1941, followed some months later by personnel from 'Little Norway'. This brought the strength to about 200. At that time the aircraft were transported by ship and, although 41 ships had been sunk in the Atlantic that month, they all arrived safely. The formidable task of assembling the aircraft from crates and bringing them into use must be recorded. On 23 June 1941, 330 became the first operational Norwegian squadron established outside the country. It also became the largest of the Allied air units stationed in Iceland.

As only one airfield existed on the island (near Reykjavik), the seaplane squadron was split into three parts: 'A' flight was to remain in Fossvagur near Reykjavik, which was also the site of the squadron HQ; 'B' flight was to be located at Akureyri to the north, and 'C' flight at Budareyri on the east coast. 'C' flight in particular suffered from extreme weather conditions as well as the difficulties of the surrounding steep and mountainous terrain.

From the outset 330 (N) Squadron concentrated primarily on the Battle of the Atlantic. After the Soviet Union had come into the war in July 1941, the defence of convoys to and from Murmansk made Iceland even more important. 'B' and 'C' flights were well situated to combat German air reconnaissance that would alert their submarines, and to do extensive escort duties. 'A' and 'B' flights could cover the Denmark Strait in particular for the same purpose and were also able to attack surface ships and submarines heading for the Atlantic. By the end of 1941, 330 Squadron numbered a total of 309 personnel, 25 of whom were British who catered mainly for communications and intelligence.

The Northrop aircraft stood up remarkably well under the most severe conditions of Icelandic climate and winter darkness, though it soon became evident from the tasks allotted that longer range and better armoury were required, and that two engines, de-icing equipment and better navigation facilities would be most desirable. Therefore in June 1942 Coastal Command provided two Consolidated Catalina for the squadron on loan, and in July and August a further three were added. These were also required because by this time the Northrop strength had been reduced by losses to 13. The personnel strength of the squadron was adjusted accordingly.

In mid-1942, after about a year of operations the squadron on Iceland had accomplished approximately 7,500 flying hours, and conducted 246 submarine searches, 379 convoy escorts, 250 reconnaissance flights and 18 ambulance flights. 15 submarines had been detected and forced to submerge; nine had been attacked of which seven sustained damages. Eight reconnaissance aircraft had been engaged and damaged. The squadron's losses amounted to ten Northrops and two Catalinas, with altogether 21 aircrew personnel. The weather not only affected the aircrews' operational tasks but also posed exceedingly harsh conditions for the aircraft servicing personnel, who to a large extent had to work outside on small tenders day and night. In both respects the squadron received full credit from the RAF.

As the struggle for the Atlantic progressed, the USA had increasingly extended its support with bases for escort groups and aircraft. Eventually this included Iceland. Thus the Coastal Command there was relieved and at the end of 1942 it was decided that 330 Squadron was to move to Oban in Scotland. There it would come under 15 Group Command and be equipped with Sunderlands. This big four-engined flying boat fully equipped required a crew of 10. In January 1943 the squadron departed from Iceland, leaving a contingent of Northrops for a time at Budareyri to guard the east coast.

After intensive training the first operations from Oban were carried out on 20 April, thus bringing the squadron back into the Battle of the Atlantic which was now at its peak. The squadron still supported the anti-submarine operations generally. However, the distance to areas further north was deemed too long and impractical. The stay at Oban was therefore short and the next base was Sullom Voe in Shetland. By 14 July the whole squadron of 13 aircraft was in place and could start operations, now under 18 Group Command. It welcomed the opportunity to operate towards and along the Norwegian coast. The extended range of the Sunderlands allowed the Murmansk convoys to be escorted far to the north and east in the Arctic Ocean. Such missions could be both demanding and tedious, but they formed a critical part of the ships' protection against submarine attacks. The weather in Shetland could be as harsh as that experienced in Iceland. Though better facilities existed in the harbour, 'gale-crews' often had to be kept on board the big flying boats to avoid disaster.

330 Squadron remained at Sullom Voe until the end of the war. With its Sunderlands it accomplished over 12,000 flying hours, and conducted 655 submarine searches, over 50 convoy escorts and 22 different rescue tasks. Fifteen submarines were seen, of which two were sunk and four damaged. Two German aircraft were damaged. Four of the squadron's aircraft were lost with a total of 46 personnel. In total the squadron lost 16 aircraft with 63 personnel.

331 AND 332 SQUADRONS IN FIGHTER COMMAND

By the spring of 1941 the training in Canada of pilots and ground crew had reached the stage where a first fighter squadron could be transferred and stationed in the United Kingdom. On 21 July 1941 331 Squadron was established at RAF Station Catterick under 12 Group, Fighter Command. In September of the same year another contingent of ground crew was transferred, which together with pilots, some of whom had already seen service in Fighter Command, made up the second squadron. This became 332 (N) Squadron, established on 21 January 1942, also at Catterick. Before 332 arrived, 331 had been moved first to the northern base of Castletown (North Scotland) and then to Skeabrae (Orkneys). On 4 May 1942 it was transferred south to RAF Station North Weald, by Epping, under 11 Group of Fighter Command. On 19 June 332 followed, and for the rest of the war the two Norwegian squadrons operated together.

331 (N) Squadron was equipped at the outset with Hawker Hurricane Mark I and shortly after obtained Mark II B. It became operational at Castletown (North Scotland) on 10 September with the primary task of providing air defence for the naval base at Scapa Flow. It also offered general convoy protection in adjacent coastal waters. To accommodate this task better the squadron was soon moved to Skeabrae – a 'difficult' and harsh airfield

where single engine operations were made more difficult by the darkness during winter and the frequent strong winds and icing conditions. Clouds unfortunately often let the enemy hide before intercepts could be accomplished. To improve coverage the squadron used to hold detachments at Sunburgh Head (Shetlands), Dyce and Peterhead (North Scotland). In November 1941 Spitfire II As replaced the Hurricanes and, as the serviceability of the squadron's aircraft had proved to be high, these were again changed for factory-new Spitfire VBs with 20 mm cannons. This was done before the squadron was ordered south to North Weald.

332 (N) Squadron at Catterick began using Spitfire II and then, like 331, changed to Spitfire VB. The squadron did mostly convoy protection and occasional air defence interceptions, partly operating out of West Hartlepool. Here the first success and the first loss were registered before the squadron joined 331 at North Weald on 19 June.

Once the Battle of Britain (August–October 1940) and the Blitz (September 1940–May 1941) were over, Fighter Command turned to offensive strategy, in cooperation with Bomber Command which so far had represented the offensive part of RAF operations. Soon the US 8 Air Force joined in with its day operations. Germany and the Luftwaffe were not to be given peace at any time. In general the task of the air offensive was to cause damage to the German war potential; in particular to cause losses to the Luftwaffe and tie up its forces in Western Europe in order to relieve the Eastern Front after Germany had attacked the USSR. Simultaneously it was to cause damage to the industries of France, Belgium and Holland that worked for Germany and to the communications in these countries that supported the German war effort.

THE NORWEGIAN WING IN FIGHTER COMMAND

Statistics pertaining to the Norwegian Wing in 11 Group are satisfying. From a total of 69 fighter squadrons in South England at the time they show the best record of serviceable aircraft, the highest number of flying hours, both in operations and training, and the lowest number of accidents per month and per flying hour. In addition, soon after their arrival, the Norwegians were placed best or among the best in numbers of German aircraft shot down and damaged per month. The RAF expressed its recognition by placing the squadrons among the first to receive upgraded aircraft and equipment as these became available, for example the fitting of giro gunsights.

Naturally the success of the squadrons was given due recognition by the Norwegian military and political authorities in London. But it was also recognised that the operations of that time, apart from air defence, standing patrols and convoy protection – i.e. all the offensive tasks – did not conform with the Governmental Agreement of 28 May 1941. This divergency in employment became all the more evident when the RAF urged that the fighter squadrons be included in the Tactical Air Force, which was in preparation prior to the invasion of the Continent (Operation *Overlord*). The Tactical Air Force was to comprise the major part of Fighter Command squadrons together with squadrons from No. 2 Group of Bomber Command. The Norwegian Wing was to form part of 84 Group linked to the 1st Canadian Army.

At this time the Norwegian Air Forces HQ was preparing for a third fighter squadron to be part of the existing wing. This must be judged in the context of the central Norwegian joint defence planning. The government had ambitions to establish forces that could join with forces being raised in Sweden. It was hoped that these would unite with the resistance groups in Norway and form a national contingent to liberate the country. This force would require air elements. In this respect the British authorities gave very little hope that any outside forces might be diverted from the main Allied task that lay ahead. On the Norwegian side the hope was nourished that the Fighter Wing of three squadrons could be equipped with Mustangs, which had a greater range than Spitfires and could be deployed from a base in Scotland.

Although the above is known, it has not been possible to document the discussions that must have taken place between the Norwegian Defence Staff, the Norwegian Air Forces HQ and the Air Ministry on this issue; an issue which must be considered rather unrealistic in view of the urgent priority for long-range escorts for the day bombers over Germany. There has been recorded, however, in regard to the Norwegian Wing in the Tactical Air Force, a calculation made by the Air Ministry that pilot losses in the invasion and the months ahead would considerably exceed those experienced so far. The approximately 750 ground crew would likewise be exposed. This led to an alternative proposal by Norway that the third squadron, in accordance with the Governmental Agreement, be established as part of the air defence forces in the UK. In the end the Air Ministry proposal for the Norwegian Wing prevailed, apparently accepted without any expressions to the contrary except that the question of a third Fighter Squadron was deferred.

The Norwegian concurrence must be deemed pragmatic as well as tolerant, though hardly popular in all of the national policy-making circles. It departed from the original Governmental Agreement yet there no longer existed a threat to Britain. It is of interest to note that the name of Norway in regard to *Overlord* is not to be found. The Wing received the decision to be part of the Tactical Air Force enthusiastically while regretting that an additional squadron was not to be formed.

One effect of the curtailed build-up was a gradual surplus of new pilots who were frustrated by being kept out of action. Eventually they were assigned to the Wing from which, to some extent, seasoned pilots were made available for other RAF squadrons.

In preparation for the invasion the Tactical Wing, called at first No. 132 (N) Airfield, was established on 1 November 1943. It formed an independent fully mobile unit, containing all the elements necessary to serve the deployed squadrons. In March 1944 it was enlarged by the addition of RAF 66 Squadron, which was supported mainly by Norwegian servicing crews. Some British Signal and Intelligence elements were also added. 132 (N) Airfield thus comprised about 70 per cent Norwegian and 30 per cent British personnel, and a joint command structure was established. Before the invasion two RAF Regiment squadrons were attached for the purpose of local air and ground defence. In July 1944 an additional RAF Squadron, No. 127, joined the 132 (N) Airfield, now termed 132 (N) Wing. The events and the variety of operations of the campaign into Europe, leading from France through Belgium into Holland, are beyond the scope of this paper. The last day of operations was 21 April 1945. The two Norwegian squadrons were then withdrawn from 2 ATAF and, leaving all equipment behind, were transferred to 11 Group Fighter Command where they were re-equipped in preparation for possible deployment in Norway. On 4 May the Germans capitulated, but the situation as regards Norway remained uncertain until 7 May. By then the Norwegian servicing echelons of the Wing were on the move towards the UK where they were also re-equipped. 36 Spitfires crossed to Norway from Dyce on 22 May; the ground personnel with their equipment followed by sea.

To sum up, 331 and 332 Squadrons of the Norwegian Wing within Fighter Command and 2nd Tactical Air Force were credited by the RAF with 180½ enemy aircraft destroyed, 25½ probably destroyed and 123 damaged, together with the destruction of much enemy equipment on the ground. The losses in operations were 72 killed, 11 held as prisoners of war (1 repatriated). Two were shot trying to escape – and as a point of interest two of the three prisoners from the Big Escape who succeeded were from the Norwegian Wing.

333 SQUADRON

In accordance with Norwegian ambitions, a unit of seaplanes was desired to operate along the coastlines and in the fjords for transporting personnel, picking up saboteurs, reconnaissance, and making attacks on shipping and submarines. The idea was supported by Coastal Command, but was initially held back by the Air Ministry until 8 February 1942 when the 'Norwegian detachment' of RAF 210 Squadron was based at Woodhaven by the Firth of Tay near Dundee. The element operated Catalina flying boats. After a year of operations and in recognition of its valuable special operations, the detachment was singled out on 1 January 1943 as a separate 1477 (Norwegian) Flight. It consisted of three Catalinas with Norwegian aircrew and servicing personnel.

Ever since the autumn of 1940 the Norwegian Air Forces HQ had pressed for the capability to attack targets along the Norwegian coast and inside Norway. The opportunity came when Coastal Command supported the use of Norwegian aircrew for such tasks. In April 1943 five Mosquitos were made available on loan, plus additional aircraft for training purposes. On the addition of another Mosquito, a separate flight was formed alongside that of the Catalina flight.

On 10 May 1943 the two flights became the 333 (Norwegian) Squadron, operationally under No. 18 Group of Coastal Command. The Mosquito operating base was RAF Station Leuchars, while the Catalinas remained at Woodhaven. Both flights were very active. The Catalinas provided a valuable means of communication to and from Norway. They also carried out anti-submarine operations, as did 330 and other Coastal Command squadrons, in the sea area between the Faeroes and Iceland, called 'Rosengarten' by the Germans. Because of the performance of the Mosquitos and the use of surprise, various new tasks were made possible. It became evident, however, that the required training for conversion to the Mosquito had been based rather too much on Norwegian impatience and over-confidence and British trust. Although there was some initial success, undue losses caused Coastal Command to enforce a temporary non-operational status for intensive training purposes. The results were encouraging and by mid-November 1943 the flight was again made operational.

The time that followed was mainly devoted to reconnaissance along the Norwegian coast, attacking German aircraft and ships, and searching for submarines that to a large extent depended on the North Sea. After the invasion of the Continent, some Coastal Command aircraft that had previously been employed in the Bay of Biscay and the English Channel were transferred to 18 Group Banff and Gallachy for strike operations against German ships along the Norwegian coast. The Norwegian Mosquitos were then deployed to Banff to assist this RAF strike force, either as 'outriders' for target search and identification, or as a guiding element for the strike itself. On such operations the crew's intimate knowledge of geography and conditions proved to be most valuable.

333 squadron ('A' and 'B' flights) was credited by the RAF with four submarines sunk, eight damaged, 18 German aircraft destroyed and two damaged. It performed 22 special missions to Norway and North Russia. Twenty-eight members of the aircrew were lost, and four taken prisoner.

R(NO)AF/45 GROUP, TRANSPORT COMMAND

The RAF had established its Ferry Command (later named Transport Command) in July 1941 at Dorval Airport in Montreal, Canada. The task was primarily to freight two- and four-engined aircraft from Canada and the USA to theatres of war on a world-wide basis. In late 1941 four Norwegian pilots formed a unit that in time came to number about 40 personnel. The unit was termed 'R(No)AF/45 Group'. Experienced pilots, navigators, wireless operators, mechanics, instructors, meteorologists and air traffic controllers made up the personnel. Many pilots and aircrew members served in the unit during periods of rest from other operational flying.

At the beginning of 1942 the aircraft commonly ferried were the Hudson, Lodestar and Venturas. The usual route taken was Gander or Goose Bay, Greenland, Iceland and Prestwick. Some B-24 Liberators went by Gander and Prestwick to the Far East. B-25 Mitchells, A-20 Bostons and B-26 Marylands were added, also C-47 Dakotas, Catalina PBYs, Lancasters, and Mosquitos. Altogether 690 aircraft were delivered overseas that had either a Norwegian crew or had individual Norwegian members as part of the crew. The losses amounted to five persons. Of the occupied countries only Poland was more strongly represented in Transport Command than Norway.

Norwegians serving in British units

BOMBER COMMAND

Aircrew members of the Norwegian Air Forces were admitted into Bomber Command from October 1942. Throughout the war 60
Norwegians flew on 4-engined aircraft ('heavies'). Of these 22 became Captains (skippers). The crew otherwise were generally a mixture of British, Commonwealth and Norwegian personnel. Nine of the 22 skippers completed the full 'operational tour' of 30. Two made one tour as navigators and then another tour as pilot/skippers. After the full tour two became Flight Commanders (one on the Pathfinder Force). One was skipper on the Mitchell two-engined bomber of RAF 180 Squadron (Two Group), and became Flight Commander. Losses amounted to 13 of the skippers and 29 of the other crew members. In addition five were taken prisoner of war.

Within the framework of Bomber Command, the 'Special Duties' consisted of two squadrons of RAF Bomber Command operating out of Tempsford. The task was to serve the underground forces in occupied countries either by airdropping personnel and supplies, or delivering or picking up agents. One Norwegian served as skipper and Flight Commander in 161 Squadron after a full tour in Bomber Command. Another, with a Norwegian navigator, completed a tour on drop-service with Halifax, then continued on delivery and pick-up service with Lysanders, mainly into France.

FIGHTER COMMAND

Many Norwegian pilots and navigators served at various periods in different RAF Fighter Squadrons. Three of these were given the function of Wingleaders ('Wingco/flying'). Four became Squadron Commanders and two Flight Commanders. In total Norwegians in British squadrons of Fighter Command have been accredited with 58 aircraft destroyed, 4 probably destroyed, 17 damaged plus a variety of ground targets engaged. In addition a number of Norwegian pilots in the course of service with RAF in Fighter Command held temporary positions in gunnery weapon training units and even had duties in operational staff. Losses amounted to 41 personnel.

The RAF No. 604 and the 85 Mosquito night fighter squadrons attracted many Norwegian aircrew members. These squadrons were at first part of the air defence force of Southern England. Prior to the invasion the squadrons were transferred to Bomber Command with the primary task of night intruder, to offer protection to the bomber stream and to attack selected targets in Germany or enemy-held territory. Altogether fifteen Norwegian aircrew members followed 85 Squadron. As a small intermezzo the squadron was brought back into Fighter Command; Norwegian aircrews accounted for eleven flying bombs.

THE 'STOCKHOLM ELEMENT'

This contingent was a separate Norwegian war effort in an area of prime national interest. It is recorded in this paper although, while assistance was rendered by operational control, it was not subordinated to any of the RAF Commands.

Air transport was required between the UK and Sweden because of the great number of refugees. By January 1941 2,851 such refugees were registered. After Germany attacked Russia, this avenue of escape was no longer available. At the same time the demands on the Norwegian forces in the UK were ever-increasing. After some endeavours to establish a separate arrangement, an agreement was reached by which BOAC allowed two Norwegian aircraft and crew to operate within its route concession between Stockholm and Leuchars. The arrangement began in the summer of 1941 although the final Anglo-Norwegian Governmental Agreement was first reached in midsummer 1942. Formally the Norwegian aircraft 'belonged' to BOAC and carried BOAC registration. The crew in BOAC uniform were paid by the company on a refund basis and carried British passports.

The Norwegian contingent was strengthened by four Lockheed Lodestars provided by the Norwegian government. Then three BOAC Lockheed Hudsons were added. However, as German defence became increasingly alerted to the activity and more effective, the Air Ministry in the spring of 1943 restricted the traffic to couriers for essential missions, using Mosquitos only. The passenger figures from Stockholm to Scotland by that time were in 1941 – 141; in 1942 – 559; in 1943 – 533.

The Norwegian authorities found, however, that transport flights for recruitment purposes were of such importance that another arrangement was essential. This was felt particularly by the Air Force which had already made arrangements to select candidates for pilot-training from refugees in Stockholm. In October 1943 an arrangement was established by which Norway would, independently but still within the BOAC structure, maintain the route to Stockholm using the Lockheed Lodestars. The British still provided airport and operating services out of Leuchars. This proved to be an effective arrangement and the traffic increased considerably. The number of passengers between Stockholm and Scotland is registered as 962 in 1944 and 1,114 up to 7 May 1945. In the last year of the war the Norwegian Air Force acquired under lend-lease 10 Douglas C 47 Dakotas, but these were introduced just as hostilities ceased. During the war 3,309 passengers were transported to the UK using the Stockholm route. The losses amounted to 11 aircrew and 18 passengers.

It is of interest to note that the Norwegian urge for transport for recruitment purposes, strongly supported by the British Foreign Secretary Anthony Eden, led to an American offer of assistance. This operation using four-engined Liberators transported 1,576 persons who had already been earmarked in Sweden for service in the Norwegian forces in the UK.

Closing remarks

Operational command by the RAF provided an effective and harmonious structure in which Norwegian fighting units and individuals could fulfil their aspirations, together with members of other Allied forces. It was marked by a friendly spirit, fairness and recognition of merit, appreciated by flying and ground crew alike. In the higher echelons of control – Norwegian Air Forces HQ in London and the Air Ministry – relations were sometimes more difficult, because political considerations, joint military planning and economic questions could complicate the use of Norwegian forces within the overall Allied war aims. Frank and open discussion, helped in my view by the generous attitude of the RAF, maintained a constructive atmosphere for solving any problems which arose. In this the traditionally close ties between our two countries may have played their part as certainly did the performance of our fighting elements.

In a message to the Norwegian Air Force at the end of the war, the RAF Air Council concluded:

> When your aircrews return to their own land, they will carry with them
> the good wishes and warm friendship of the Royal Air Force who
> earnestly hope that the links which have bound our two air forces in
> adversity and war will be maintained and developed in peace'.

It was not only the common cause and the sharing that had cemented our air forces. For the Norwegians in exile the RAF stations became their true home. This again led to the forging of many close and lasting links between the local population and our personnel of all categories and ranks. A sign of the relationship from our side may be judged by the large volume of membership of all branches held by the Norwegian branch of the Royal Air Force Association. The Royal Norwegian Air Force in its post-war structure owes a great deal to the example and traditions demonstrated by the Royal Air Force during the war.

11 Operation *Jupiter* and possible landings in Norway

H.P. WILLMOTT

> It is necessary to continue to press on with such preparations for operations on the continent this year [that] will
>
> (a) lead the enemy to think that we propose to attack this year and
>
> (b) not lead the Russians to think that there is no chance of our attacking this year.
> We are considering how these conflicting considerations can be reconciled.
>
> Memorandum of 7 July 1942 from British Chiefs of Staff to Churchill (PREM 3.257.5, PRO).

IN 1940 and again in 1941 British forces found themselves expelled from the continental mainland, but in the latter year, and some two years before COSSAC began its detailed planning for *Overlord*, work began on the doubling of the single-track rail line between Didcot and Southampton. It is not hard to deduce the reasoning that formed the basis of this development: if British forces were to land in northern France, they would be obliged to draw upon the resources of the industrialised North and Midlands through a secure and adequate line of communication running through the ports of southern England. In effect 'the ports of southern England' meant Southampton and northern France meant Normandy, and the relationship between strategic choice and what was administratively possible is obvious. It is perhaps surprising to note, therefore, that German Intelligence failed to appreciate the significance of a development which would seem to accord with one reality: that the fate of Europe for some three centuries had been decided neither south of the Alps nor in Scandinavia but on the North European Plain. Translated into the terms of the two great wars of twentieth-century Europe, what this has meant is that Germany's quest for the domination of the continent could only be broken as a result of the defeat of German armies in the field.

In the Second World War the road that led Allied forces north the length of peninsular Italy was a road that, in strategic terms, led them nowhere: Italy proved to be a liability to whichever side occupied her. In this same conflict Scandinavia, and specifically Norway, proved very similar, *mutatis mutandis*. Her conquest of Denmark and Norway in spring 1940 and her later association with Finland provided Germany with no significant or long-term strategic advantage yet imposed upon her obligations that she could ever less afford as the tide of war turned against her in those theatres where her fate was to be decided. Yet almost until the end of the war Germany maintained unreduced a major garrison in Norway and, at various times, Norway paraded across the stage provided by British and Allied strategic deliberations seemingly with an importance that was never hers to command. She was to suffer the indignity of occupation, repression and exploitation by a rapacious enemy for five years but, as a strategic backwater, after June 1940 no major campaign was fought upon her soil as Allied attention focused elsewhere and thus ensured that, at least in terms of the treatment she was to receive from her western friends,

> *she never felt the tread of countless men,*
> *Her breast was never scarred by nameless graves, Her face was never*
> *marred, despite her fears,*
> *By ruthless hordes of Allied engineers.*[1]

Oslo, in short, was to share the fate of Prague, not of Warsaw and Manila.

There were, however, two periods when events might have unfolded to a very different purpose, or, perhaps more accurately, there were two occasions after June 1940 when Churchill sought to carry the war to Scandinavia in the form of major offensives. The first and better known occasion was in mid-1942 and was to take the form of the *Jupiter* initiative and the second, one year later, came between the *Trident* (Washington DC) and *Quadrant* (Quebec) conferences as the British high command sought to settle national priorities in readiness for the consultations with the Americans that were to settle the Anglo-American programme and timetable for the European war. Nothing came of either attempt, and in Churchill's failures is evidence not simply of the fact that in these matters Britain lacked the power of decision but the perils that present themselves to the historian by use of such terms as 'high command' with their overtones of singleness of purpose and intent. Moreover, in Churchill's failures is the evidence of a good faith towards the United States on such issues as *Overlord* that was questioned both at the time by certain members of the American high command and subsequently by many American historians.

The *Jupiter* initiative has its origins in the German attack upon the Soviet Union, specifically with Stalin's telegram that Churchill received on 19 July 1941. Stalin suggested a British naval and air effort that would complement Soviet military operations in northern Norway. This was a proposal which foundered upon certain unalterable facts that are as well known as Stalin's initial suggestion. In 1940 and 1941 Britain had been reduced to a military position that bordered upon impotent irrelevance, obliged to fight where she could rather than where she would and unable to deal effectively with the weak German corps that made its appearance in North Africa after February 1941. Certainly in these years with forces within the United Kingdom that did not constitute either by size or by quality an adequate strategic reserve, there was no question of Britain considering a major military commitment in Norway; and after its 1940 experience the Royal Navy, having been mauled off Greece and Crete, could not have contemplated a return to Norwegian waters with equanimity. In short, Stalin's suggestion was doomed by two calculations, that

Britain could not commit forces to a campaign in Norway at the expense of home defence, and that the Royal Navy could not sustain itself off a beachhead in hours of perpetual daylight within range of enemy shore-based air power. These facts of life, moreover, were underpinned by another: that any effort in Norway was essentially irrelevant because such an effort was very unlikely to draw German forces from other fronts (i.e. against the Soviets) either on a scale or at a time to be to Allied advantage.[2]

Such considerations, plus the obvious difficulties involved in staff consultations with the Soviets, were clearly the factors behind the British *sotto voce* treatment of planning in the second half of 1941. It would appear, moreover, that whilst hard-headed military considerations dictated caution, the desire not to offend the Soviets by an obvious rejection of Stalin's suggestion kept the Norway option in being – certainly until the time of Eden's visit to Moscow in December 1941.[3] But at the first of the Anglo-American conferences to be held after the United States' entry into the war, *Arcadia* at Washington in December 1941 – January 1942, Churchill made no reference to Norway in his opening examination of the European war. An operation against Norway was cited as an option open to the western Allies, but the priorities identified by the British at this conference were offensives first against French North Africa and then north-west Europe.[4] Under such terms of reference Norway would naturally fall by the wayside. If an offensive into Norway could not be undertaken in 1940 and 1941 because Britain could not afford to weaken the forces held for home defence, then in 1942 and 1943 she could not consider an offensive into Norway that could only be staged at the expense of the forces needed for these two other undertakings.

This paper is not the place to trace the tortuous process whereby the American high command, very reluctantly, came to accept the greater part of this British argument. It is sufficient for our purposes to note that in spring 1942 the British high command, at American insistence, accepted the principle of landings in north-west Europe in 1942 (*Sledgehammer*) and/or in 1943 (*Round-Up*) and thereafter set about extricating itself from the consequences of this commitment. As part of this latter endeavour the Norwegian dimension, more or less in limbo after the Soviet refusal in January 1942 to proceed with *Marrow*, was revived. In February the British planners had passed two heavily doctored plans, one for an attack on Stavanger and the other on Narvik, to Norwegian staff officers for their consideration and in March discussed with Norwegian representatives plans for operations against Spitsbergen and Bear Island.[5] But with the *Sledgehammer/Round-Up* commitment the pace quickened and in May staff studies extended to an examination of the terrain and climate of northern Norway – in no small measure based upon the Shell Tourist guidebook of the area – which was passed to Churchill on the 29th/30th.[6] His enthusiasm no doubt suitably fuelled, on 1 June the prime minister directed that the planners examine *Jupiter* as the 1942 alternative to *Sledgehammer*.[7] By the 7th the S. Section's initial efforts had resulted in a draft proposal that was circulated for critical comment. This proposal envisaged a descent upon Finnmark, specifically upon Kirkenes and Banak, and Petsamo in Finland, by some four divisions, and drew from MO8 the observation that any offensive against northern Norway necessarily had to involve an assault on Narvik which, all but by definition, would involve a very different operation – against a much superior enemy – than envisaged by the Joint Planning Staff.[8] But it was the original proposals that were the ones presented for Norwegian comment on the 15th though by the 22nd, as MO8 later noted, second thoughts had led to the E. Section being ordered 'to prepare an appreciation to decide which areas of northern Norway must be occupied'.[9]

With the British high command determined, for very good reason, not to proceed with *Sledgehammer* the prime minister's initiative of 1 June, despite *Jupiter's* dubious operational credentials possessed some merit especially when tied, albeit inconsistently, to the belief that an abortive *Sledgehammer* in 1942 was very likely to jeopardise a 1943 *Round-Up*. But on 13 June the prime minister issued a second directive to the planners under the terms of which *Jupiter*, which through an unfortunate choice of words was 'to roll the map of Hitler's Europe down from the top,' was to be 'the convenient prelude and accompaniment to *Round-Up*'. Here was a confusion of priorities and inconsistency of purpose that was to persist over the next weeks, but after it was agreed in Washington on 21 June that the American staff should examine *Gymnast* and the British *Jupiter* in order to provide against the possible cancellation of *Sledgehammer*,[10] Churchill moved to the position that if there was no *Sledgehammer* in 1942, then the Americans should undertake *Gymnast* at the same time as *Jupiter* was launched by the British. This somewhat incredible formula – that one ally should undertake an operation that it did not want whilst that operation's sponsor undertook another operation that it had reasoned was beyond its means – was endorsed by the War Cabinet and passed to the Americans on 8 July.[11] Churchill repeated this proposal in his telegram to Roosevelt on the 14th.[12] Thereafter a heavy if belated dose of realism plus, no doubt, an abundance of American antipathy towards peripheral operations, ensured that in 1942 the western Allies did not commit themselves to two separate and scarcely converging offensives at a time when between them they barely had sufficient resources for one.

Perhaps surprisingly, however, *Jupiter* survived the authorisation of *Gymnast*. Having been revived as part of a search for an alternative to *Sledgehammer* it now displayed a tenacious hold upon life, clearly in part because of the Soviet connection at this desperate stage of the war and, presumably, in part because of Churchill's patronage. For whatever reason, it did so in the face of the evident hostility of a sceptical planning staff that even as early as 15 June discounted any thought of 'rolling up' the map of Hitler's Europe from the north and never deluded itself into believing that *Jupiter* could ever possess anything but 'limited military value'. The basis of this scepticism is not hard to find. With Banak some 220 miles from Murmansk and thus beyond the range of Soviet close-support aircraft *Jupiter*, even without a Narvik dimension, would necessarily involve a carrier commitment which in turn would involve the reinforcement of the Home Fleet at the expense of the Mediterranean. With no prospect of freeing forces from this theatre or of raising the number of escorts needed for a Norwegian venture,[13] *Jupiter*, by the least exacting standard, was a non-starter, but at their meeting with the E. Section on 24 June, as MO 8 noted, 'The Directors of Plans . . . although they agreed in principle with our conclusions . . . decided that an outline plan was to be prepared for the original Operation *Jupiter* – the capture of the Banak-Kirkenes-Petsamo area.'[14]

It is clear, therefore, that amongst the planning staff there was a widespread conviction after 24 June that *Jupiter* was mere window dressing. Certainly within another month, with the *Gymnast* commitment in place, *Jupiter* was afforded 'deception-purposes' status only by the planners[15] – though whether the enemy to be deceived was Churchill or the Germans is a moot point. It would appear that after the 24th the staff was prepared to examine *Jupiter* on the basis that 'the Prime Minister will react much more rationally to hard facts and figures if he feels that we here are really doing our best to make (the operation) possible.' Lest this somewhat jaundiced view of proceedings should be disputed reference to two developments should be made. First, on the 28th, just four days after their meeting with the Directors, the planners submitted a paper that flatly stated that it was not possible to produce a realistic, sensible, practical *Jupiter* plan.[16] Second, after the Chiefs of Staff and War Cabinet meetings of 5 and 7 July that in effect killed *Sledgehammer* and resulted in the *Gymnast–Jupiter* combination being placed before the Americans,[17] the Chiefs of Staff entrusted the planning of *Jupiter* to General McNaughton whose Canadian troops had been earmarked for this operation. Had the service chiefs, their directors and planners been in earnest with respect to *Jupiter* at this stage of proceedings, there is little doubt that they would have ensured that the planning process remained wholly under their own collective hand. Conversely, a Canadian disparagement of *Jupiter* could not but weaken Churchill's political argument in favour of this operation. Thus it proved. After a distinctly bleak interim report on 25 July, McNaughton's report was completed on 5 August and finalised as a Chiefs of Staff paper on the 7th with its conclusion that *Jupiter* 'is an extremely hazardous operation . . . and the result might be a military disaster of the first magnitude . . . [Its] risks would only be acceptable if politically the results to be achieved were judged to be of the highest importance.'[18]

The McNaughton paper was passed to Churchill's office on 15 August and was discussed by the Chiefs of Staff on 11 September. Such delay could be regarded as tacit notice of *Jupiter's* fate, and, indeed, the Chiefs of Staff on the latter date in effect administered what proved to be the *coup de grâce*. But the delay in dealing with McNaughton's paper must have been related to the fact that during August there were two 'Operation *Jupiter*' papers in existence. The second document was remarkable by any standard. It was an unusual paper in that it contained a number of hand-painted maps, including one of Copenhagen, within its nineteen pages – of frenzied, infantile nonsense. A 'Great Allied Front' was to be opened by a British descent upon Finnmark, Jutland and the Danish islands after an attack on Kiel *à la* Pearl Harbor. With the resultant collapse of Finland and of the U-boat offensive in the Atlantic the Allies, aided by a popular uprising in Norway and by Sweden, would secure control of the whole of Scandinavia and then be in a position to support the forces that had established themselves in Denmark – though these forces were expendable if Norway was secured. The entire operation, however, would be conducted on a scale that would enable it to be written off as a raid if it miscarried.[19]

Against the cold, remorseless military logic of the McNaughton paper, with its assessment that carriers 'would be exposed to risks . . . which would not be commensurate with the protection which their aircraft could afford' and its very dubious assessment of *Jupiter's* chances of success simply because of weather conditions, what was obviously Churchill's last attempt to keep the Norwegian option alive foundered. The Chiefs of Staff accepted the logic of the McNaughton paper but not two observations that the Directors brought to their attention. The calculations that the last date for the authorisation of a 1943 *Jupiter* was December 1942, and that even if there was no other operation in 1943 it remained improbable that *Jupiter* could be effected, were discounted by the Chiefs of Staff,[20] though in the event the accuracy of the second soon became self-evident. As it was, Churchill had to be content with the issuing of another directive to the planners[21] that led to a reconsideration of the administrative overheads involved in this operation,[22] but thereafter *Jupiter* was allowed to fade from the scene. The momentum of the *Torch* enterprise and the hypnotic effect that all great enterprises exude in their final stages of preparation were too powerful to be deflected by any proposal that, in reality, had never hung by more than a thread.

American resistance to the *Gymnast* proposal in the spring of 1942 had been based upon a number of calculations, the most pertinent being that an invasion of French North Africa was likely to lead to a widening commitment in the Mediterranean theatre that would end any prospect of an invasion of north-west Europe in 1943. If so critically important an endeavour as this was to fall by the wayside as a result of *Gymnast* then so, too, would so marginal an operation as *Jupiter*, and events confirmed the accuracy of this American assessment. For *Jupiter*, therefore, 1942 presented the 'go-now-or-never' choice: 1943 thus saw the realisation of the implications of the decisions taken at its expense in the previous year. This, however, did not prevent Churchill returning to his demand for *Jupiter* in the course of 1943, but the logic of the *Gymnast* decision, the widening of the Mediterranean commitment and the priority afforded *Overlord* in 1943 ensured *Jupiter's* demise. In this process the logic of 1942 repeated itself, though in a slight different form and with one addition. If in 1941 and 1942 a want of resources and the overriding priority of the defence of the United Kingdom doomed a Norwegian venture, then in 1943 this same venture had to be discounted because of the need to prepare for *Overlord* in 1944. Moreover, though 1943 saw the release of British fleet carriers from the Mediterranean with the surrender of Italy the priority afforded the strengthening of the Eastern Fleet in readiness for an intensification of the British naval effort against Japan ensured that British carriers would not find themselves gathered off North Cape for Operation *Jupiter*.

★   ★   ★   ★   ★

Between January and April 1943 *Jupiter* did not figure in British deliberations. These concentrated upon the situation in the Mediterranean, and the premise upon which British calculations were made, set down in a paper of 18 February and discussed by the Chiefs of Staff two days later, was that the decision to proceed with *Husky* – the invasion of Sicily – after the clearing of North Africa precluded any option outside the Mediterranean.[23] For the staff the only unfortunate consequence was not that *Jupiter* would fall by the wayside but that the operations in the Bay of Bengal then under consideration would have to be abandoned with no possibility of replacement.[24] It was not until mid-April that these calculations were challenged in a directive, issued by Churchill, that ordered the re-examination of *Jupiter* with a January 1944 schedule.[25] The prime minister's ostensible reasoning was that the operation had to be reconsidered in order to guard against the prospect of there being no invasion of north-west Europe in 1943.[26]

Such a formula was agreed with the Americans in August 1943 at the *Quadrant* conference, though it was one that applied not to the 1943 but to the 1944 timetable.[27] The significance of this agreement is easy to miss. Having been persuaded against its better judgement to accept the North African and Sicily commitments in successive years and having seen the north-west Europe commitment delayed as a result, by the second quarter of 1943 the American high command was not prepared to be diverted for a third year from northern France: at *Quadrant* the principle and at least some of the detail of *Overlord* were settled. Though much remained to be done before the *Overlord* commitment and plan were finalised, the *Jupiter* provision agreed at *Quadrant* was without meaning other than to represent the destruction of Churchillian hopes for *Jupiter à la* 1943 *ou* 1944.

In preparing for *Quadrant* the prime minister had instructed the planners to reconsider *Jupiter* because

> I have no doubts myself that the correct strategy for 1944 is
>
> (a) Maximum post-Husky exploitation certainly to the Po, with an option to attack westwards in the south of France or north-eastwards towards Vienna, and meanwhile (to seek) the expulsion of the enemy from the Balkans and Greece.
>
> (b) *Jupiter* prepared under the cover of *Overlord*.
>   It is important . . . to make every preparation with the utmost sincerity and vigour but . . . it is essential that we should have this other considerable operation up our sleeves.[28]

Given the state of relations with the Americans with reference to the *Sledgehammer/Round-Up/Overlord* saga, on reading this note one is left to ponder the accuracy of the view that if the French vice is lechery then the British vice is treachery.

What followed the issuing of this directive is interesting. The Chiefs of Staff discussed the directive on the 21st and the planners prepared a report in accordance with their instructions. In their report's two pages was a modesty that reflected their patent lack of enthusiasm for an operation that, in their view, would end any prospect of executing *Overlord* in 1944. Thereafter, despite Churchill's insistence that the operation be discussed immediately and then *en route* to Quebec, *Jupiter*, in the words of Ismay, 'was crowded out by more immediate business' with the result that, not having been discussed by the British, a 1944 *Jupiter* was never discussed with the Americans at Quebec.[29] After the ill-tempered *Trident* conference in Washington in the spring of 1943, it is perhaps just as well that this was so. *Quadrant* was difficult enough without the trouble that would have been provoked had the British sought to shelve *Overlord* in favour of Churchill's 18 April logic. As it was, the *Jupiter* formula agreed at *Quadrant* outlived the conference by less than a month. The British staff, clearly irritated by what was no more than a sop to Churchill's prejudices, reported that there was indeed no alternative to *Overlord* in 1944 and that even a delayed *Overlord* was more relevant to Allied needs than a timely *Jupiter*. Moreover, given *Overlord's* current schedule for May 1944 the planner's statement that *Jupiter* had to take place in summer 1944 but could not be executed before May 1944 possessed a significance that demands no elaboration.[30]

One can see from the events of 1943 that *Jupiter* died – if indeed it had ever lived – in September 1942 and that thereafter it was merely its spirit that haunted Whitehall and Downing Street. But the western Allies had not finished with Norway as a result of the *Overlord* decisions at *Quadrant*. The pre-*Quadrant* studies initiated by Churchill's search for an alternative strategy had examined the conflicting claims of Finnmark and the Stavanger-Bergen area, and had raised the possibility of using the Special Force then awaiting employment in the Aleutians in the winter of 1943–1944 in northern Norway. It was noted that the latter would add credibility to the deception plans that would be needed for *Overlord*.[31] Herein, indeed, was Norway's future role in the unfolding of Allied strategic policy, and herein was an obvious irony. In considering *Jupiter* the British did not seek to liberate Norway; though Norway, either in whole or in part, would be liberated in the process. But Norway's role after autumn 1943 as cover for the Normandy landings (or more accurately as the cover for the Pas de Calais landings that were the cover for Normandy under the terms of the double-deception plan prepared for the Allies) lay in ensuring that the German garrison in Norway was unreduced, that German mastery of the country was uncontested. The German defeat in Norway in the Second World War was one inflicted by time and distance and the drain these imposed upon German resources, and not one that was registered in the field.

As part of the Allied deception and distraction effort there was an increasing naval commitment in northern waters which reached its peak in April–May 1944 with attacks on airfields, shipping and the battleship *Tirpitz* at Kåfjord on 3 April. The continuing need to distract German attention after the Normandy landings led the Royal Navy in July to execute its first three fleet carrier offensive operation of the war when aircraft from the *Formidable*, *Furious* and *Indefatigable* unsuccessfully sought out the *Tirpitz*. In what remained of the year the *Indefatigable* and her sister-ship *Implacable* were involved in four more strikes against the enemy in Norway, but if these attacks formed part of a continuing deception effort and part of the attempt to complete the collapse of German seaborne lines of communication, they also served another purpose, scarcely less important to the Royal Navy – that of working up the newly commissioned *Indefatigable* and *Implacable* before they made their way to the Pacific and Operations *Inmate, Iceberg* and *Downfall*.

This process had long been anticipated. Even before July 1943, when Churchill made his bid to resurrect *Jupiter*, the Royal Navy's planners had turned their attention to the question of the employment of British fleet carriers once the Italian fleet surrendered, and in July 1943, when this question took a pressing form, they considered the question without reference either to the Norwegian theatre in general or to *Jupiter* in particular.[32] There was never any question that with Italy's elimination from the war British carriers, after Sicily and refit, would proceed to the Far East – and after *Quadrant* and his insistence that British forces make their way to the Indian Ocean, the prime minister did not dispute the schedules devised by the Admiralty for the overhaul and departure of its ships.[33] If for no other reason, the Far East priority and the carriers' schedules rendered *Jupiter* impractical, though in truth the *Jupiter* tide had ebbed before July 1943. In short, and with only a very minor distortion of what was written, by March 1943 the British military's interest in the Scandinavian countries did not extend beyond the reading of telegrams about them.[34]

There remain only two matters concerning Norway that stand between the reader and the end of this paper. The first concerns the Soviet liberation of North Norway in October 1944. In this process there was another irony. What in part had taken the Wehrmacht into Norway in 1940 was fear of British intentions, and what had shaped much of subsequent German defensive policy in Norway was this same fear of British intentions. Yet the invasion of Norway was to come not from the sea but overland, not by the British but by the Soviets, and in the process the British could do little more than try to help the Norwegians ensure that token national forces would be involved in the liberation of eastern Finnmark.[35] Of course the British were not beyond using token forces of their own when it came to the liberation of Norway, but not before May 1945. It is perhaps worth noting that this eventuality was foreseen by the planners in June 1943 when, of course, *Jupiter* was under consideration.

The second and final point is to raise the obvious question of whether there was any realistic prospect of *Jupiter*'s adoption at any time. *Jupiter*, in various forms, was on the desks of British planners for some sixteen months, and for most of that time it led a furtive, harried existence. It was battered as much by Churchill's rash enthusiasm as by the planners' scepticism,[36] and there can be little doubt that both in 1942 and 1943 the planners quite deliberately allowed *Jupiter* to be overtaken by events. Those events consistently worked against *Jupiter*. At very best Norway was marginal to the outcome of the war, and after 1942 Allied possession of Norway would not have yielded bases for air and amphibious operations that would have justified the effort needed to secure them.[37] At no time in the war, even at the time of their greatest strength, did Britain and the United States possess the administrative margins that would have allowed them to indulge themselves in Norway; and an operation against a powerful enemy in a country suited to the defence, in the final analysis, was probably in the interests of none – Norwegian, occupier or would-be liberator. In such a situation, the search for a Norwegian strategy within the British high command was futile. The *Jupiter* search was nevertheless proof of British good faith, evidence that at the end of the day Britain would not write off the lesser states of Europe as being of no importance. That the search was unsuccessful, that the Norwegian commitment was resisted within the British high command, does not detract from this.

References

1   Amended by the author of this paper, from a poem, undated and unsigned, that in April 1944 closed the operation *Culverin* planning files, WO 203/1624. All documents cited are in the PRO.

2   J.M.A. Gwyer and J.R.M. Butler, *History of the Second World War. Grand Strategy*, vol. III, *June 1941–August 1942* (London, 1964).

3   Ibid., p. 323.

4   Ibid., pp. 325, 335 and xxx.

5   CAB 119/26. Minutes of staff discussion of 20 March 1942.

6   PREM 3/257/2. Draft report on Northern Norway submitted by DDMI (1) to VCIGS on 29 May 1942 and forwarded to Churchill on the same day, PREM 3/257/1. The booklet 'CB 4096(Q)4. ISIS Report on Northern Norway and Arctic Finland, Vol. II, Part IV, Photographs, Geography, Resources and Communications.' was sent to Churchill on the 30th.

7   PREM 3/257/2. Memorandum D.106/2 from Churchill to Ismay, 1 June 1942.

8   WO 106/2006. Note on JP(42)578(S) (Draft) by MO8 of 7 June 1942. The JPS had three sections, the Executive Planning, Future Planning and Strategical Sections. These sections conducted studies, prepared and examined plans and liaised with service planners.

9   PREM 3/257/2. Memorandum D119/2 from Churchill to Ismay, 13 June 1942.

10 PREM 3/257/5. Minutes of Chiefs of Staff meeting of 6 July 1942.

11 PREM 3/257/5. Minutes of War Cabinet/Defence Committee meeting of 7 July 1942. Noted despatch of signal by teleprinter at 0120 on the 8th.

12 PREM 3/257/5. Telegram from Churchill to Roosevelt of 14 July 1942.

13 WO 106/2006. Briefing paper prepared for Chiefs of Staff meeting of 15 June 1942.

14 Ibid. Summary of proceedings in MO8 paper of 6th July 1942.

15 This observation was made nearly two years later about a plan for an invasion of Simular (off Sumatra) that was under consideration at Churchill's insistence: it seems appropriate comment on these proceedings. (See CAB 119/17/86. Memorandum of 6 April 1944 from Hollis to Capel-Dunn.)

16 WO 106/2008. Papers EPS (42)328 and JP (42)648(E) of 28 July 1942.

17 PREM 3/257/5. Memorandum 125/2 from Churchill to Ismay, 5th July 1942. Minutes of Chiefs of Staff meeting of 6 July 1942. Memorandum from Chiefs of Staff to Churchill, 7 July 1942 (From this document comes the quotation that opens this paper). Minutes of War Cabinet/Defence Committee meeting of 7 July 1942.

18 PREM 3/257/3, WO 106/2004 and WO 106/2008. COS (42)222(0). 7 August 1942. Operation *Jupiter*.

19 CAB 119/26. Unclassified paper 'Operation Jupiter', dated August 1942.

20 WO 106/2008. Briefing paper for the Chiefs of Staff meeting of 11 September 1942. These comments were struck through in green pencil, which indicates that Brooke personally deleted them. It seems, however, that for technical reasons these observations were correct: see note 23.

21 Ibid. Memorandum 154/2 from Churchill to Ismay, 15 September 1942.

22 PREM 3/257/4. COS (42)278(0)(Final). 24 September 1942. Operation Jupiter. Certain of this paper's conclusions were somewhat surprising and deserve some consideration *en passant*. It gave 1 February 1943 as the earliest possible date for *Jupiter* and noted that postponement would decrease its chances of success. It pointed to the need for an American involvement in the operation because of naval and amphibious deficits, which, in fact, were remarkably small. It assessed the

requirements of *Jupiter* as a single fleet carrier and four battleships, and whilst the latter figure would not seem unreasonable, the calculation that just one carrier would be needed would seem to be as unrealistic as the assertion that in 1943 two would be available. The paper also pointed to the fact that freeing warships for *Jupiter* would involve slowing the convoy cycle with the loss of between 400,000 and 500,000 tons of imports. Despite its carrier calculation, the drift of this paper is very clear: leaving aside an American dimension to the operation and a major loss of imports, a lead time of four or five months pointed to a 1943 *Jupiter* having passed its sell-by date even in September 1942.

23 CAB 84/53. JP (43)81(S). 18 February 1943. Re-examination of 1943 strategy against Germany. Minutes of Chiefs of Staff meeting of 20 February 1943.

24 CAB 84/53. JP (43)140(S) (TofR). 1 April 1943. European strategy 1943–1944.

25 PREM 3/257/5. Memorandum from Churchill to Ismay, 18 April 1943.

26 Ibid. Telegram from Churchill to Dill, 25 April 1943.

27 CAB 84/55. CCS 319/5. *Quadrant* agreement.

28 PREM 3/257/4. Memorandum D. 134/3 from Churchill to Ismay, 19 July 1943.

29 Ibid. Memorandum from Ismay to Churchill, 17 September 1943. Summary paper of 19 February 1944.

30 CAB 84/55. JP (43)296(Final). 9 September 1943. Operations against Norway.

31 CAB 80/70. COS (43)320(0). 18 June 1943. Operations in Norway and Finland.

32 This comment has been made on the basis of the author's recollection and notes of JP (43)202(TofR) and the subsequent report. These documents, consulted in the course of his work on planning and preparations for the despatch of British carriers to the Far East, are no longer in the PRO files in which they were found by the author.

33 Churchill's behaviour in this matter was not quite as simple and straightforward as this account would suggest: see the first chapter of the author's PhD thesis 'Grave of a Dozen Schemes: The British Search for a Naval Strategy for the War against Japan'.

34 WO 106/2008. MO3 hand-over notes of 11 March 1943.

35 CAB 84/53. JP (43)178(Final). 21 June 1943, Operations from the United Kingdom – plans in the event of German disintegration.

36 It may be noted, if only in an aside, that this scepticism stood in sharp contrast to the estimation of British capability of both Churchill and Hitler after 1942.

37 CAB 84/55. JP (43)268(S) (Draft). 26 July 1943. Norway.

12 Operation *Jupiter*: a Norwegian perspective

EINAR GRANNES

TO do justice to *Jupiter*, the operation that never came into being, it is necessary to evaluate it from three distinct angles:

1 The Allies, i.e. prime minister Winston Churchill versus his military advisers and the Americans.
2 The enemy.
3 The Norwegian Home Front.

The Allies

To appreciate the following, it must be stressed that Operation *Jupiter* was Churchill's 'own constructive plan'. Mr H.P. Willmott used the term 'futile existence' of Operation *Jupiter*, and it seems valid, as far the Allies were concerned, because none of the many plans were realised. However, for a surprisingly long period *Jupiter* was a shuttlecock between Churchill and his chiefs of staff, part of the time involving President Franklin D. Roosevelt and his political and military advisers. The Americans never showed any interest in the project. Considering the odds, one keeps wondering at the longevity of *Jupiter*, both as separate plan(s),and as alternative(s) to other large-scale operations. Studying *Jupiter* files at the PRO in 1983, I was struck by the operation's 'chronological persistence'. No sooner had its fate been sealed by the Joint Planning Staff (JPS), than it rose to the surface, weeks or months later, at the demand of Churchill.

It has been suggested, that the prime minister's partiality was roused after reading a John Steinbeck novel of occupied Norway. Moreover, while France was not highly esteemed by Churchill at that time, as a result of the 1940 defeat and the succeeding political confusion, his fertile imagination may well have been stimulated by learning of young Norwegians, crossing the North Sea to join Allied Forces in the UK. Churchill seems to have had exaggerated and romantic ideas of what people in occupied countries could – or would – do to assist Allied landing forces. Naturally, the open revolt in which he seemed to believe was out of the question.

It must be acknowledged that Churchill ordered his chiefs of staff to prepare plans for an invasion of North Norway *before* the German attack on the Soviet Union, though at the same time he warned against hunting for prestige to compensate for the defeat of 1940. The first British studies for an invasion of northern Norway are dated 1 July 1941. On 18 July Stalin sent a telegram to Churchill demanding that he immediately establish two fronts, one in the north of France and one on the Arctic Ocean. It was in the interest of Britain, as well as of the USA, to help the Soviet Union fight the Germans. In August the UK started sending war material to Murmansk by way of the hazardous sea route in the north, at the same time stationing aircraft and crew members there, first of all to cover the last part of the perilous sailings. From September–October 1941 the USA joined in, and in November President Roosevelt applied the Lend-Lease Act to the Soviet Union.

As long as inferior striking power prevented an invasion of the continent, Norway appeared to be an option for the British. Operation *Jupiter* acquired a new dimension after the USSR became an ally. It was now a matter of great importance to secure safe passage of supplies with the Arctic convoys. This could be done by taking part of North Norway from the enemy. To this end, Churchill hit on many ideas, but they all lacked 'military soundness'. An example of poor judgement was *Ajax* in October 1941, when he was taken by the notion to capture Trondheim with the help of a rather mysterious Norwegian underground army, pushing through to the Swedish border and hoping for that country to join the Allies. Of course, there was no more a secret army in Norway at that time than there was a so-called French 'secret army' in unoccupied Vichy. *Marrow*, in November 1941, was a more sensible project. It entailed a seaborne assault on Petsamo and Kirkenes using Soviet troops and the Norwegian contingent in Scotland, supported by British warships and transports, plus a hundred aircraft. On 5 January 1942 the USSR rejected the idea of participating in operations in Finnmark. But Churchill did not abandon Operation *Jupiter*. Neither did SOE. While the Chiefs of Staff (COS) complied with Churchill's orders, scrutinising details and appraising the strategic value of his roughly outlined plans, SOE seems to have pursued its own course in order to build up armed and trained groups among local people in Norway and other parts of occupied Europe. From the beginning of 1942, SOE's activities in Norway were coordinated with Norwegian policy in the Anglo-Norwegian Collaboration Committee.

Sooner or later, German-occupied Europe had to be invaded, and while Britain stood alone, it was important to incite people to give armed support to invading forces. In June 1941, the British considered that only Norway, Czechoslovakia and Poland had sufficiently high civil morale, with nuclei of military organisations to bring about patriotic uprisings in the event of an Allied invasion. Later, the priority list was altered, with Yugoslavia and France being placed on top. It was decided, however, that the equipping of Milorg in Norway should be maintained, as long as it could be done by sea transport and did not interfere with the arming of British troops.

While *Jupiter* still shone brightly in its hidden cave two of its offspring, *Anklet* and *Ascot*, had short lives in December 1941. Both were planned in cooperation between the Royal Navy, DCO and SOE. *Ascot* – to cut the north-south overland communications in Helgeland, central Norway – was turned down. Strutting with borrowed feathers from *Jupiter*, *Anklet* proved to be an ill-devised plan, rather than the 'raid' it has been termed. The most aggressive planners wanted permanent bases in the southern part of the Lofoten Islands, with 9,000 soldiers supported by naval and air forces. I draw attention to these two plans because they were the prelude to a protracted engagement by SOE in the Helgeland district, where the local military resistance (Milorg) was activated.

At Churchill's request on 3 June 1942, the Chiefs of Staff Committee instructed the Joint Planning Staff (JPS) to work out a general evaluation of a possible landing in Troms, Finnmark and northern Finland. During a meeting of the War Cabinet on 11 June, Churchill emphasised the advantages of *Jupiter*, especially when *Sledgehammer* was rejected. Evidently, it was on this occasion that he observed: 'In fact, we could begin to roll the map of Hitler's Europe down from the top!' On 13 June he reopened the question and ordered the JPS to evaluate two alternatives for northern Norway and Finland, *Viceroy* and *Jupiter*. Discussing Churchill's memorandum two days later, the British military chiefs concluded that as a second front, *Jupiter* was of minor military importance, and that with the poor north-south communications there would be small chance of success in taking Norway from the enemy. Shortly after this, Churchill went to the United States. In the White House on 21 June, Churchill prevailed upon President Roosevelt, who promised that the Combined Chiefs of Staff (CCS) should make a thorough study of *Jupiter* parallel to *Torch*. Further sanction than this *Jupiter* never received within Allied strategy, and it was not mentioned in the decisive memorandum of 24 July 1942.

Like the British generals, the highly esteemed American Chief of Staff, George C. Marshall, had no liking for *Jupiter*. On the British side, however, military, political and economic aspects of *Jupiter* were studied in accordance with Churchill's wish. On 27 July he wrote to Roosevelt that *Torch* could only be kept secret by developing deception operation. This, allegedly, was why he went on with *Jupiter*. To keep the enemy in suspense, Canadian troops in the UK would be issued with winter equipment.

Jupiter reached a peak of attention in the summer of 1942, when Churchill kept the COS busy with planning for six weeks. The Commander-in-Chief of Canadian troops in the UK, Lieutenant-General A.G.L. McNaughton, was appointed to direct operations. After having studied the plans thoroughly he – like the British military staffs – gave them the thumbs down, and in September 1942 Churchill finally granted that *Jupiter* could have no priority, considering *Torch* and *Overlord*. He assured Roosevelt that from then on he would look on *Jupiter* only as a deception. Still, there may have been more to it. It is recorded that McNaughton considered the second week of December (1942) to be the best choice, in order to take the enemy by surprise. So *Jupiter* lived on, obviously not only as a deception, through 1943 and even into 1944. In a report from Combined Chiefs of Staffs' meeting of 24 August 1943 the following conclusion was drawn:

> If the circumstances make it impossible to carry out *Overlord* in
> Normandy, it might be necessary to view *Jupiter* as an alternative. Plans
> to this end, with special attention to South Norway, should therefore be
> worked out and kept up to date.

To prepare for the invasion of the European continent the Allies established a new supreme command, COSSAC. On 9 September 1943 the JPS recommended that COSSAC should work out plans for the occupation of Norway as an alternative to *Overlord*, and to do the same for Denmark, using the south of Norway as a basis. The advantages of taking Norway from the Germans were evaluated strategically, militarily, economically and psychologically. On behalf of the COS, General Alan Brooke, chairman of the Committee, said that by March 1944 it ought to be clear whether *Overlord* could be launched. COSSAC stated that *Jupiter* could in no way be a substitute for *Overlord*, and suggested that planning for Norway should be restricted to starting a campaign in the event of a German withdrawal (Allied planning for the liberation of Norway, *Rankin B* and *Rankin C*).

It can thus be ascertained that *Jupiter* had three 'faces', at least in the imagination and terminology of Winston Churchill:

1 *Jupiter* as an independent operation, 1941–2.
2 *Jupiter* as an alternative to *Torch* and *Overlord*, 1942–4.
3 *Jupiter* as deception, 1942–1944.

No doubt, the long – if not charmed – life of *Jupiter* can be ascribed to the persistence and influence of Mr. Churchill. To the present commentator it seems likely that the great man's views affected SOE's activities in Norway, which – at least in the central parts – were stubbornly aimed at making preparations for an Allied (i.e. British) invasion. The fact remains, that Churchill obtained no approval for *Jupiter* either from his (British) military staffs, or from the Americans. None of the plans he put forward turned out to be militarily sound. It should, however, be taken into account that the option of *Jupiter* as an alternative was held open almost to the end of the Second World War. As for Churchill, he observed in February 1944, that Norway should of course have been liberated in 1943 (!).

The enemy

Strange to say, as early as the autumn 1940 the Germans carried out anti-invasion manoeuvres in central parts of Norway. Grossadmiral Raeder warned his Führer of 'the constant threat' of a British invasion in Norway and found him attentive, as this notion was in accordance with his own. Hitler's obsession with Norway as the Second World War's 'field of destiny' made him strengthen his northern flank with the largest warships, submarines, aircraft, coastal fortifications and soldiers. The transfer to northern waters of submarines and powerful 'raiders', like *Tirpitz* and *Scharnhorst* eased the pressure on the Atlantic convoys. In the early summer of 1942, the number of enemy troops in Norway was increased from 100,000 to 250,000. When the C-in-C of *Armeoberkommando Norwegen* (AOK Norwegen), Generaloberst Nikolaus von Falkenhorst, lamented the antique equipment of his army, he received 52 artillery batteries. Following heavy losses at sea, Hitler lost faith in the Kriegsmarine's surface fleet and ordered guns of large calibre to be taken from ships and mounted in coastal forts in Norway.

On 12 May 1942, Falkenhorst declared that one must not be deceived by the calm in the Norwegian operational theatre. Before the end of 1942 one might well meet with Anglo-Saxon operations in Norway. During the last weeks of 1942, and at the beginning of 1943, Hitler directed more troops to Norway, especially to the northern and central parts, from Germany and from the Eastern Front in Finland. AOK Norwegen's counter-espionage constantly received reports of an imminent invasion, and Falkenhorst (Wehrmachts-befehlshaber Norwegen = WBN) took rumours of an alleged landing in the 'Bodø area' more seriously than before. In a report of 19 November 1942 he mentioned a 'credible piece of intelligence', claiming that the Allies would undertake major operations in Norway, when tonnage had been released after the landings in North Africa (*Torch*). Information from several sources indicated that the invasion would come in a weak spot between Narvik and Trondheim in the darkest season, despite the likelihood of rough weather during landing operations. WBN's counter-intelligence also reported that Norwegian officers with local knowledge were being flown from Sweden to the UK. The British landings in North Norway were supposed to be coordinated with an offensive on the Murmansk front by the Red Army, supported by winter-trained soldiers coming from Iceland. To counter this menace, WBN instructed 33. Army Corps in Trondheim to move the army reserve from Bergen to Mo-Bodø. It included several special units. The first body was to reach its positions before the end of November. The securing of airfields, and of barring lakes with chains, for instance Røsvatn in inner Helgeland, the second largest lake in Norway, was to be discussed with the Wehrmacht Territorial C-in-C, residing in Mo. WBN concluded his orders of the day with the following instructions:

a) Keep watch on the coast.

b) Swift reports from reconnaissance units, especially Luftwaffe.

c) Abwehr should oversee the Norwegian population, cooperating with Sicherheitsdienst.

d) WBN's staff should temporarily move to the operational theatre in northern Norway.

While the 196. Inf.div. (offensive) had long been present in Mo (1,500), 60 miles north of Mosjøen (2,000), it now also became the HQ of 14. Luftwaffen-feld Division. In the first half of December 1942 the 121st Inf.div. was transferred from Germany via Stettin to Norway. To strengthen 25. Panzer div. in Norway, several panzer and pioneer units were moved from Finland to Norway.

In late autumn 1942, the Germans sounded the alarm several times along the entire Norwegian coast. The warning system was changed, to distinguish between raids, landing operations of limited extent and full-scale invasion. Commandants of coastal forts complained of lacking searchlights for the observation of small vessels, which could be heard, but not seen, near land in the dead of night. The Wehrmacht and Organisation Todt built strong fortifications close to the sea (from the Bay of Biscay to the North Cape), with trenches, minefields, barbed wire and guns. Along a sixty-mile stretch of the

Helgeland coast in central Norway, 55 pieces of artillery calibre 75mm –
155mm were positioned to repel assaults from the sea. Admiral Norwegen,
Generaladmiral Boehm, contemplated locating torpedo batteries, cut out of
solid rock, in the approach to Namsos. Other, similar plans were indicative of
the German apprehension, regarding the intentions of the Allies. With
hindsight, the many premature warnings of invasion appear 'hypochondriac'.
The Luftwaffe was responsible for most, as when its long-range reconnaissance
aircraft 'spotted' the embarkation of British troops in the Clyde and other
Scottish ports, ostensibly heading for northern waters. On another occasion in
late 1942, British destroyers steaming eastwards from Iceland were suspected
of spearheading an invasion of Norway. The enemy's uneasiness about Allied
landings probably reached its highest level directly before *Torch* in North
Africa 8 November 1942. Another critical time seems to have occurred in
connection with *Overlord*. In May 1944, AOK Norwegen kept a sharp look-out
for Allied airborne troops in Helgeland. Shortly afterwards, when German
secret police rolled up SOE's clandestine activity in the same area, AOK
Norwegen launched an offensive which, in the words of the Army chief of
staff, was 'extensive'.

    In a report on the situation of 20 September 1944, the occupying army's
Chief of General Staff stated that the Norwegian population was completely
dominated by the Norwegian government in exile, and that every order from it
was obediently executed. He declared that the secret military organisation,
Milorg, was directed from London, and so well trained and armed as to be
reckoned with in due time. The report stated that Mosjøen was one of the main
points (*Schwerpunkte*) of military resistance in Norway. By this time the
Wehrmacht in Norway amounted to 335,000 personnel, not counting members of Organisation Todt. There were also 67,000 starving POWs, mostly
Russians.

The Norwegian Home Front.

Jupiter was as 'real' to the Milorg men as it was to the enemy. For the
embryonic, militant underground cells, which sprang up in the wake of the
defeat in 1940, the idea of a possible British invasion was paramount to morale.
Subsequently, the goal of taking an active part in liberating Norway, by
assisting landing forces, was the motive power behind the building up of a
secret military organisation of some 40,000 men under joint command. It was a
question not of if, but when an Allied invasion would take place. Counterba-
lancing the frustrating feeling of helplessness was an almost fatalistic faith in a
just outcome of the war. On 20 November 1941 the Norwegian Defence
Council in London adopted Milorg as an integrated part of our armed forces.

    Norwegian military instructors and W/T operators bringing tons of
supplies, plenty of fighting spirit and a firm belief in an imminent invasion,
were heartily welcomed by the local inhabitants in enemy infested Norway.
Those involved often displayed excessive optimism, as the following example
shows. On 31 March 1942, the Archer mission W/T operator in Helgeland sent

one of his very few telegrams, which in its simple-mindedness must have given his superiors at SOE's London HQ a start: 'Can we have the approximate – or preferably – the exact date for the invasion in Mosjøen?'

In May of the same year a telegram to Home Station from the recently arrived Heron mission, integrated with Archer, reported that Captain Skaar, shadow leader of Milorg in Helgeland, estimated that ten thousand men could be recruited from Nordland county alone. On 27 May, Home Station replied coolly: 'Captain Skaar must realise that nothing is going to happen in the near future'. Still, the non-committal answer appeared to contain half a promise. However that may be, when General von Falkenhorst warned in May 1942 of possible 'Anglo-Saxon operations in Norway before the end of the year', Milorg had long prepared for such an occasion. Forty tons of supplies were ferried from Shetland to Helgeland from December 1941 to April 1942. By May 16 tons, mostly arms and ammunition, had been carried over steep mountains to selected caches near enemy camps, to be used by Milorg during an Allied invasion. The inland transport was suspended, as snow-melting and flooding of rivulets prevented skiing, and spring farming had to be done. But in July, the carrying of weapons revived, and at the end of the month long-awaited hand grenades arrived in a smack. Milorg men busy with haymaking got the message, and threw away scythe and rake. The grenades must be fetched at any price. Feelings were running very high, and persistent rumours indicated invasion when the nights grew darker. In London the leader of SOE's Scandinavian section, Colonel J.S. Wilson, wrote on 25 July 1942 to Professor Captain Leif Tronstad, at the Norwegian Military Office IV :

> It seems to me a matter of real importance for the C-in-C to have one or more representatives in North Norway, who can be used at present for our joint purposes and who will be in a position to act as local leaders when the time comes.

Rumours found favourable conditions, where hope survived. Among the most militant, wishful thinking hardened into 'invasion psychosis'. The spark of anticipation kindled the fuse of conviction which crackled towards its anticlimax. The increasing rates of arms transport, and the organising of fighting groups, produced a sense of dramatic haste. In its elusive nearness, *Jupiter* was the basis for underground military activities.

When the weapons transport was disclosed to the Germans by a notorious gang of traitors, resulting in the execution of 23 Milorg men in October 1942, and the imprisonment of many more, it did not deter the remainder. At the same time, in Trondheim, ten prominent citizens were executed as reprisals for the generally hostile attitude of the population. While these deeds of darkness aroused conflicting emotions, they did not subdue the resistance. Abroad, the shooting of hostages caused disgust and condemnation. The *Daily Telegraph* wrote that it would be an insult to the civilised world if those responsible for this outrage should remain unpunished. Following appeals from legal authorities in exile, President Roosevelt solemnly promised to punish the German war criminals and their Norwegian lackeys. Nazi atrocities in Norway aroused anti-German sentiments in Sweden, where reputable newspapers denounced the executions with strong words. Thus, unwittingly, Milorg's preparation for a British invasion had an important psychological effect in Sweden and in the USA.

It is interesting to note, that while Lt.-Gen. McNaughton considered the second week of December 1942 to be most suitable for an invasion, in order to take the enemy by surprise, Lt. Sjøberg, on the spot in Norway, expected the invasion to materialise any time. To this end he kept logging tracks open for the would-be invading forces. As leader of the SOE-sponsored missions to Helgeland, Archer/Heron (1941–42), he reckoned on 36 hours' notice of an invasion. I have not been able to find out who fixed this deadline, whether it was Sjøberg himself, or someone with inside information in the UK. It seems likely that Churchill was kept informed of SOE's ambitious activities, at least until summer 1942, and it is hardly too imaginative to suggest that the prime minister's prejudice in favour of *Jupiter* leaked to officers in command of missions preparing for invasion in central Norway.

Despite broken illusions, and apparently useless loss of lives, most Milorg men stuck to their belief in Allied landings within the space of weeks or months, rather than years, and the need to prepare for them. After their arrests by the Gestapo and SD in the summer of 1944, well known men from the older generation were firmly convinced that invasion was near at hand. After the war ended a former prisoner told me that during his captivity in central Norway, in summer 1944, he expected any morning to wake up hearing English-speaking soldiers outside the barrack windows. When even prisoners conveyed the impression of being firmly convinced of Allied invasion, it certainly did not ease the strain on a predisposed and nervous enemy.

To all appearance, the Germans were perplexed as to Allied intentions towards Norway, and they were unable to challenge Churchill's 'paper tiger', either with missiles or marching orders. All in all, it is my opinion that Operation *Jupiter* – though playing its essential part behind the scenes – had great strategic value to the Allied cause during Second World War.

Discussion

Listening to Professor Riste's paper, *Professor Robert O'Neill* was struck by the parallel with the experience of Australia as a minor ally (though of course not occupied). Britain was good at recognising Australian sovereignty, but all higher command posts went to British officers. Australians were therefore good at tactics, bad at strategy. The war also improved Australia's diplomatic representation. Did it leave Norway's armed forces and foreign service in a similar position? *Professor Riste* replied Yes to both questions. One of the problems in having a Western element in the liberation of North Norway was that Norwegian units could not operate on their own because the whole support function had been done by the British. They could operate in the field very well but they did not have the rear echelons. There was, however, a growing staff element in London concerned with planning for liberation which could only be done by Norwegians. This staff eventually amounted to 700 people and the planning effort must have helped to give the Norwegians a clearer idea of strategy. The Norwegian foreign service, too, developed enormously during the war. Before the war it was very small, concerned mainly with looking after Norwegian commercial and maritime interests. International politics were 'dangerous'. But close relations with the British and the very international environment of wartime London greatly widened Norwegian perspectives.

In answer to a question about the relationship between king and government, Professor Riste answered that it was of great importance that there was complete and undivided cooperation between the two. The king stood by the government through thick and thin – especially in the early period when the Nygaardsvold government was not popular with Norwegians either at home or abroad. A telling episode occurred in February 1941 after reports from Stockholm that Norwegian circles there had appealed to the king to take personal power and dismiss the government. The king took the opportunity to call the government together and to state that he was wholeheartedly behind it. *Professor Archer* pointed out that this unity was also cross-party, since the Conservative leader and President of the Storting Carl J. Hambro stood by the government however much he disagreed with it. Professor Riste said that Hambro was *outwardly* loyal, though in his frequent letters to London from America he often disagreed with their policies. He became a troublemaker by making speeches in the USA – mostly supportive of the Norwegian war effort but also propagating his special foreign policy line – a small-state philosophy, criticising all great powers almost equally. He therefore became an *enfant terrible*, and certainly *persona non grata* with the British government.

Sir Alexander Glen opened the discussion of Dr Thowsen's paper by remarking that he knew at first hand virtually all the personalities and a large part of the transactions, and had never heard a clearer description of these negotiations both in London and New York. He emphasised the professional expertise of the British team in the Ministry of War Transport. Sir Cyril Hurcomb, the permanent secretary, had occupied the same position in the First World War. He was a skilled negotiator and, at difficult moments, was also a great ornithologist. At meetings in Berkeley Square he would open the window and casually enquire the identity of a particular bird. 'His capacity for muddying the waters was infinite. Gilmore Jenkins, the Number 2, was just about as skilful and Bill Weston was a real hit-man. A formidable team.' The Norwegian shipowners were determined that Norway would enjoy after the end of the war a merchant fleet capable of earning Norway her keep. This was an absolutely legitimate aim. The British and Norwegian negotiators had great mutual respect, though it was not always a cleanly fought fight.

In reply to a question about disagreements within the Norwegian Shipowners' Association, *Dr Thowsen* said that the problem was that most of the shipowners were back in Norway. Very few leading shipowners wanted to leave the country. Lorentzen and Hysing Olsen were not leading, or even very successful, shipowners. After the war there were tensions between those who had left and those who had stayed. But during the war there were good connections between Norway and London, especially via Stockholm. Shipping policy was dominated at first by Nortraship. Then came Minister of Shipping Arne Sunde who thought *he* should have a say and started to interfere. Up to 1942 the conflict was between Nortraship London and Nortraship New York. After 1942 it was between Nortraship and the Norwegian Ministry of Shipping.

Asked whether Norwegian shipbuilders managed to drag their feet while building for the Germans, Dr Thowsen replied that not many ships were built owing to shortages of raw materials, sabotage and going slow. Most ships built were delivered after the war, only two or three during the war. Dr Thowsen then raised an important question: did this amount to economic resistance or economic collaboration? 'If you build slow, you still earn money but the Germans don't get their ships.' So what is it? *Joachim Rønneberg* offered an amusing sidelight on this question. 'Our district,' he said, 'had no road connection with Oslo. They built it during the war. On 7 May 1945 they blew the last rock, and on 8 May the first car passed.'

The authors of the two papers on Operation *Jupiter* were asked whether, in their opinion, Churchill regarded it as a genuine option rather than merely as a feint to deceive the Germans. *Dr Willmott* saw Churchill as a 'true believer' who was handled by his staff in such a way that he could be diverted from such schemes. *Dr Grannes* agreed that Churchill was sincere and emphasised the importance of morale as a factor in Churchill's calculations. Boosting the morale of occupied Europe might ultimately help an Allied invasion force. *Professor Riste* did not disagree with Dr Willmott's assessment, but emphasised that one must be aware of the psychological context of *Jupiter's* origins. In 1941 Churchill had a desperate need for action to show that Britain was not defeated. He was looking for places on the map where Hitler could be hit without disastrous losses. The Norwegian coastline was so long that it *was* possible to find such places – where one could run away if opposition became too strong, such as the Lofotens in March 1941. There was also the Russian factor: in June–July 1941 there was a need to show the Russians that Britain *was* fighting. In 1941 *Jupiter* was a morale booster. In 1942 it slid over from being a plan that *might* be carried out to being a deception plan.

Asked about the intelligence dimension of *Jupiter*, *Edward Thomas* replied that scarcely a week passed without German naval decrypts sounding the alarm somewhere on the Norwegian coast, or reflecting the high command's fear of raids: 'Whenever they sighted a Russian convoy, the first reaction was "Is it an invasion?" '. *Ragnar Ulstein* added that the home front, too, earnestly believed that there was a landing ahead. Resistance groups were formed in Norway by agents arriving from London, and the purpose was to prepare for invasion. Many men were lost in 1942–3 because they expected an invasion, exposed themselves and were caught and executed. The home front reacted the same way as the Germans. Deception inspired the Norwegians to rebel and organise themselves. *Sir Brooks Richards* pointed out, however, that there is no evidence that SOE used resistance as a conscious element in deception. Sir Robin Brook (Sir Brooks's regional director in western Europe during the war) was very clear on this point.

PART III

Intelligence and Resistance

13 Norway's role in British wartime intelligence

EDWARD THOMAS

FOR the purpose of this chapter, the term intelligence is used only in the sense of information gathered and analysed in support of those making operational and strategic decisions. I will be discussing the role of SOE and the Norwegian resistance only inasfar as they were sources of this sort of information.

Sharing Sandy Glen's great admiration for the Norwegian people I would be less than human if I did not start by saluting some of the fine Norwegian naval officers I had to do with during my two years as naval intelligence officer in Iceland: the celebrated Captain Ullring, then in command of the gunboat, HNMS *Fridhof Nansen*, who shared my office when he came ashore; Commander Brinck and his brave squadron of young Kvartermester who flew dangerous patrols in single engined Northrop float-planes over the fog and ice of the Denmark Strait on the look-out for German raiders – and gave me a taste of their work; and Commander Brekke who commanded HNMS *Honningsvåg*, an armed trawler captured from the Germans in circumstances calling for great courage and presence of mind. I sailed with him in fair weather and foul, learning to like 'Labskaus' and to say 'Fand steke meg'!

It was in Iceland in 1940 that I first experienced the workings of Ultra, though I was not then party to the secret. *Fridhof Nansen* did important – and largely forgotten – work in frustrating early German attempts to land meteorological parties in Greenland and Jan Mayen. These were organised by the Abwehr whose cypher had just been broken at Bletchley Park. The decrypts revealed their intentions and the fact that Goering attached great importance to them, as did the Germans to their subsequent met. activities in the Arctic. What intelligence made of them is chronicled in our history.[1]

Ultra played no part in the *Altmark* incident, the German naval Enigma not being broken till a year later. Coastal Command followed up reports from agents run by the French, and these led to her interception in Jøsingfjord. If the Nelson touch was displayed there it was Nelson's intelligence methods that led to the first battle of Narvik. Captain Warburton-Lee and his destroyers were sent there on the strength of no more than a solitary Reuter report saying that a single German warship had reached Narvik, and wisely sought confirmation from a pilot station in the Vestfjord. There he was told that six destroyers, 'bigger than yours', had passed by, steering north. This was to prove a sorry underestimate.

The failure to give warning of Hitler's invasion of Norway was a disgrace to British intelligence and to Whitehall in general. Many clues pointing in the right direction had been received. But they went separately to the three Service Departments and the Foreign Office, none of whom individually thought them conclusive. For example the report of 4th April of a German photo reconnaissance flight over Norway's west coast – a unique event – went to ground in the Air Ministry, while the operational significance of Abwehr decrypts about the activities of a German spy ship in Norwegian territorial waters well before the invasion went undetected in the Admiralty. In those days there was no effective machinery for bringing all the evidence together and thinking about what it might mean. Had there been it is scarcely credible that it would not have dented the prevailing view in Whitehall that the Germans would never dare send an expedition acrosss the sea in face of British naval power. As it was, sightings of Germany's big warships were thought to presage a break-out into the Atlantic.

The short campaign taught the British quite exceptionally valuable intelligence lessons. One arose from the breaking of the first operational Enigma. This was the version of the cypher used by the German Army and Luftwaffe throughout the campaign. Bletchley poured out decrypts about the strength, intentions and whereabouts of the enemy. No one had expected the Enigma to be used in this way or on this scale. No arrangements had been made to send its highly secret yield to the battle zone, and none could be improvised. So it served only to keep London informed of what was going on and laid an immensely important foundation for future understanding of the organisation and workings of the German forces. But a manner in which it might in future be sent to operational commanders was suggested during the retreat from Oslo to the north by King Haakon and the British Embassy staff. The Oslo representative of the SIS succeeded in keeping in touch with London throughout the perilous journey by means of his secret radio channel. In all future campaigns, from France onwards, the SIS's signals network was used for passing operational intelligence direct from Bletchley Park to Army and RAF commanders in the field. The Admiralty used its own network. After Iceland I worked for a time at Bletchley translating and editing, at breakneck speed, decrypts revealing the instructions sent to U-boats in the Atlantic, the activities of the German navy off Norway, and very much else besides.

The British Embassy in Oslo had already, in the first days of the war, been the scene of a sensational intelligence coup. The 'Oslo Report', pushed through the letter box by a German who was to remain anonymous for fifty years, was one of the most remarkable intelligence documents of the war. It set forth so much about German scientific and technological advances – radar, navigational beams, guided missiles, rockets and other experimental weapons – that at first practically everyone believed it to be a hoax. But Dr R. V. Jones – that redoubtable scientific intelligence officer – thought it probably genuine and used it throughout the war as a touchstone for interpreting often fragmentary evidence about German scientific innovations. In the end its truth was to be proved in almost every particular. Dr Jones now tells us that its author was Professor Hans Ferdinand Meyer, wartime head of Siemens Central Laboratories.

Returning to Ultra, the Enigma of the Luftwaffe had been broken in 1940.

But the versions of the cypher used by the German Army and Navy proved much more difficult. That the German naval Enigma was broken, and an immense contribution to winning the war thereby achieved, owes much to Norway. By April 1940 Bletchley had made good theoretical progress, and was then helped by the few papers remaining in a German patrol vessel captured and looted on its way to Narvik. But to make the further decisive step Bletchley needed further and more systematic captures. The Lofoten raid of March 1941 was planned primarily with this end in view. Material captured from the armed trawler *Krebs* set Bletchley well on the way to a decisive solution which was completed soon afterwards by three further captures. Two, from weather ships on the high seas (but based in Norway), were planned operations. But the third – the famous U-110 – was fortuitous. With this invaluable help Bletchley read the Home Waters settings, which carried 95% of the traffic, from March to the end of May, albeit with some delay: but from then on it broke the daily changing settings with little or no delay until the end of the war. The December 1941 raid on Vågsøy yielded further valuable cryptographic material. So the high price exacted by German reprisals was not wholly in vain. Ultra made a very great contribution to winning the Battle of the Atlantic – a battle on which all depended – and was thus responsible for saving perhaps hundreds of Norwegian merchant ships and the lives of their crews. Its illumination of the sea war off Norway included regular testimony to the German's constant fear of Allied landings.

The Enigma played a part in the early stages of the *Bismarck* episode. The Luftwaffe was flying abnormal reconnaissance of the ice edge from Trondheim/Værnes, and decrypts revealing this were the first warning that something was afoot. They caused the C in C, Home Fleet, to refuel his shadowing cruisers. But what set British forces in motion was information from the Norwegian military attaché to his British colleague in Stockholm to the effect that two large German warships – the other was *Prinz Eugen*, later to be torpedoed off the Norwegian coast – had been sighted steaming through the Kattegat by the aircraft of a Swedish cruiser. The rest of the story is well known. But the part played by the Norwegian MA is insufficiently acknowledged.

It was not until 1942 that Hitler's fear of invasion – he said that every ship not in Norway was in the wrong place – and German knowledge of the successful passing of convoys by the Arctic route to north Russia sent their big ships to Norwegian bases. The intelligence story revolved largely round their movements and intentions. But not exclusively. In June 1941 Ultra from north Norway had finally dispelled doubts in Whitehall as to whether Hitler really intended to invade Russia. Because the Germans had to resort exclusively to radio communication with remote Finnmark their traffic, in the Luftwaffe Enigma, could be intercepted and decrypted. This was not the case on other fronts. From 14 June it furnished clear indications that Germany intended to push forward in Finnmark, and to do so on 22 June. That they failed to capture Murmansk and the Kola Inlet – a failure pregnant with significance – was helped by the disruption of their supply shipping off north Norway by British and Russian submarines. The British were guided by authorities in

London who now had good information from the Enigma about German convoy movements, routes, escorts and patrols.

Ultra was to provide information of this sort right up to the end of the war. But it was seldom complete and often late. That the information needed for Allied air and naval operations in coastal waters, and for the activities of SIS and SOE, was so extraordinarily full sprang from the enormous amount of information that came to hand to supplement the Ultra. Ultra was, in any case, only distributed to very few recipients and was mostly used as background. Photo reconnaissance played a big part. But most of the non-Ultra information came from Norwegian sources. The Norwegian High Command in London had its own sources, and collaboration between them and the SIS almost entirely lacked the friction experienced with other governments in exile. They agreed on an early division of labour, the SIS obtaining information from the ship-watchers, and the Norwegian government political, military and static information. This filled out the information about the German army of occupation received from Ultra. The OSS had no difficulty in accepting the Anglo-Norwegian system of control I seem to remember that it was OSS agents who warned in early 1941 of the German intention to renew their attempts to establish met. stations in Greenland.

Even the SIS and SOE got on with much less than their normal friction. So there must have been something special about Norway. All information about the Resistance came, of course, from the SOE. But they also gathered enormous amounts of information about the German occupation. Since, by a ruling at the highest level, this was circulated by the SIS as CX reports it is impossible – as is the case with other occupied countries – for historians to tell precisely what information came from SOE. A further valuable non-Ultra source was the systematic and informed interrogation of escapees from Norway and elsewhere at the London Reception Centre in Wandsworth which was run by naval intelligence. Captured, or stolen, documents were always another valuable source. Perhaps the biggest coup of this kind was the capture during the Vågsøy raid of maps showing the coastal defences not only of Norway but of all occupied Europe. All this is the sort of information which, evaluated against the background of Ultra, was used for the planning of *Jupiter* and the re-occupation of Norway.

One very important supplement to Ultra was the establishment by the SIS of its ship-watching stations from the Kattegat to furthest north which was in action from early 1942. One subject on which Ultra could not be relied on to provide timely warning, or sometimes any warning at all, was the movement of Germany's main naval units. Reports from the ship watchers were often the first to be received in London. The movements of these ships between Germany and their Norwegian bases were often accompanied by dramas in which I became involved when I later joined the Home Fleet. But today I must concentrate on *Bismarck's* sister ship, the *Tirpitz*. Her sucessful destruction, wrote Churchill, 'would alter the entire naval situation throughout the whole world. She thus became an intelligence target of the highest priority. After Bomber Command's three unsuccessful attacks on her in the Trondheimsfjord in early 1942 she sailed north for Altafjord and the notorious PQ 17 operation –

one which demonstrated the frailty of Ultra. The ship-watchers played no part in this as it was not until a year later that the SIS, after many attempts, succeeded in establishing an agent overlooking *Tirpitz's* anchorage at the base of Altafjord. I could say more about PQ 17 since the view we take in our history differs from that generally propagated. But now is not the time.

After PQ 17, in July 1942, *Tirpitz* returned, not to Altafjord but to Narvik. It was against her that one of the most daring attacks of the war was planned. It is not generally known that Leif Larsen's attempt to bluff his way to her vicinity had to be switched at the last moment to Trondheim. Ultra had revealed, on the eve of his planned departure for Narvik, that *Tirpitz* had arrived, completely unheralded by any sources, at Trondheim on 24th October. Larsen sailed as scheduled on 26th October having had barely 24 hours in which to re-jig his attack. The sad outcome of this has already been related at this conference. He was in the mould of the great Norse heroes. Another Leif Eiriksson.

Another Norwegian, no less brave, figured in the next attacks on the *Tirpitz*. This was the SIS's man in Altafjord – the famous Torstein Raaby who was to re-appear after the war as radio operator on the *Kon Tiki*. After a refit in Trondheim *Tirpitz* sailed again for the north in February 1943, her departure having been reported by the ship-watcher in Trondheimsfjord. Thereafter she lay in Altafjord while the next attack was planned. This was to be by RN midget submarines, or X-craft, towed north by six fleet submarines. This attack had also to be planned for both Narvik and Trondheim in case *Tirpitz* moved. RAF photo reconnaissance from north Russia kept watch on her, making sure she didn't. I leave to your imagination the vast amount of all-source intelligence needed for the planning. The operation succeeded – though not fully. One of the X-craft had difficulty in getting through the battleship's net enclosure and this hampered its attack. What proved to be correct information about the depth of the net enclosure had been provided by the British naval attaché in Stockholm who had received it from 'young Norwegian resistance men'. Goodness knows how they obtained it! But their information was unfortunately, not to say scandalously, rejected by Admiralty's boom-defence experts.

The first damage reports came from Raaby. They were the first he sent. Thereafter both he and Ultra kept up a running commentary on the repairs to the wounded battleship. In fact, Raaby was to transmit daily for ten months. By this time, September 1943, I had been posted to HMS *Duke of York* as intelligence staff officer to that great and much-loved Admiral of the Fleet, Lord Fraser of North Cape, who on Boxing Day 1943 brought about the destruction of Tirpitz's stable-mate, the *Scharnhorst*. She had sailed into the Arctic night, reported only by Ultra, on Christmas Day completely unaware of the presence of the *Duke of York*. It is a proud thing for us all to know that a memorial to the event, and to Bruce Fraser, now stands on Nordkapp. The Norwegian fleet destroyer, HNMS *Stord*, played a notable part in the battle.

In the spring of 1944 Raaby reported that *Tirpitz* was once again fit to travel and a further attack was planned. It was to be made in April by carrier aircraft of the Home Fleet and they required intelligence of a different sort, notably about anti-aircraft defences. Again it came from all sources and was valuably supplemented by Raaby and PR from north Russia. All this was put together by the excellent Inter-Service Topographical Department in Oxford where many Norwegians were present to lend realism to the intelligence. It had been set up in consequence of the pitiful dearth of this sort of intelligence which had hampered the British forces in Norway in 1940. The *Duke of York* was present at the fly-off and nothing more beautiful, or professional, could be imagined than the sight of the entire fleet racing into the wind in Arctic sunshine against the backdrop of Norway's snow caps.

The attack disabled *Tirpitz* for three months and this time the navy had to depend entirely on Raaby for information on the progress of repairs. Follow-up attacks were attempted by the carriers for which Raaby, with utmost daring, transmitted hourly weather reports. All were frustrated; and in July, Raaby having by now been forced to flee into Sweden, another agent from a safer place in Altafjord reported *Tirpitz* again on the move. A further large-scale attack was planned and this time, at my suggestion, we took Raaby with us in the *Duke of York*. Alcohol meant no more to him than mother's milk: and my mess bill soared.

This attack also failed and *Tirpitz* was finally sunk off Tromsø by RAF Bomber Command. By this time intensified attacks aimed at German merchant shipping in the Leads had been in progress for over a year. Sadly, innocent Norwegian ships sometimes suffered. These attacks were carried out by RAF Coastal Command, carrier aircraft and submarines of the Home Fleet, and the Norwegian motor torpedo boat flotilla based in the Shetlands. Again a large intelligence effort was called for. These attacks had grown in importance. Despite the fact that economic intelligence estimated that ore shipments from Narvik had grown considerably during 1942–1943, it was of the opinion that Germany was suffering from a grave overall shortage of shipping in northern waters. This strain was increased by the restrictions on shipping progressively imposed by Sweden from 1943 and, after the Finnish armistice, by Germany's having to withdraw her northern army through Skibotn and the Inner Leads. The anti-shipping campaign was also intended to reinforce *Fortitude North*, the Allies' pre- D-Day deception plan. This succeeded in tying down a large force of U-boats in southern Norway, while it was not until six months after D-Day that Germany started to withdraw ground forces from Norway to other fronts. These movements were reflected in Ultra and in reports from Norwegian sources.

The anti-shipping campaign contributed materially to the strategic weakening of Germany at this time. During 1944 economic intelligence showed that sinkings were outstripping new construction, while ore shipments declined from 40,000 tons in October 1943 to 12,000 tons in November 1944. Bombing of Norwegian ports assumed high priority towards the end of 1944 when Ultra and PR showed that the Germans intended to continue the U-boat war from Norway after the evacuation of their French bases, now employing a new type of ocean-going U-boat whose formidable characteristics were disclosed by decrypts of Japanese messages from Berlin to Tokyo. These revealed the high hopes pinned on these monsters by Hitler and Doenitz and were among the reasons why some thought that the Germans would continue the war from Norway after the collapse of Germany. Intelligence in London, while lacking intelligence either way of such an intention, confessed in March 1945 that such a development could not be ruled out, but thought that any resistance must be short-lived because of Germany's chronic shortage of oil and of the difficulty of moving stocks of any description to Norway. Of this there was, in any event, no evidence. Indeed Ultra had shown that oil was being moved from Norway to Germany to ease the shortage there. The Allied bombing of the huge concrete shelters for the new U-boats in Bergen and Trondheim was most regrettably accompanied by many Norwegian deaths. Ultra showed that the start of the new Atlantic offensive, originally planned for the autumn of 1944, was being progressively delayed, largely because of the bombing of Germany by Bomber Command and its mining of the Baltic, and the first of the new monster U-boats did not sail from Bergen until a couple of days before Germany's capitulation. She achieved nothing.

I will conclude, as I started, with scientific intelligence. Our history describes the intelligence background to the famous raids on Norsk Hydro's heavy water plant at Vemork, near Rjukan, of which I can give you now only a compressed summary. In early 1942, when the feasibility of constructing an atomic bomb had been accepted and work on a British one approved, nothing definite was known of a German programme, or even if there was one. That the Germans were in some way active in the nuclear research field was known to Allied intelligence from, amongst other sources, the testimony of Swedish scientists – and one Norwegian scientist – having contacts with German scientists known to be interested in nuclear research. This could, in any case, be safely conjectured from SIS and Norwegian reports of mid-1942 that the Germans attached importance to increasing the output of heavy water from Vemork. Opinions differed among the Allies as to whether heavy water could be used in making a viable military weapon within the likely time span of the war. Given the lack of firm intelligence either way, however, SOE was ordered in mid-1942 to plan the destruction of Vemork.

Much information was collected from well-placed Norwegians; but the attack by Combined Operations personnel of November 1942 ended, as is well-known, in dismal failure. There followed Joachim Rønneberg's brilliant attack of February 1943. This time Norwegian Army volunteers were employed backed by much fuller information from PR, the Norwegian High Command and local SIS sources. This destroyed several months' output of heavy water and put the plant out of action. Further stocks were destroyed, by a separate SOE action, while being moved to Germany.

In August 1943 SOE reported that small-scale production had been re-started and in the light of this, and of other information that the Germans were bent on restoring the position, Vemork was finally razed to the ground by the US Air Force. Some have claimed that this put an end to German attempts to produce an atomic bomb. But the British had long thought that the Germans were interested in heavy water for some other purpose – perhaps for the production of fission weapons less than an atomic bomb proper. Some Americans thought differently. In the end the British were proved right. Just as well they were. Otherwise we might not be here today.

References

1   F.H. Hinsley, E.E. Thomas, C.F.G. Ransom and R.C. Knight, *British Intelligence in the Second World War* (4 vols., London, 1979–88)

14 Norwegian intelligence in the Second World War[1]

RAGNAR ULSTEIN

12.5, 1944. Specification of milk deliveries in M6, April 1944.

UNDER this innocent heading there is a listing of milk deliveries to all German billeting areas, hospital wards and military barracks in Nord-møre, the district south of Trondheim. The intelligence organization XU designated the area M6. Rations per soldier amounted to a quarter of a litre of skimmed milk per day. Soldiers in hospital wards were allocated three quarters of a litre per day.

Statements of this kind were provided monthly to the local XU commander by dairy contacts. Similar statements arrived in XU districts throughout Norway. Other statements which showed force levels were deliveries of beer and bread. Taken together, these listings turned out to be a good basis for the counting of troops. Information on force levels was dispatched on microfilm or otherwise well hidden in the care of couriers on board trains headed for Stockholm. The material was picked up there by members of the Norwegian Intelligence Service and forwarded to London.

XU was not the only intelligence gathering organization which kept an eye on the Wehrmacht in Norway, but it was the largest with approximately 1500 agents spread throughout South Norway, and a day-to-day leadership in Oslo. Similar organizations based in Oslo were 830S, RMO and SB. All of them sought to chart and pass on information of military interest. In North Norway, strategically the most important part of occupied Norway, there were similar groups organised by couriers who had come from the Intelligence Office in Stockholm (E-Kontoret). Established in the summer of 1943, they operated from bases close to the border on the Swedish side. In the course of that year, the Swedish policy of neutrality had changed radically in favour of Norway and the Allies. The Swedish intelligence service allowed the Norwegians to establish these bases, and in exchange they were given access to intelligence gathered in Norway.

It is estimated that some 1,400 Norwegian intelligence agents were spread around North Norway. They were farmers, drivers, workers on German construction sites, doctors and teachers and people from other professions and trades. As a rule, they were familiar with the locality and organised in cells which covered specific areas. Couriers transported the intelligence material on the long routes across Arctic mountain regions to the bases on the Swedish side.

Norwegian radio agents, operating along the 2,650-kilometre coast from

Kirkenes in the north-east to Kristiansand in the south, constituted the single most important element of the intelligence-gathering network that was set up in Norway. With undercover hosts and other helpers they numbered 1,800 persons. Radio agents numbered about 200 and operated directly under SIS/FO II (FO II was the Norwegian intelligence office in London). In most cases, they were sent from the British Isles by ship or aircraft, but quite a few came from Sweden. These agents frequently returned to London via Stockholm. At one stage, 50 agents were simultaneously in active service along the Norwegian coast. Their primary task was to report on ship movements. Their primary intelligence target was German warships. Starting in January 1942, when *Tirpitz*, escorted by heavy and light cruisers, steamed northwards to Norwegian bases, this fleet was the prime target for all operational intelligence on the North Norwegian coast.

From the autumn of 1943 the intelligence units in Norway covered the Wehrmacht on land and at sea, with or without radio transmitters. The Gestapo frequently infiltrated the networks which had been built up in various sectors, though in most cases invisible hands were able to repair the damage and reestablish functioning networks. Tragedies occurred all the time. Successful German penetration was invariably followed by arrests, torture, despatch of prisoners to concentration camps in Germany or summary executions. Still, the record of triumphs compensated for occasional setbacks. During long periods of the war, no ship could pass through a coastal district without shortly afterwards being reported to operational commands. In a note to the Norwegian High Command, Lieutenant Commander Eric Welsh, head of the Scandinavian section of SIS, gave an example of the speed and effectiveness of the reporting system which had been developed. The note concerned two SIS agents operating along the coast north of Florø, a small town between Bergen and Trondheim:

> This station is providing most useful information. I may refer to a telegram No.8 dated 5 February (1943): Time of observation 1100. Time of Dispatch (message to SIS) 1312. Received at HQ 1342. Received in Admiralty 1348. Content of message was that one battle cruiser, one cruiser and three destroyers had passed in a southerly direction. The message was supplemented on the same day at 1400, received here at 1617 and sent to the Admiralty at 1630. It confirms that the ships involved were HIPPER, KÖLN and three destroyers.

The 'E-groups' (intelligence-gathering groups) which covered the Wehrmacht on land were no less efficient than those operating along the coast. Gradually, German fortifications and military units were described and their location mapped, while changes and movements were recorded continuously. The age of the soldiers and their fitness for combat were all reported. News about Hitler's secret weapons, one-man submarines or torpedoes, quickly reached the Allies over the radio or via Stockholm. The agents along the coast and throughout the country became the eyes and ears of the Allies, and were probably the most significant contribution which the resistance movement made to the victory in 1945.

There is a wide gap, however, between the nation-wide coverage which the intelligence service provided in Norway in 1943–5, and the patch-work of 'rescue groups' set up in 1940. Practically all of these initial groups were destroyed by the Gestapo in the weeks or months that followed. They lacked experience in secret operations and knowledge of the Gestapo. The first Norwegian Gestapo collaborators were up and running as early as the first illegal groups. Gradually, however, the knowledge acquired by members of the resistance leaked out of their prison cells: the secret German police and Abwehr agents, disguised as 'good Norwegians', were seriously underestimated. Later, knowledge about the torture, which very few could resist, also came out.

The British intelligence service and the inexperienced Norwegian one which was established in the summer of 1940 started from scratch. Both the groups in Norway and the leadership abroad had to go through the painful process of learning from experience and mistakes. The first SIS station came from England in the summer of 1940, but did not last long. 'Hardware', as it was known, operated from Haugesund, south of Bergen, and lasted eight weeks before it was uncovered by a collaborator disguised as an 'Englandsfarer'. The transmitter 'Oldell', which came to Oslo in July 1940, survived remarkably long, until March 1941, when it was uncovered, not by collaborators, but by the second major enemy, the 'peiler'(radio direction finder).

There were many individuals who, in the year of defeat and without a mandate, decided to leave Norway and establish links with the Norwegian and British leadership in London. Many of them were endowed with exceptional energy and courage. A great number of them returned as intelligence agents, saboteurs and instructors. Most of what was initiated in Norway from the outside was based on these people. Very often the districts where they came from, and to which they were sent, became the first points of support for the operational intelligence gathering service. Other points along the Norwegian coast might have been at least as interesting. But, so far, no refugees had come from these areas. This accidental, personal choice of individuals and operational areas lasted far into the war, typically enough for a population under occupation, where the overwhelming majority doubted that their contribution could make a difference one way or the other. They were spectators of the global drama, which, to a very great extent, also concerned them.

Perhaps it was not such a haphazard choice, after all? The individuals who came in the hour of defeat did represent a special category. That they risked their lives by reporting to the authorities abroad, may be indicative of this. Other individuals, with similar qualities, had, simultaneously, started some sort of illegal activity at home in Norway. The intelligence service, like Milorg and all other resistance activity, was developed by people of this kind. Many of them committed grave blunders during the first two years. First and foremost, they were too open and optimistic, and many of them paid dearly for it. But later generations of resistance people were to stand on their shoulders. What distinguished the intelligence service from much other resistance in occupied

Norway was that it was at war from the outset. Signals and reports from stations and groups formed the basis for operations on Norwegian territory, either there and then or subsequently. One should add that those who were involved in intelligence gathering – Allied espionage – risked heavier punishment than most others if they fell into the hands of the enemy.

It is necessary to distinguish more clearly between two kinds of military intelligence: operational and static intelligence. The operational, which might form the basis for rapid operations, was transmitted by radio stations. The static emanated from groups that transmitted reports by courier, and provided the basis for future operations. Groups that provided static intelligence grew up largely without outside initiative. They established contacts with the authorities abroad and subjected themselves to their leadership. Radio stations were, as a general rule, established on the initiative of SIS/FO II in London. Orders were passed on from the Defence Command (Forsvarets Overkommando – FO) in London, mostly through MI II in Stockholm to the static intelligence gathering groups, which were financed by the Norwegian defence ministry. SIS had a corresponding authority over the Norwegian radio agents.

From 1941 to the summer of 1943 half a dozen Norwegian-Russian radio groups had been established along the coast of Finnmark and North Troms. Their tasks were roughly similar to those of the SIS agents, except they were under Russian leadership. In the course of July–August 1943 these groups were broken up and practically exterminated by German forces.

The Lines of Command to Norway

The Intelligence Office of the Norwegian Ministry of Foreign Affairs had been established in London in the summer of 1940 on the initiative of three refugees, who were its first three officials. The office was in close collaboration with the (British) Secret Intelligence Service. In January 1941, the office was absorbed into a new Intelligence Office, which the government established under the Ministry of Defence ('E'-Office). This office was responsible for recruitment and, together with the British, for the training of radio agents. The British had operational command in the field. Sources show that the British operators were working closely with the Intelligence Office, which was later dubbed FO II. Static intelligence material from Norway was initially dealt with by British experts. But as the Norwegians gradually acquired officers from different districts in Norway, they were themselves able to handle the material, analyse it and pass it on to military planning staffs.

In April 1943, FO in London wanted to decentralise the XU organisation in South Norway, in order that each district might report directly to the XU chief of the military office at the Stockholm legation. London felt it was too risky to have the leadership of the largest intelligence organisation remain in occupied territory. If it were to be captured, the whole organisation might be destroyed. XU chief Arvid Storsveen, who stayed in Stockholm, travelled to Oslo to explain the matter to his successor. It turned out that the latter disagreed with the plan. While Arvid Storsveen negotiated with the resident leadership, he was taken by surprise by the Gestapo and killed. Arvid Storsveen's successor as XU chief, based in Stockholm, was his brother Erik, who had formerly been regional chief in Trondheim. XU South Norway – outside Trøndelag and Inner East Norway – continued under the leadership of the chief in Oslo, Øistein Strømnæs. Conditions were ripe for discord, which erupted in the autumn of 1943 with a declaration from the XU chief in Oslo to stop furnishing intelligence until certain conditions were met, among them replacement of personnel at MI II in Stockholm. FO accepted these demands because the alternative was to sack the XU chief in Oslo. The consequence might have been that the XU organisation, which consisted of experienced leaders and collaborators, would disintegrate. The authorities did not venture to take such a risk. The struggle between the XU leadership and FO/MI II flared up again later and reached a climax just before the war ended. This affair throws light on the dilemma a defence command in exile faces when it is charged with running secret military activity in occupied territories.

Section II of the Defence Command, FO II, was, from February 1942 onwards, charged with responsibility for static intelligence gathering. FO IV was responsible for Milorg, and SOE was charged with a large number of operations in Norway. These were gradually coordinated with Milorg. In the autumn of 1943 this division of responsibility between Milorg and the intelligence service was implemented in Stockholm, with MI II for intelligence and MI IV for Milorg.

In the field there were a number of instances when the intelligence-gathering aspects of the secret services clashed with Milorg and SOE. Often this simply could not be avoided, owing to the secret nature of the service and fact that the recruitment of collaborators and contacts was limited. But there were also tensions between different groups and organisations at home and the secret services based abroad. By the nature of things intelligence-gathering services could never be coordinated in the field. In principle, radio agents who came in from Britain or Sweden were to keep away from other resistance groups. In practice, it often turned out that agents needed help from people who worked for one or more of them.

Offices in charge of intelligence operations and organisations were spread out, in London, Stockholm or Oslo. This led to problems of cooperation and often to strife, but, under the circumstances, it was an unavoidable price to pay. Norwegian and Allied authorities in London and Stockholm learned that it was practically impossible to interfere in the structuring of the intelligence networks at home against the will of the leaders there. Consequently, the XU Centre in Oslo kept its chief until the end of the war. The large illegal organisations, with their links to parallel and subordinate groups and contacts, were given an authoritarian structure because of security considerations. The need for protection against the Gestapo created an exclusive circle of initiates at the top, and a corresponding sense of loyalty from the many local leaders who never saw the supreme leader.

The flow of operational and static intelligence from occupied Norway increased from year to year. Operational intelligence continued to be provided in all essentials by the radio agents, who worked for SIS/FO II. The SOE agents usually had main tasks other than intelligence-gathering and are, consequently, not dealt with here. But from them, too, there was a steady stream of intelligence reports and signals.

Four SIS stations were operational during the second half of 1940. In 1941, the number was 6, in 1942, 11, in 1943, 24, in 1944, 51, and in 1945, 46. Few of these stations were operational for more than a year. At times, coverage was far less complete than the figures would indicate. At the end of April 1945, SIS/FO had 27 operational radio stations in Norway. Of these, 14 were located along the coast of Trøndelag and North Norway. Although the number of operational stations was low in this period, the overall impression of rapid growth is nevertheless correct. The loss of stations in the spring of 1945 would have been more than compensated for by new or planned stations when the war came to an end. With respect to the Russian-Norwegian stations in Finnmark and Troms, Norwegian, and to some extent Russian, sources, indicate that these were operational from the end of 1941; there were 7 operational stations between 1942 and the summer of 1943. After that only one or two were in operation.

The number of radio messages varied from month to month. Some stations had technical problems, others were exposed and were taken by the enemy, or were closed for a while, and then disappeared. Overall, however, the quantity of operational radio messages increased sharply. As regards the SIS stations, there are reports of only 19 messages from these in 1940. This number is probably too low. The 'Oldell' station in Oslo despatched more than 600 signals from July 1940 to March 1941. During its eight weeks of operation the station 'Hardware' at Haugesund despatched 70 signals. However, probably only 19 signals from these stations had real operational value. The reason may be that our source, FO II, was insufficiently informed about the British-led activity so early during the war, and before the Norwegian administration was established. The author has not had access to the SIS archives, which are, regrettably, still closed to researchers.

Three years later, in 1943, the number of operational messages had reached 1,100, and in 1944, 3,017. During the last four months of the war there were reportedly 878. According to the final report of FO II, the system had handled 5,600 reports in the course of the five war years. The number of reports that provided static intelligence, mostly from groups without radio transmitters, also increased markedly. FO II's record of registered reports via Sweden to London from May 1942 to May 1945, shows that 1,796 messages arrived during the latter half of 1942. The number shot up to 3,664 in 1943 and to 10,400 in 1944. During the last four months of the war, 4,250 messages arrived in London. Altogether, this amounted to some 20,000 reports. At times, XU's contribution reached more than 1,000 typed pages in the course of one week.

In the period 1940–42, refugee and interrogation reports, especially from people who came from coastal areas, were judged to be of particular importance. Added to this, as noted above, were the 'E'-telegrams despatched from the SOE-Milorg stations. In the spring of 1945, there were 69 of them in Norway. Many intelligence reports, sketches and pictures were given added value when compared with photographs taken by Allied and Norwegian aircraft during thousands of missions over Norway. FO II developed an archive of aerial photographs which made it possible quickly to find pictures that were needed for operations in Norway. A number of offices under FO II took care of individual districts in Norway. Others specialised in various subject areas, Navy, Army, Air Force, artillery, railways and other scheduled traffic.

On 1 July 1944, the Intelligence Office of the Ministry of Defence, FD/E, was merged with F0 II. Leaders, district specialists and desk officers were still, with few exceptions, veterans from intelligence groups in Norway. The principal task of FO II was, as before, to process all reports about German military activity in Norway in order to obtain a picture of their forces at any given time, their combat strength and readiness. These estimates were developed jointly by five sections covering the German Army, the Navy, the Air Force, Norwegian industry and Norwegian topography respectively.

FO II became a provider of intelligence reports for Norwegian and Allied staffs. The section produced detailed district books for some counties in West Norway, and for some thirty towns, with sketches of all fixed German defence installations, billeting and stocks. The books were produced in accordance with a loose-leaf system and were continually kept up to date. They formed the basis for all military planning of operations in Norway. Similar surveys were put together for oil storage tanks, industrial plant, telecommunications, roads, bridges, harbours and Norwegian ships under German control. On average, FO II prepared 20–25 major reports a month, most of them written in English and based on intelligence which was continuously pouring in from Norway.

FO II's office responsible for covering troop formations and strength, gradually developed an archive of German forces in Norway. The archive included files for each division, every naval command along the coast – there were ten of them – and for subjects that were to be studied more closely. There was an index of more than 5,000 German officers in Norway, a listing of army postal service numbers and of the number of Germans who were billeted at 2,000 localities throughout the country.

The Losses

The total loss of life in the intelligence gathering groups was, according to the author's records, 267. One hundred and two were executed, 94 died in prison or camps, 67 died in combat or under arrest, and four died as they attempted to escape. Altogether some 800 persons escaped, and about as many were arrested. The casualties of the Norwegian-Russian groups, which operated on the coast of Finnmark and Troms, were far greater than in all other intelligence groups. Out of more than 100 persons, 52 were arrested. Of these, 23 were executed, 10 died in combat, two died in accidents and 11 escaped. This represents 35 dead, and a total loss – if prisoners and refugees are included – of nearly 100 per cent. Loss of life in the radio groups that were directed from London was comparatively small. Out of some 1,800, about which there is more detailed information, slightly more than 50, or some 3 per cent, lost their lives. The approximately 200 SIS agents in this group took a loss of 26 men, i.e. some 12 per cent. The static intelligence gathering organisations had the lowest casualty figures. Sources with detailed information on 1,200 persons from the whole country indicate that 23 lost their lives.

There are several reasons why the losses were nearly total for the Soviet-Norwegian groups. Most important, perhaps, is that the occupier dealt far more harshly with prisoners who had been directed from the Soviet Union than from Britain. Some of these groups were also located in areas on the coast of Finnmark and Troms which made it very difficult for them to hide from the local population. To some extent they were victimised by gossip and informers. The accounts also show that the operational intelligence service with radio transmitters was more prone to suffer casualties than the static groups.

The leadership in London considerably underrated the dangers of radio bearing in Norway. Reports from the field about sudden arrests and loss of stations were incomplete, and it may at times have been difficult to provide a reliable reason as to why a radio station was taken. Might it be the work of informers, loose talk, radio bearing, or simply an accident? We must assume that all of these potential reasons were investigated. The available source material does not indicate that London was particularly concerned about radio bearing, even though signals from stations and reports from telegraph operators often referred to determined direction-finding boats and aircraft and soldiers with antennas that protruded from their rucksacks. As early as the spring of 1941, there were reports suggesting that radio bearing was the probable reason for one of the first losses of a radio transmitter and an operator ('Oldell'). In the autumn of that year, the bearing of another station was taken ('Skylark B'). The same fate befell other stations later. Nearly all of the stations – twelve in all – taken in 1944 were exposed by direction-finding equipment. Most losses in 1945 were attributed to the same reason. It seems that, until the end, the SIS leadership was of the opinion that their equipment was difficult or impossible to locate with direction finders. The operators at the Sabor station in Rogaland learned by bitter experience, as the last in line of a long row of colleagues, that SIS erred in this vital area.

SOE, the sister organisation of SIS, which directed the many Linge and Milorg stations, was far more on its guard against direction finders. The operators usually had orders to move to new bases after a few weeks. Moves of this kind were in themselves risky, but it was thought to be less risky than to operate in the same location for long periods. This is precisely what most of the SIS stations did. This practice had obvious advantages as it relieved radio agents of the difficulties and dangers of providing new contacts. It also, however, increased the dangers of exposure.

Resistance groups at home and the leadership abroad learned from experience in the field. That also goes for SIS/FO-II in other contexts, but in this important area they do not appear to have learned very much. A memo from FO-II, signed by General Hansteen and Lieutenant Colonel Roscher Lund in December 1944 to MI II substantiates this. It states *inter alia*: 'As regards the risks from direction finding equipment, it is, of course, true that every station can be located, but, as a rule not to the extent that the location can be pinpointed. Quite possibly, some stations may have been taken as a result of direction finding, but it is not known to us . . .'

The Illegal Structures

From 1943 onwards, the intelligence-gathering groups were, like other military units in occupied territory, secured externally against one another. They were also secured internally through intermediaries who would have to bear the brunt when someone was arrested, and slow down or render exposure impossible. In reality, precautionary measures were often poor. Many agents knew about one another. At times, the situation was so transparent that security rules could not be put into practice. But also in bigger cities there were too many who knew too much. There was a considerable number of cross-contacts between groups and organisations, which developed as the need arose or as a result of the agents' and leaders' zeal for work. Having once specialised, intelligence-gathering became a trial of patience for agents who had been given tasks that did not require much time. Many agents wanted to do more, but in that event this had to be done inside other groups, and that was against the rules.

The British commander of the Scandinavian section of SIS had a motto which he reportedly tried to imprint upon Norwegian SIS agents in the field: *Little, but good*. There were many SIS agents, and even more in the other intelligence gathering groups, who did not manage to live up to that motto. The rough winds of war forced them into ever wider fields. The SIS chief himself violated this motto when, in 1944, he let one of his best radio agents organise a network of stations between Stavanger and Bergen. This agent did an outstanding job. Reports from his transmitters provided the basis for several successful attacks on German convoys. Yet when this lone agent was accidentally arrested, everything collapsed throughout the large district.

The organisation of the network of agents around the battleship *Tirpitz*, with nearly ten stations along the coast between Alta and Ofoten, suffered from a similar weakness, but it did not result in a catastrophe. The operators knew about the nearest neighbouring station, and often more than that, and many of them had joint contacts. Four of the stations were taken, but none of the neighbouring stations were exposed.

The security of radio stations in the Oslo area was generally poor for most of the war. The majority of operators and leaders knew about one another, and some helped, or were stand-ins, for others. Some of the contacts were so infiltrated into neighbouring groups that the Gestapo, given some luck and skill, might have broken up most of it. But when they were provided with an opportunity, they shot and killed the principal agents and got no further. Several radio agents in the Oslo area had, incidentally, contacts high up in the Sicherheitsdienst, Abwehr and Stapo, and took their precautions as far as possible.

The author's records show that many intelligence agents had already been working for other organisations, especially Milorg, but also in export activity and illegal newspapers. Nearly all intelligence leaders had started their illegal career in other illegal groups. When someone was arrested in some of these 'older' groups, former members were exposed to danger. It was conceivable that prisoners under torture might reveal names of persons who had left the group in the belief that they had opted out of illegal work. In this manner a person or a group, otherwise well secured, might face disaster.

Generally speaking, most intelligence-gathering groups developed a proficiency which rivalled that of the opponent, the Gestapo. The amateurs who survived 1940–3 eventually turned professional. They knew much about the Sicherheitspolizei and knew that, subjected to torture they might sooner or later be opened like a book. The guiding principle was therefore that contacts were to hide or flee when one of their own had been arrested. Nonetheless, there are many examples of contacts who did not escape in time.

Some prisoners endured torture longer than others. There were those who broke down immediately out of fear or confusion. Evidence was either overwhelming, or the prisoner was confronted with others who had already been forced to talk. No member of the underground who knew of the Gestapo's methods could pass judgment on those who cracked in prison. In spite of this, there was throughout the country, and in most groups, people who thought that *they* would put up with torture, at least for a few hours. And we know that some of them managed just that, while others succeeded in misleading the interrogators long enough for the contacts to escape.

The Achievements

It is impossible to assess with complete accuracy the achievements of the intelligence-gathering service throughout the five years of war. We know that hundreds of signals about *Tirpitz* and the German strike fleet from January 1942 onwards contributed, together with other sources, towards either destroying the fleet or effecting its withdrawal from Norway. As such, they also contributed to the resumption of the massive Allied logistical effort to Murmansk in late autumn 1943, which was kept going until the end of the war. The Russian-Norwegian radio agents along the coast of Finnmark and North Troms, as well as the radio agents from the west along the coast of Nordland and South Norway, contributed to the sinking of many supply ships. During the final war months German shipping was practically paralysed by losses.

With respect to the static intelligence-gathering groups, we know that they carefully mapped the Wehrmacht in Norway, its installations, forts and fortifications, air fields, camps and military stores. They furnished information and kept Allied staffs up to date on bridges, roads and harbours. When Germany pulled the Lapland Army out of Finland and into Norway and started to send military units to the Continent, the intelligence groups covered their movements southwards from district to district to ports of shipment in Østfold, Oslo and Vestfold. Reports about the quality of the troops in the country were provided. Reinforcements to Norway of mini-submarines in

1944–5, one of Hitler's secret weapons, were soon discovered, and their subsequent movements were reported continuously.

Civilian and military supplies were registered. Hundreds of agents furnished information about German readiness against Allied landings, about plans for the blowing up of bridges, quays and other installations. SIS agents in Oslo had moles high up in the Wehrmacht command and in the Abwehr. XU had a source in Gestapo's headquarters at Viktoria Terrasse. There was a steady stream of information about Wehrmacht officers and officials of the Sicherheitsdienst, about Norwegian and Allied prisoners and casualties.

During the final months of the war there was uncertainty as to whether the Germans would fight in Norway following capitulation on the Continent. The information that 5,500 intelligence agents provided about the Wehrmacht was an important factor in drawing up Allied plans. The wealth of information that had been gathered during the war also proved most useful when the Wehrmacht finally capitulated in Norway on 8 May 1945, and Allied and Norwegian forces moved in to take control.

References

1   This article is based on a three-volume work by the author on the Intelligence Service in Norway, 1940–45. The third volume was published by Cappelen Forlag, Oslo, in October 1992. The sources are Norwegian, British and German and have been annotated in the book.

15 Milorg and SOE

ARNFINN MOLAND

MY subject for this chapter is the relationship between the Norwegian Military Organisation and the British Special Operation Executive – henceforward 'Milorg and SOE'. The evolving relationship between the two ad hoc organisations followed a pattern familiar in occupied countries during the Second World War. It was one of growing together from point zero through a period of reluctant acceptance, and then finally entering an almost frictionless stage with virtually no discord at all. The wartime period can thus be divided into three phases. The first may be labelled *the phase of non-collaboration*, to put it somewhat dramatically. This attitude, which was mutual, lasted from the summer of 1940 throughout the year 1941 and into the best part of 1942 as far as the rank and file of the two organisations were concerned. At the leadership level, however, one aspired to do better, and consequently a *period of coexistence* and even *cooperation* developed from the autumn of 1941 onwards. It was, however, the last two years of the war that constituted the *time of cooperation* on all levels.

In order to understand this development, it is necessary to sketch the events from 1940. Having recovered from the shock created by the German attack on 9 April, different groups of people in Norway began to plan for some sort of resistance. By the end of 1940 an organisation for military resistance – Milorg – existed, though at an embryonic stage. It was founded, inspired and directed by Norwegians in Norway, and was recognised as part of the Norwegian armed forces under the command of the Norwegian government and the Norwegian High Command in London on November 20, 1941. During this premature stage, Milorg was joined by an unknown, but large number of men. The aim was to build up a secret army in the most careful manner, avoiding actions and even weapons, and to prepare for the day of liberation.[1] Milorg wanted to 'go slow, lie low'. One should not attract German attention and thereby jeopardise the lives of civilians and have the fragile Milorg nipped in the bud.

As for the British, their military intelligence had jumped the gun and dispatched a few men to Norway a few days before the German attack.[2] The man who later became head of SOE, Major-General Sir Colin Gubbins, participated in the campaign in Norway in the spring of 1940. These men established contacts with quite a few Norwegians, and when SOE was established in July 1940, they became the core of the Norwegian component in the British effort to hamper the German exploitation of the country. SOE's aim was to carry out acts of sabotage in German-occupied countries. Its Scandinavian Section, began to develop under the direction of Charles (later Sir Charles) Hambro. Norwegian refugees were happy to be asked to go on special training courses with the purpose of becoming British agents in Norway. Gradually, this resulted in the formation of the Norwegian Independent Company No. 1, later called the Linge Company after its leader, Captain Martin Linge. In December 1940 the important Shetland base was established as a joint base for SOE and the Secret Intelligence Service (SIS). Norwegian refugees, who had crossed the sea in their fishing boats, were recruited as agents. These agents joined the Linge Company and Shetland base, and adopted the British view of active resistance policy in occupied countries, which corresponded roughly to their own. It is therefore evident that this group of Norwegians was bound to clash with their Milorg colleagues – in spite of their having the same goal, a free Norway – as their ways of achieving this objective differed so much.

What, then, was SOE's resistance policy for Norway? While the Milorg leadership wanted to build up a centralised secret army, slowly and carefully over a long period, avoiding activities that might endanger the work of the organisation, SOE's leaders were in a hurry. They had a great need for activity that would produce results to present to MEW. The idea of a 'secret army' was not too popular in the Admiralty, in the War Office or among the Chiefs of Staff. 'Irregular warfare' could easily become a war fought by amateurs. But SOE had Churchill on its side as he favoured any offensive strategy, especially in Norway. SOE's solution was raids and sabotage, contrary to the policy of Milorg. Furthermore, inside SOE's Norwegian Section, both in London and Stockholm, there were 'several Britons who took the absolute standing' that SOE should conduct its work without interference from Milorg. Colonel J.S. Wilson, head of the Section, put it like this:

> There was still amongst its staff the inherent British attitude of kindly –
> but none the less galling – superiority to the foreigners. There existed
> . . . a distrust of Milorg's ability to take ordinary security precautions.
> The arrests in the autumn of 1941 gave apparent reason for this distrust.[3]

Wilson concludes that 'the tendency of the British officers concerned was to demand that all S.O.E. organisation should be independent of Milorg'.

It is fair to say that the British view on the lack of security inside Milorg was based more on facts than on a condescending attitude to foreigners. Members of Milorg and their leadership were of course amateurs in the field of clandestine activities. Some British officers claimed that Norwegians in general were too talkative and open. But then again some Norwegians commented on certain British officers: for instance the Milorg pioneer Paal Frisvold remarked on Major Malcolm Munthe: '. . . to carry out secret military missions in Norway, I don't know anyone who is less suitable than him'.[4] I shall not elaborate on this quotation, but as for the British view, it is indisputable that Milorg had to learn 'the hard lesson of security' and they had to learn it 'in the bitter school of experience', as the British put it. And, it may be added, they *did*.

SOE decided to carry out its resistance activities in Norway independently of Milorg and the Norwegian government and other Norwegian authorities in

London. SOE's important document pertaining to this decision, 'Norwegian Policy' of 11 December 1940, gave directives to those Norwegians who worked for SOE in Norway; it also reflects the importance that the British attached to Norway. Although the document stated that the liberation of Norway would most probably come as a result of an Allied invasion, it was also necessary that SOE boost the Norwegian morale by means of propaganda and sabotage. The key phrase here is that through SOE, Norway was to become 'a thorn in the German side'. The ultimate aim was a general rising in Norway. This could only be achieved by having a separate SOE organisation in each district. The document stated finally that SOE had a 'long-term programme' and a 'short-term programme'. The former aimed at building up a Secret Army, trained in guerrilla and sabotage, and assisting an Allied invasion. The 'short-term programme' aimed at raids and sabotage, so-called 'tip-and-run landings and air raids', carried out in association with the Directorate of Combined Operations (DCO).

One such raid was the *Claymore* operation against the Lofoten Islands on 4 March 1941. The British evaluated this raid as a great success, 'a classic example of a perfectly executed commando-raid'.[5] I do not intend to go into details about these raids as such, but it is obvious that the British attitude was not shared in Norway. The Germans took heavy reprisals: homes were burnt, people arrested. Besides, the targets destroyed were regarded in Norway as Norwegian property, not as a blow to Germany's capacity to wage war. It even struck a jarring note among the participating Norwegian soldiers who began to doubt whether it was right to operate under British orders and carry out British plans, perhaps even without the knowledge of the Norwegian Government.[6] SOE, however, was thrilled by the success of Operation *Claymore*. The result was a document entitled 'Scandinavian Policy' of 16 April 1941, in which SOE expressed its wish to do things its own way and get things going in Norway's fight for freedom. In doing this, however, SOE definitely overestimated the Norwegian willingness to fight the German occupation regardless of the consequences.

Why then this concern for the consequences? The answer is that the Norwegian resistance leaders felt a heavy burden of responsibility. Norway had lived in peace for 126 years: they were not mentally prepared for war. In their report of 10 June 1941, which was addressed to King Haakon, but ended up with SOE, Milorg's Council emphasised that they did not want weapons and that they resented any sabotage acts, whether carried out by SOE or by any other organisation. It was this attitude that provoked the famous remark from one of the Milorg pioneers in London: 'Military Sunday School'. The Milorg leaders received a reply from SOE in August of the same year, but it contained no changed attitude. On the contrary, SOE stressed the need for a more active policy: sabotage, training and arms drill. Last but not least, the reply implied that Milorg must take orders from the British.[7] This was not at all reassuring to Milorg. Besides, they were not at all convinced that the Norwegian government was kept informed about SOE's activities in Norway. When the problems and misunderstandings concerning their own attempt to make contact with the government were solved in October 1941, they learnt that their letter of 10 June had never reached its destination. Their suspicion that SOE was keeping the Norwegian government in the dark was proved. To avoid further calamities, the Norwegian government recognised Milorg in November 1941.

SOE responded quickly with a memorandum entitled 'Anglo-Norwegian Collaboration regarding the Military Organisation in Norway', written by Sir Charles Hambro and sent to the Norwegian minister of defence, Oscar Torp. Hambro expressed a wish to cooperate with the Norwegian government and other Norwegian authorities. But Milorg must work along the same lines as SOE had drawn up for resistance in other occupied countries, based on mutual confidence and harmonious cooperation between British and Norwegian resistance leaders in England. Torp accepted the invitation and, with his personal assistant Thore Boye, met Sir Charles Hambro. He assured Hambro that 'not only was he in favour of continuing the arrangements that existed between the Norwegian authorities and S.O.E., but that he wanted to facilitate them'.[8] In return he personally expected to be taken into SOE's confidence 'absolutely'.

In the meantime, a report on the raid against Måløy, Operation *Anklet* in December 1941, stated that the year 'ended on a sad note', with Captain Linge himself being among those killed. This time a group of twelve Linge soldiers took action. They felt they could not go on fighting, feeling almost like mercenaries as they did not have the blessing of Norwegian authorities.[9] Though in a minority, their view was soon approved, after a short period of internment. The principle at stake – full information and approval of the Norwegian government – was guaranteed in the year 1942.

There were no more raids. Instead, SOE concentrated on the long-term programme. On 1 January 1942 a special Norwegian Section, headed by Wilson, was established within the SOE to direct SOE's work in Norway. In addition, the talks between Sir Charles Hambro and Oscar Torp resulted in the establishment of the important Anglo-Norwegian Collaboration Committee (ANCC). Thirdly, on 6 February, Torp established the Norwegian High Command (FO). On 16 February the first meeting of the ANCC was held, with representatives of SOE and FO. One may say that the two organisations now entered the phase of cooperation, and one might consequently conclude that this goes for SOE and Milorg as well. However, though these organisa-tional improvements at the top marked a great step forward, the problems in the field were far from being solved. The gap between word and deed was in fact at its greatest in the year 1942, as the policy of non-collaboration continued among the rank and file. Agents were still sent to Norway with strict orders to avoid contact with members of Milorg. I therefore choose the expression 'coexistence' to characterise the relationship at this time.

As for SOE's relation with the Norwegian legation in Stockholm, which also had an important link to Milorg, the legation was, according to Wilson, more reluctant to adopt the new policy of 'complete trust and co-operation'. As a result, Major John Rognes, who had assisted SOE activities from Shetland in 1941, was sent by Minister Torp to Stockholm. His mission helped to improve relations between the legation and SOE, Norwegian Section in Stockholm.

The main issue for the SOE-Milorg relationship in 1942 was the question of their role in the reconquest of Norway. A Norwegian committee in Great Britain had drawn up the main tasks for Milorg, and their view was then evaluated by SOE. Lack of space prevents me from elaborating on this theme, but an important Norwegian claim was that Milorg should only be fully engaged in case of an invasion aiming at a permanent reconquest of Norway or part of it. This meant, according to SOE, that SOE could not carry out its 'short-term actions'. A meeting was held in Stockholm in February to coordinate the view of the Ministry of Defence with that of the Milorg leaders. Finally SOE delivered its report in April on 'The Reconquest of Norway. SOE's Role'. Here they summed up their activity and expressed their will to cooperate. However, it would still be necessary to maintain separate SOE organisations in the districts in Norway, which would have no contact with their Milorg colleagues. The formal expression for this 'apartheid' policy was 'certain lines of parallel action'. SOE and Milorg should, however, let these lines fuse 'when the proper time for amalgamation comes'. SOE considered the establishment of radio communications between Norway and Great Britain, between Sweden and Norway, and inside Norway, to be SOE's main role in the future, together with supplying Norway with weapon and explosives, training and transporting Norwegian agents. Finally SOE would do the utmost to help with 'long-term planning with a view to the reconquest of Norway'.[10]

During the year 1942, the policy of 'parallel action' often led to grave episodes. At Lillehammer, the agent 'Anvil', suspected of being a traitor, was nearly killed by Milorg. Careless agents jeopardised Milorg's regional resistance network, and the crises piled up as the year progressed. The process began when 'Penguin' and 'Anchor' got into a fight with the Gestapo, leading to the German reprisals at Televåg in April 1942, 'the greatest shock that Resistance in Norway had yet encountered'.[11] This community on the western coast of Norway was destroyed and its inhabitants deported. In addition, eighteen men were shot as a reprisal. The military resistance on the west coast of Norway received a heavy blow through these arrests and executions. To add to the problems, SIS played a part in the same area and 'contributed in part or in whole to the disaster'.

The next SOE operation, *Redshank*, in Trøndelag in May 1942, was more successful. It was the first coup-de-main operation against an industrial target: a transformer station was destroyed to slow down the delivery to the Germans of the valuable pyrites from the Orkla mines. The drawback was of course sharpened vigilance against resistance work in the district. But the year 1942 continued to produce disasters. The capture of the *Anchor* organiser in Drammen in May resulted in a series of arrests two months later. Added to the seizure in Østfold of the SOE agent 'Crow', this was a heavy blow to Milorg in eastern Norway. The Milorg leader Knut Møyen wrote in a contemporary report that had it not been for the standing order given to the SOE agents to avoid Milorg, this would not have happened:

> The difficulties and the situation as a whole change every week, so to speak, and it is therefore necessary that all who arrive get thorough

additional briefing, no matter how well they have been instructed in England.[12]

In September and October, the time had come for Trøndelag and northern Norway. To make a long story short, the first joint SOE-DCO coup-de-main operation ever, *Knotgrass-Unicorn*, against the Glomfjord Power Station and the SOE operation *Kestrel* against Fosdalen Mines, both carried out entirely without the knowledge of Milorg and with no information about the activities whatsoever, led to a fervent search for resistance people in the district. From 6 to 12 October, a state of emergency was inaugurated in Trøndelag and 29 persons were executed.

As this tragic year in the history of military resistance in Norway progressed, the Milorg leaders were on the verge of giving up their work. New meetings were held at the highest levels. To solve the crisis of confidence, not only between Milorg and SOE, but also between Milorg and Norwegian authorities in England, FO in June 1942 sent Jacob Schive back to Norway. A Milorg pioneer highly respected by the organisation, Schive returned to London with a report which slightly exaggerated Milorg's strength. Together with the disastrous effects of the 'certain lines of parallel action' pertaining to SOE and Milorg and the continuing process going on inside the ANCC, it resulted in a new document issued by SOE on 21 September 1942. Written by Wilson himself, this amounted to nothing less then a new programme called 'SOE Long-term Policy in Norway' in which SOE finally gave up its independent course. SOE admitted the mistakes that had been made on both sides, including the 'lines of parallel action' and declared that a 'drastic revision' was necessary. Wilson's attitude played a great role in this process of mutual understanding:

> . . .in time all realised that it was impossible to run two independent
> para-military underground movements side by side. Inevitably it would
> lead to crossing of lines and to the two cutting each other's throats.[13]

Major Leif Tronstad, one of the leading resistance pioneers, now in London and member of the ANCC, and 'whose memory as "The Professor" will be held in reverence by all in S.O.E.',[14] expressed it this way:

> We have experienced that it is impossible to maintain two separated
> military organisations without intermixing and complications that may
> trigger off the worst consequences. We must therefore go for *one*
> effective organisation with *a mutual strong* leadership.'[15]

Directives were issued by both SOE and FO aiming at securing good relationship on all levels. SOE and FO agreed on what were to be their respective responsibilities and duties. Initiative, planning, education of agents and instructors, transport, supplies, were all to be taken care of by SOE, in cooperation with FO. Milorg should roughly speaking provide the rank and file. Resistance policy should be a matter for the ANCC, whereas the everyday performance in Norway should be handled by the Milorg leaders. To quote Wilson again:

> Taking it all in all, FO IV/SOE/OSS seemed to have come through most of their childhood's ills, and to be gaining in strength and, possibly, in wisdom.

One should, however, bear in mind that SOE had been established for the purpose of coordinating the irregular military resistance with the Allied war effort. Consequently, it was important for the Chiefs of Staff Committee that SOE's hegemony as the only 'co-ordinating authority' in these matter was recognised.

Though there are sources indicating that 'especially from December 1943 . . . the cooperation has had an intimate character',[16] it is fair to say that the period of non-collaboration in the field and coexistence at the top level was transformed into full cooperation on all levels from the beginning of 1943 onwards. Contact between Oslo and London was improving, followed by a better understanding between the Central Leadership of Milorg and FO and SOE in their joint capacities. An important factor in this process was Milorg's own decision concerning the future character of the organisation. Was it to be a poorly trained resistance group, built on the organisational principles of the prewar army and not armed until the very day of an allied invasion, or a decentralised, fully trained and armed guerilla organisation? In the spring of 1942, the Central Leadership of Milorg through its 'Directive No.1 to the District Leaders' chose the latter alternative.[17] This did not mean, however, that resistance policy in Norway was settled once and for all. The decisive battle was fought in the autumn of 1942 and in the spring of 1943 at the top level of Milorg and its civilian equivalent, Sivorg. The Central Leadership of Milorg gave an unconditional answer to FO in London in January 1943: Milorg wanted weapons, indeed their whole existence depended on it. Sivorg protested, but shortly afterwards, its leaders realised the necessity of this decision. This acceptance of the reality of war, and of military resistance as such, made it of course easier for Milorg to adjust to the British activity and to appreciate SOE's new policy of cooperation *in the field*.

Wilson attributed much of the improved atmosphere in the field to the instruction of local Milorg leaders by SOE agents. He explicitly mentions the two *Gannet* instructors dropped in Gudbrandsdalen in November 1942. When they returned to Great Britain two months later, they had held eleven separate courses, training 59 men in lonely mountain huts in guerrilla warfare, small arms, demolitions and unarmed combat:

> Men from the United Kingdom were no longer looked on as dangerous interlopers, but as friends and allies who were recognised as well-trained and secure . . . F.O. IV and S.O.E. were over the top of the hill.[18]

During this period, SOE intensified its sabotage activities and Milorg was little by little engaged. The usual pattern was for Linge soldiers to be dropped in the vicinity of the target, or even sometimes in Sweden. They would then launch the attack, often helped by local Milorg men. Three groups of targets were hit: ships, industry and railways. It is impossible to go into detail about these operations here. The most famous, Operation *Gunnerside* against the heavy water plant at Vemork in February 1943, is, however a good example of thorough Anglo-Norwegian planning, the use of Norwegian agents who knew the area like the back of their hand, and, in the sinking of the Hydro ferry carrying semi-finished heavy water, in cooperation with the local Milorg group. It is also an example of the effectiveness of coup-de-main operations as compared with heavy bombing, in terms of both casualties and accuracy, a theme that was often on the agenda in Anglo-Norwegian meetings and in which SOE, FO and Milorg took a unanimous view in favour of the former.

From the turn of the year 1943, the Supreme Headquarters Allied Expeditionary Force (SHAEF) decided the lines of policy to be followed in Norway. In other words, the joint British-Norwegian resistance had to adjust itself to the framework of SHAEF. Because of the plans SHAEF had at that time for the invasion of the Continent, no commitment in Norway was wanted, and Milorg was strongly warned that it should not encourage any rising in Norway. Ironically, the old Milorg slogan 'lie low, go slow' now had a renaissance. The idea was to grow in strength and wait for the day to come. Any untimely rising, like that of the French maquis in the Vercors, would not be supported. Nevertheless, the more than 30,000 men in Milorg waited eagerly to do something more than mere training, and after the Allied invasion on the Continent they were allowed to attack and sabotage German shipping, lines of communication, industries etc.[19] This was quite important as the restlessness amongst the rank and file increased. The sabotage of the offices for labour conscription in the spring of 1944 represented a little outlet of steam. However, when the above mentioned directive came in June, the opportunities for action increased. Regular clashes with the Germans were still to be avoided. Usually, the attacks were planned and launched by combined groups of Milorg and SOE personnel. But even before this new directive, Milorg's role in these joint British-Norwegian operations had been steadily increasing. In fact, *Feather II*, which crossed the border from Sweden on 22 April 22 1944 to attack the Thamshavn railway, was the last British operation planned *outside* Norway. Henceforward, it was the Central Leadership of Milorg that decided on these issues. Meanwhile, Milorg grew in strength and numbers. Supplies, equipment, instruction and training were provided by SOE and FO in London. This was no easy task considering Norway's topography and climate.

All in all, Allied aircraft flew 717 successful sorties out of a total of 1241, dropping 208 agents, 9662 containers and 2762 packages with arms, munition, explosives, radio equipment, uniforms, medicine etc. In addition, supplies were sailed from the Shetlands: in 194 trips, 190 agents and 385 tons of arms and equipment were landed in Norway and 345 agents were brought back to England. Instructors were sent to train members of Milorg, together with W/T operators. It was mainly in the last year of cooperation between SOE and Milorg that the figures grew to such proportions and thus gradually increased Milorg's striking power.

The SHAEF directive of June 1944 was based on the assumption that it would be easier to let the Germans retreat from Norway and defeat them in central Europe. However, as the situation in this part of Europe changed towards the end of 1944, SHAEF changed its strategy. In a directive of 5 December 1944, Milorg was told to attack the railways in Norway on a large scale to prevent the Germans from withdrawing their fresh troops from Norway and sending them to the central European theatre for use against the Allies. Milorg was naturally very pleased to get this opportunity. After the surrender in Finland, an enormous number of troops were withdrawn into Finnmark in northern Norway and thence southwards. In close cooperation with SOE parties which had been held in readiness, Milorg attacked railways and bridges on a large scale. So well did Milorg carry out its task that, according to the head of SOE, Major-General Sir Colin Gubbins, 'From Norway, there was a reduction in rate of movement from four divisions to less than one division a month'.[20] However, German documents such as the *Kriegstagebuch*, do not support such an unreserved conclusion. Eleven divisions were withdrawn from June 1944 until the end of the war, seven of these in the first four months of 1945.[21]

Despite sabotage activity, the main objective for Milorg in the last year of the war was protection against German destruction of communications, transport, industries,
ports etc., in case of a German withdrawal accompanied by the scorched earth policy practised in Finnmark in the autumn of 1944. The detailed plans were made in London and a total of 110 officers were sent in from Great Britain to lead this work. In addition, a considerable number of Linge officers already in Norway on various other missions were directed to such tasks in the last phase of the war. Milorg also established a few bases – groups of specially handpicked men placed in camps far away in the forest and up in the mountains – ready to strike if the signal was given. The leaders and instructors were SOE personnel.

At this stage, in the spring of 1945, approximately 40,000 Milorg men, equipped, trained and well disciplined were prepared for the worst alternative, a German last stand in Norway. The equipment as well as the training and partly, I should say, the discipline, could be attributed to the fruitful cooperation with SOE which in turn had at its disposal some of the best specimens of Norwegian youth. Milorg obeyed SHAEF's order not to provoke the Germans but could not avoid a few clashes as the Germans attacked. On these occasions, Milorg proved their capability to defend themselves and even strike back. Their losses were small compared with German casualties.[22]

As we all know, the German Commander in Norway, General Boehme, signed the German surrender in Norway on 8 May 1945. Milorg did not have to fight at all. Their role in this rather risky period of transition was to stand guard, protect buildings, arrest traitors etc. They were finally demobilised in July 1945. As for the Linge Company, they were inspected by Colonel Wilson on 30 June and demobilised.

These few pages are of course only a rough survey of the relationship between Milorg and SOE. However, I have tried to show how two ad hoc organisations, with basically the same goal, operating side by side, at the outset virtually as antagonists with an attitude of non-collaboration, managed gradually to adjust themselves to each other's course and, in the last years of the war, to achieve such a high degree of cooperation that the SOE phrase from the spring of 1942, 'amalgamation' may be used. 'Basically the same goal': yes, but the inherent contradiction in the SOE programme made the first two or three years difficult: the building up of a secret army *combined with* offensive actions. The former required an attitude that did not attract the attention of the Germans and thus agreed perfectly with Milorg's policy. The consequence of offensive actions, on the other hand, was precisely the opposite, and this was Milorg's constant worry. For reasons already described, SOE had to concentrate on the offensive part early in the war. As the war developed, SOE toned down this aspect of its activity. At the same time, Milorg adjusted its policy to the harsh reality of war. In this way the two lines met and converged. Although this pattern may not have differed much in outline from that which developed in other occupied countries, there was perhaps one important difference after all: the *degree of success* achieved by the partnership, or 'amalgamation', between the two organisations.

References

1 Weapons are not desirable . . .': Report from Milorg Council to HM King Haakon VII on 10 June 1941.
2 See the discussion at the end of Section I above.
3 J.C. Wilson, *S.O.E. Norwegian Section History*, p. 23 (unpublished manuscript, Norway's Resistance Museum (NRM)).
4 14 July 1941. MiIV-archive, No. 79, NRM.
5 Christopher Buckley, *Norway, the Commandos, Dieppe* (London, 1951), p. 184.
6 But for a more positive assessment of the value of the raid see Edward Thomas's contribution to this book.
7 'Norwegian Policy', 17 July 1941.
8 Wilson, *S.O.E. Norwegian Section History*, p. 21
9 Diary belonging to Birger Fjeldstad, one of 'the Twelve'. Copy at NRM.
10 Sverre Kjeldstadli, *Hjemmestyrkene* (Oslo, 1959), pp. 180–1.
11 Wilson, *S.O.E. Norwegian Section History*, p. 35.
12 Kjeldstadli, *Hjemmestyrkene*, p. 162.
13 Wilson, *S.O.E. Norwegian Section History*, p. 24
14 Ibid, p. 23
15 FO IV archive, NRM.
16 'FO, Rapport, Del 1', p.16, NRM.
17 Ivar Kraglund and Arnfinn Moland, *Norge i krig*, vol. 6, *Hjemmefront* (Oslo, 1987).
18 Wilson, *S.O.E. Norwegian Section History*, p. 64.
19 SHAEF directive, 'Resistance in Norway', of June 1944.
20 Sir Colin Gubbins, 'Resistance Movements in the War', *Journal of the Royal United Service Institution*, May 1948, p. 219.
21 *Kriegstagebuch* db IV2, p. 1332ff.
22 Paul M. Strande, *Fallskjerm over vassfaret* (Oslo, 1977).

16 The Linge Company and the British

JOACHIM RØNNEBERG

I landed in the UK at Balta Sound (Shetland) in March 1941. Having been the only one on board with no feeling of seasickness, I was determined to join the Navy as the quickest possible way to active service. After a few days internment at Victoria Patriotic School I found myself in London – at that time a nightly target for enemy bombing. I remember I was deeply impressed by the way the inhabitants reacted to the agony of falling bombs. After having met Captain Martin Linge for a short interview, followed by an invitation to lunch, I forgot my intention to join the Navy.

Captain Linge, a Norwegian reserve officer who had been attached to the British Expeditionary Force in Gudbrandsdal/Åndalsnes in 1940, had gone back with the British to the UK in May 1940. Now he had been invited through friends in SOE to assist in building up a special military unit consisting of Norwegian volunteers, both young and not so young, to be trained by British experts at British special paramilitary schools at British expense to wage war in German-occupied territory. I had no reservations about joining up. Linge was to be our leader. He had been in charge of a group of Norwegian soldiers, who went to the Lofoten Islands as a small part of a British military expedition in March 1941. He was a man of great charisma and great fighting spirit, and was an inspiring leader. He assured me it would not be long before I was in active service. He made it clear to all who joined that earlier experience (military background) might be an asset, but his 'work' called for quite other qualities too. 'Forget everything about promotion (stars). Concentrate on fighting the Gs', was his message to all of us.

Early in April I marched up the alley leading to Stodham Park near Petersfield wearing a battledress of Norwegian Independent Company No. 1 (NIC 1). I was on the first official course in the company's history, together with twenty other Norwegians; and we were wondering what we would encounter. We were met by Major Tynan, CO of the school, and were introduced to the training staff. We met two other British officers whom I later learned to value highly as friends: Lieutenant Chaworth-Musters and Captain Boughton-Leigh who both worked in the SOE administration.

The next day we certainly registered a new way of life. Training was concentrated – a mixture of PT, military instructions, fieldcraft, weapon-training and silent killing: irregular but very useful methods for putting an enemy out of action. I gladly admit that it was not always easy to fall asleep while reflecting on the day's instructions and my future life as an 'irregular'. The British provided very good instructors, the right types who convinced us of our ability to survive in all situations. I later realised that the toughness and brutality of the training was meant to scare us, to make us think and perhaps ask for a transfer to a more 'normal' type of service. It was in the common interest to sort out people whose personality did not suit such special work, and the sooner the better. During the whole period of training we were under constant observation.

Those who remained with the group went from Stodham Park to Arisaig in Inverness-shire in the west of Scotland for more advanced training. Again we met friendly and expert instructors, with whom we became close friends. We always felt they did their very best to qualify us to meet future situations with self-confidence and calm. We never felt that were either Norwegian or British: we were allies in the deepest possible sense. After three weeks of intensive training we went to the south coast for three weeks of 'Finishing School' which gave us insight into codes, cover stories, knowledge of the enemy, his methods and weapons; in other words, how to become the best possible spy. We were told frankly that once in the field 'you were the loneliest person imaginable. Your future would depend on your ability to use what you had been taught during training – and a fair amount of good luck.'

After a week of parachute training at Ringway we were ready for 'take-off'. We were transferred to the holding school Fawley Court near Henley. Here we might be selected to be sent to other special schools for special training: e.g. wireless operator, demolition/sabotage, propaganda. Wherever we went there was always the same friendly reception from officers and staff. We certainly were made to feel at home!

In June 1941 Captain Linge collected me at Henley. I was to act as accompanying officer to a new group of students at Stodham Park and Meoble Lodge (Arisaig). The administration of the schools had asked for this arrangement. I went through a second round at the main training schools during which I acquired closer ties to the training section and the staff officers. When the training was completed at Meoble, I waited for a new group to arrive from Stodham Park. From then on I was attached to the training staff at Arisaig, as a result of a request from the Meoble administration. By the time I had been through the programme three times, I was urged to take responsibility for the training and for planning practical target exercises. I took it as a sign of the close cooperation between our two nations.

We often went on leave to London and met friends. Sometimes I was asked questions about my training, but I never had trouble giving a general answer: military training in Scotland. When on leave I sometimes heard Norwegians, both military and civilian, talk of a 'gang' of young Norwegians, out of ordinary control, trained by the British and also under their command. It was quite obvious that Norwegian army circles did not applaud the idea. Captain Linge once told me of the problem he often had with Norwegian authorities in London. The temperature between the SOE and the Norwegians was at times very low, early in the war and especially after the Lofoten raids in 1941. The main reason was lack of information and lack of mutual trust. Our unit and Captain Linge were blamed. I do know that Captain Linge felt this as a personal burden and, because of it, he insisted on going on the raid at Måløy in December 1941. The British could not stop him and he never came back.

After the raids in December 1941 at Måløy and in the Lofotens, the feelings between the Norwegian authorities and SOE rose to boiling point as the Germans took heavy reprisals in Norway, and at the same time launched a propaganda attack on the Norwegian government in exile, accusing them of being under British rule with no influence whatsoever. It added to the problems that Norwegian participants came back disillusioned as a result of the quick withdrawal. At the same time several smaller groups were training in sabotage against power plants and industry in Norway. On leave in London they had heard the reactions to the recent raids and now they demanded to know if their planned operations had Norwegian approval. For security reasons members of three groups were 'interned' in the Arisaig district; the fourth group (Høyanger) continued with their training. After a motoring accident on the way to 'ST 61', which resulted in the deaths of some of the members, the operation had to be cancelled. I met the 'interned' groups while on an exercise at Inverarie and heard the bad news of Linge's death at Måløy and of the situation in the unit in general. In February 1942 I was transferred from the Arisaig training unit to our new holding school at Aviemore to take over the sabotage/demolition training. When I arrived I found a unit in uproar!

A new leader from Norwegian HQ in London, Major E. Hjelle had just arrived. Unfortunately he knew very little of the very special and complex unit he was to command, and he was obviously under orders to bring us under Norwegian control! The older members of the unit who favoured Linge's line of action felt unhappy and wished for even stronger British influence. Major Hjelle represented the Norwegian view: wait and see; train for some future day far ahead! He had a following of pre-war officers and youngsters who saw a possible military career ahead. Apparently consultations on the highest level were going on between the British (SOE) and Norwegians. We felt we were pawns in a struggle for influence that was tearing the unit apart. Everything was in a mess! We nearly forgot the Germans. Since I belonged to the staff, I was asked one day to inform the British CO (Hampton) that the older members of the company wanted action to bring back the fighting spirit of Linge as soon as possible, otherwise they wished to be transferred to more active service (Navy, merchant fleet etc.). The threat reflects the desperate situation at the time. How we and the British felt the loss of our leader, Captain Linge!

We had several visits from Norwegian HQ in London, one from the minister of defence, Oscar Torp. The 'Høyanger' group put on a show at Drumintoul Lodge to demonstrate the planned attack on the works at Høyanger. They intended to cut the pipeline after putting the valves out of action. The free flow of water would result in a landslide, thus putting the power station out of use. When told this by one of the group, the minister of defence remarked sarcastically that the result would be lots of water in the valley below. A quick reply from the attacker: 'OK, I will stop at the valve house and close the valves when a message comes from the factory'. A roar of laughter underlined the difference in opinion and the minister of defence made his exit, a bit insulted. The Norwegian policy was to stage attacks anywhere but in Norway. We also had representatives from Milorg who warned us against acts of sabotage etc. They would endanger clandestine work in Norway. Returning SOE personnel should never leak information to the British – only to the Norwegian authorities! No wonder the older members with experience in the field reacted promptly on behalf of SOE. The other members wanted the British out and the unit altered to a special Norwegian training school. I was even asked to make new pamphlets for sabotage/ demolition in a new organisation . . . Something had to be done!

Norwegian representatives from both sides had to start negotiations to improve the situation. Major Hjelle was replaced. When he left, quite a few of the 'rebels' followed him to begin as students at a Norwegian military college in London. Things returned to normal. A depot leader was appointed. Most people felt happy again. The nights grew darker and the time for action drew nearer.

In 1942 the Norwegian military organisation was altered. Forsvarets Overkommando (FO) was established and and our unit was placed under FO IV, its leader being Bjarne Øen. Our new leader was Major Leif Tronstad. From now on no operation was to be launched without consultations between SOE and FO IV. Cooperation grew better and better as time went on, not only between SOE, the US Office of Strategic Services (OSS) and Norwegians in exile, but also with the Milorg leadership inside Norway. All of those involved did their best to hit the enemy and cause as little trouble as possible to the civilians in Norway or to Milorg. Agents went in and out by air and by sea, as did tons of military equipment for Milorg. Blows were struck at industrial and other targets of value for the Germans. 'ST 26' Aviemore took over training of new recruits, and also of updating groups of non-army officers for service with Milorg inside Norway.

Reflections on Special Operations in Norway

Norway is a very difficult for any responsible military planner because of its climate and topography. Missions in towns and populated districts could be compared with those in other European countries, but very often the operational area called for special insight and knowledge. Very few Norwegians in FO IV had this expertise, nor did any of the British in SOE. Their understanding of living conditions for groups on jobs in desolated mountainous districts was nil! When planning for *Gunnerside* (Vemork) I had to take the responsibility of procuring quite a lot of special equipment myself: sleeping bags (specially made on advice at a bedding firm's factory in London), ski-boots (from Rob. Lawrie & Co. in Newark – makers of footwear for climbing and Arctic expeditions – whose address was given me by a climber I once met in Scotland), and a variety of winter equipment collected and specially made after a private visit to the Norwegian army depot (Major Myrset) in Dumfries in Scotland. I urged strongly that a Norwegian specialist should be appointed to a new job as 'Equipment Adviser'. He never came! Lack of insight and understanding of special living conditions often resulted in long dispatches being sent to groups in remote areas. It meant waste of batteries, waste of time, and a real danger of being detected by the enemy.

Security

1) During training we were again and again reminded of the importance of security. One could never be careful enough! Nevertheless, SOE allowed quite a few staff members to be sent into occupied territory: people like Linge, Leif Tronstad and J.C. Adamson. They all knew too much and could endanger the situation for groups in the field, if they were caught and tortured by the Gestapo. It was a grave mistake.

2) Signalling routines when receiving drops. The *Fieldfare* operation was positioned on the German flying route Bergen – Værnes. We very often saw planes passing and at night heard them flying past. We asked to have procedure altered. We thought it would be safer if the plane sent a morse signal when nearing the dropping point, and we sent a signal as confirmation. Otherwise we might send our signal to a German aircraft. The reply from RAF was: 'You follow procedure, or we drop the visit!' We had to run the risk of signalling to a German plane, thus giving ourselves away.

Navigation

When going home by air we were in the hands of RAF. They refused any help or advice when deciding on the flying-in route. On the *Gunnerside* operation we were landed blind 25 kilometres from pinpoint. Fortunately we detected it and managed. On the next operation it happened again. During the first flight for Operation *Fieldfare* in October 1943, our offer through SOE to guide the plane in was refused. The flight was unsuccessful. The second attempt in February 1944 was also unsuccessful. Pulling up a blind and looking out, we immediately registered our position south of Ålesund. We guided the plane out to sea, avoiding several 'ack-ack' batteries. The pilot was impressed by our local knowledge of the countryside and German fortifications: 'Why were we not in the cockpit as guides?' We asked him to mention the episode in his report. For the third attempt, in March 1944, the RAF finally accepted guiding assistance. I was in the cockpit on the last part of the flight. There was no difficulty in checking the positions as we flew in. Pinpoint was picked out and agreed upon by the pilot. We were dropped ten minutes later. He had obviously lost pinpoint. When my parachute opened at 2,500 metres I took my position. We had been dropped 25 kilometres from where I had pointed out! We had a very bad landing indeed, but fortunately no casualties.

Morning drops (no moon period): Owing to the desperate food situation just before we were ordered into action (railway sabotage) we begged to have an early morning drop. The RAF refused. We blew up a railway bridge, causing a three-week delay in traffic and forfeited our security, expecting

German air activity to find us. Three days after the attack the RAF came to their senses and offered a morning drop. Although this was very risky we accepted the offer and got a drop on our doorstep. Only two days later, after a short snowstorm, German planes came searching, but by then all traces of the drop had disappeared.

Supplies – or rather lack of them

We landed in March with enough supplies for two months. Due to an error in the destined drop site, we asked for fresh supplies. We were told we had to manage until June–July. Flying in bright summer light meant that all security regarding the plane's safety would be put aside – in other words, we thought, invasion. We planned accordingly and stole food from a neighbouring tourist hut to keep us going. At the end of May a new message altered the situation – and showed a great lack of understanding: 'No supplies can be sent this side of summer. You must not leave the area. Hope you can manage?' We had to steal more food. In the middle of July another message came: 'Can you take a drop?' We had food stocks for six months on order and decided to risk a drop although it was now the middle of the tourist season and hikers abounded. The drop contained weapons and explosives, but only very little food (rations for 30 days). We continued to wait for drops in early September – living on stolen food. Autumn arrived with bad weather and all drops were cancelled. We had no choice but to live on stolen and scarce supplies. Our next drop was in mid-January 1945. By then we had been in Norway for ten months, living 1,200 metres above sea level, miles from the nearest farm, with UK supplies for only four months. We felt we were 'out of sight, out of mind'. We survived thanks to our own initiative, the inspiration that came from positive news, and an undiminished fighting spirit.

Conclusion

The internal cooperation between SOE and the members of the unit was extremely good: full of respect and friendliness, full of intentions to do the best at all times. The RAF might have improved matters all round by accepting offers of assistance in finding the best possible way to the target, as well as by listening to advice from agents in the field. SOE – the experts in clandestine work – might sometimes have lent an ear to suggestions about equipment for operations in Norway. A strong and willing cooperation between the different elements in an operation was imperative: the agent, the planning sector, equipment, training, transport. Mutual trust and the dissemination of information were vital to success. Looking back: serving with SOE was a very friendly, uplifting and valuable experience. I never regretted my choice of service in 1941. The British made me feel that I had two homelands. When stationed in Britain we talked of going home on a mission; in Norway we talked of going 'home' to relax or to new appointments.

PART IV

Special Operations

17 Britain and Norwegian resistance: clandestine sea transport

SIR BROOKS RICHARDS

NORWAY is reputed to have a coastline as long as that of the rest of Europe put together. The Germans never attempted to fortify or control it as they did by building the 'Western Wall' in France and the Low Countries: clandestine operations by sea from British ports to Norway flourished from 1940 to 1945 in conditions that could, apart from the ever-present risk of bad weather, hardly have been more favourable. But although the deeply-indented coast of Norway lends itself to work of this nature, the mountainous hinterland made travel inside Norway difficult under German occupation for agents and others who did not wish their baggage or their passes to be closely examined, since the number of ferries and bridges across which travellers must pass made control an easy matter.

At the outbreak of war, Norway possessed some 50,000 fishing vessels and boats of all sizes, ranging from the big steel-built whale catchers that worked in the Arctic and Antarctic to little 30 ft coastal smacks. The greater part of this large fleet consisted of wooden-built drifters, usually 60–70 ft long, with semi-diesel engines and speeds between 6 and 10 knots. A number of such boats arrived in the Shetlands early in 1940 and a constant stream of refugees continued to arrive there throughout the next twelve months. This meant that a large number of Norwegian boats from all parts of that country were available in the United Kingdom for reversing the procedure and landing parties of agents or saboteurs along the Norwegian coast. Owing to the difficulty of travel inland, however, such agents had to be maintained with supplies of all sorts and the number of operations called for was high, as each group needed to be serviced individually.

Realising the advantages of the situation in the Shetlands, the British Secret Intelligence Service (SIS) sent an Army officer named Captain L. H. Mitchell to Lerwick in the summer of 1940, where ten of the best refugee fishing vessels were collected and formed into a flotilla for clandestine work, manned by Norwegian volunteer civilian crews recruited amongst the refugees themselves. The procedure for operations was simple enough: an agent who had been recruited and trained to return to Norway would want to be sent to his own district. He would know of a local pilot for that area, if indeed he were not himself qualified in that respect. The expedition would then be built up on a 'family' basis – the skipper being chosen by the members of the crew – and would sail from the Shetlands in the most suitable ship. The ship would sail

straight into the fjord nearest the agent's home and remain there openly while
he made enquiries on shore. If these were satisfactory, the agent returned to
the Shetlands. This happy state of affairs continued throughout the winters of
1940–1 and 1941–2.

During the winter of 1940–1 SIS-sponsored intelligence organisations
were built up and the new Special Operations Executive (SOE) began to
establish, in conjunction with its Norwegian counterpart, FO IV, a series of
sabotage and para-military resistance groups. In March and April 1941 SOE
launched an extensive series of operations from the Shetlands. In the course of
some of these, Norwegians were recruited in Norway itself and brought over to
the Shetlands for sabotage courses before being returned to their own homes
with arms and explosives. SIS viewed these heavily-increased SOE commitments as a considerable security threat to SIS-sponsored agents passing
through Lerwick. Rightly or wrongly, they considered that the Norwegians
had the highest alcohol consumption and the worst sense of security of all our
Allies. Though steps were taken to deal with the worst offenders, SIS had by
then decided that a second operational base was desirable to avoid the
inevitable mixing of agents delayed by weather in the Shetlands.

In July 1941 an SIS expedition was sailed from Aberdeen with a Royal
Norwegian Naval crew in a newly-acquired fishing vessel and arrangements
were made to establish a small base for SIS needs at Peterhead under the
direction of the British Naval officer-in-charge. This base developed rapidly
into a flotilla of five fishing boats with Norwegian Naval crews. The base was
subsequently put under the command of Commander J.B. Newill, DSO, RN,
a Norwegian speaking officer, and this small flotilla, reserved for SIS ventures,
continued to operate under his control until its administration was turned over
completely to the Norwegian Naval Mission in October 1942.

At the SOE Shetlands base a certain amount of trouble was encountered
with the civilian crews: special bonuses of £50 per head per trip had been paid
to the first crews. This proved an expensive precedent when the scale of
operations increased very greatly in 1941 and eventually all crews were
formally entered into the Norwegian Navy, put into uniform and paid at
standard rates. The question of 'danger money' did not arise after this,
especially when it became known that the crew of one of the Peterhead craft,
which failed to return to its Scottish base after encountering a heavy westerly
gale, had been made prisoners of war and treated in accordance with the
normal rules of war.

The SOE base at the remote Lunna Voe in the Shetlands was run by
David Howarth, another Norwegian-speaking officer, and there was a series of
successful SOE-sponsored operations from this base to Norway in the second
half of the 1941–2 winter. Four areas – (i) the island of Stord, south of Bergen;
(ii) the Ålesund area; (iii) the island of Træna on the Arctic circle and (iv) the
island of Bremanger in the mouth of the Nordfjord – all had three, four or five
visits between January and April 1942 and most of these operations achieved
their objectives. In April the five Lunna ships completed ten operations and
for two or three days in the middle of the month they were all at sea or in
Norway at once. During the 1941–2 winter this small flotilla made 40 trips to

Norway, in the course of which they landed 43 agents and picked up nine; landed 130 tons of arms and equipment and brought out 46 refugees. But this proved to be the high point of operations to Norway by fishing boat: as stocks of diesel oil fell, fishing off the Norwegian coast decreased. At the same time enemy air patrols increased and the first casualties resulting from this enhanced enemy vigilance became inevitable as soon as the nights became too short to allow the slow-moving fishing vessels to make an offing of 100 miles or more in darkness. In April 1942 the *Aksel* was twice attacked by aircraft but landed six men and 14 tons of material and returned safely. However, during that month the *Mars*, veteran of nearly twenty voyages, and the *Froya*, were both sunk by enemy aircraft while on operations for SIS and in May operations were halted for the summer months. Three other vessels had been lost during the 1941–2 winter, two being driven ashore in Norway by gales, and one sunk without trace in heavy weather with 35 passengers on board.

Against this background, the winter operating season was started in September 1942 with some misgivings. Owing to unsatisfactory refits in Scotland, only half the SOE boats were ready for operations, but in October four big new boats (*Bergholm*, *Brattholm*, *Andholmen* and *Sandøy* – Arctic whalers which had escaped to Iceland in 1940) were handed over. From a new base at the little Shetland village of Scalloway, where a slipway and an engineering workshop were built, the fishing boat operations for SOE were resumed; but although Howarth recorded in his book *Shetland Bus*, published in 1951 and recently reissued in paperback, that the first dozen trips to Norway were successful – 'good routine trips to land agents and dump stores' – the records now available tell a more chequered story. The open boat *Sjø* which set out on a reconnaissance trip to Norway on 22 August did not return and it was later learned that her two-man crew had been captured by the Gestapo. At the end of October, Leif Larsen set out in the *Arthur* with two submersible 'Chariots', hidden under a cargo of peat, and six Royal Naval personnel for a planned attack on the *Tirpitz*, then lying far up the Trondheim Fjord. This was frustrated after they had successfully passed through a German inspection and the 'Chariots' had been put into the water and were being towed submerged; when only five miles short of the target *Arthur* rounded a bend in the fjord and ran into a strong head wind and rough water: the tow-ropes snapped and the 'Chariots' were lost. Larsen scuttled the *Arthur* according to plan and the crew, with the exception of one British Naval rating who was killed by a frontier guard, returned safely via Sweden. Then in December, as Howarth wrote, the disaster which had earlier struck the SIS boats befell the SOE flotilla. The *Aksel* was lost 200 miles north of the Shetlands on her way back from the far north. She was sighted in sinking condition by a Catalina flying boat in weather too bad to land. A destroyer was sent but found nothing. Only a few days later the *Sandøy*, which had made some half a dozen trips to Træna, was sunk with all hands and without trace or report on her outward journey, probably as a result of an attack by aircraft. Then the *Feie*, which completed three successful trips between December and February, was, again according to Howarth, lost on the short crossing to the islands south of Bergen. (Curiously enough, this is not shown in either of the available detailed official records of operations).

Twenty-four out of a total of sixty men serving in the Shetland flotilla had been lost in three months, but still volunteers came forward; and still the run of disasters continued. On 17 March Larsen sailed from Scalloway in the *Bergholm* to Træna. They were attacked by aircraft on the return trip; the wheelhouse was shot to pieces around the intrepid and imperturbable skipper but, before the ship sank, Larsen patched up the holes in the lifeboat and transferred the surviving members of the crew to it. They were 350 miles north of the Shetland and 75 miles from the Norwegian coast. Larsen headed for Ålesund, 150 miles away, which they reached by rowing: they were later picked up by MTB. On 24 March the *Brattholm* sailed to the Tromsø area to land four men and an arms cargo. She was intercepted and sunk on arrival by an enemy war vessel. Only one member of the crew escaped.

SIS, whose operations were accorded priority by the British Chiefs of Staff, carried out four fishing boat operations from Peterhead successfully during the 1942–3 winter season, but they used submarines as often as could be arranged (four times) and also the Norwegian MTB Flotilla then based at Lerwick (also four times). SOE used the French Submarine *Rubis* on one occasion. In November 1942 four French ratings from the French Submarine *Junon* were, in the course of an SIS operation, left ashore in Norway as a result of an accident to their rubber boat and remained in the hands of the agent concerned until March 1943, when they were successfully re-embarked at the third attempt. SIS's Naval Section recorded that no small credit was due to the agent who hid them during these four months: the ratings were far from easy to control and proved a source of considerable embarrassment to their hosts.

Operations were again suspended during the summer months – from May to September 1943. Everyone had decided that the days of the fishing boat were over and the search for alternatives was on. When the 1943–4 season began, SOE had obtained, through the good offices of the American OSS, three 110-foot US submarine chasers. Manned by Norwegians, and based at Lerwick, these vessels took the place of fishing boats for SOE traffic. They proved excellent sea boats, somewhat slow by MTB standards but far faster, of course, than the fishing vessels previously employed. Their reliablity and high endurance were outstanding, while their armament meant that, though often inspected by enemy aircraft, they were never attacked. These qualities, together with the available knowledge of the Norwegian coast, made operations relatively easy. During their first winter season they completed 34 operations, two of which were for SIS. SIS employed the Norwegian MTBs for two others while two further voyages to the far north – beyond the range of the submarine chasers and MTBs – were carried out by the Norwegian submarine *Ula*. One fishing vessel executed a successful operation for SIS from Peterhead in October 1943, but this method was by then considered out of date and employed only in rare cases.

At the very end of that season, in May 1944, MTB 718, a British D-Class boat which had been working with the 15th Motor Gun Boat flotilla on clandestine transport between Dartmouth and the north coast of Brittany, was brought round from that base post-haste in three days and sailed on the fourth day to Norway to embark a party of agents on the run. The whole operation was carried out in daylight, there being no darkness in these latitudes at that time of year.

After the usual summer close season, a sudden spate of SIS operations came forward in August and September 1944 and continued until the spring of 1945. Twenty seven of these missions were carried out by the submarine chasers which, according to the most detailed list available, performed a total of 75 operations during this last winter of the war (Howarth made the total 80). Four further SIS operations were done by the British MTB 718, one by a British destroyer, HMS *Venturer*, and one by the Norwegian whaler *Narvik*. The 33 SIS voyages were mainly to revictual or rescue various intelligence stations. Four stand out as exceptional: these were Operation *Aquarius III*, to rescue four agents from a small island in the southern approach to Egersund; *Lola*, to land two agents on an island near Mandal; *Selma*, to land two agents near Egersund – all carried out by MTB 718 from Aberdeen – and Operation *Synnove*, to rescue twenty agents and families from the Lofoten Islands – performed by the Norwegian whaler *Narvik*. Whether measured by the risks from the enemy or the navigational hazards of the long voyages involved these were recognised at the time as outstanding performances. At such distances from base special navigational aids did not function: weather forecasts were imprecise and unreliable; and no W/T contact could be maintained. There was also the wintry sea. From Operation *Lola*, MTB 718 just managed to return in a Force 8 sea with over 3 feet of water in the engine room and a hull so severely strained that it took over a month to repair. From Operation *Synnove* the *Narvik* came back with a cramped cargo of men, women and children, together with their belongings, which included trunks, perambulators and even two bedsteads, against a south-westerly gale, wind Force 10 and high seas Force 8.

But it was the three submarine chasers *Hitra*, *Hessa* and *Vigra*, which carried the bulk of the traffic: the 114 operations they carried out in the last two winters of the war – 29 of which were for SIS and the rest for SOE – were completed without casualties. The Scalloway base, handed over to Norwegian Naval control in 1942, had some difficulty in settling down to naval ways, such was the fiercely independent and egalitarian spirit of the fishermen who manned the ships and who were used to electing their own skippers. But in the end even Larsen, the finest, but most independent, leader of them all, was commissioned as a sub-lieutenant to entitle him to use cyphers. It made no difference to his ways. As one of his obituaries in the British press put it, 'he knew no man as master and he was conspicuous in never altering his behaviour whether addressing a Commander-in-Chief or a lowly Shetland labourer'. On the British side, Captain Mitchell of SIS had been replaced in 1942 by an SOE officer, who called himself 'Major Rogers' but whose real name was Arthur Sclater, a member of a long-established Anglo-Norwegian family. David Howarth, though to his great regret never allowed to go on operations, looked after the maintenance of the Shetlands flotilla throughout. He pointed out in his book that though the Anglo-Norwegian Scalloway base ran quite formidable war vessels over great stretches of ocean, they remained until the end quite independent of the Royal Navy. He also recorded that though the boats operating this sealine to Norway steamed 90,000 miles in the last four winters of the war, in all that time only four strange vessels were sighted.

It was, of course, providential that the American submarine chasers became available at the point when German air patrols had made the use of fishing vessels all but impossible: neither submarines nor Coastal Forces MTBs could have carried the traffic needed in the last two winters of the war. And Norway was uniquely dependent on clandestine sea transport: her weather being what it is, communications by air – so important in other parts of German-occupied Europe – were on a very limited scale during the years of the occupation, when aircraft de-icing equipment was still at an early stage of its development.

The ships involved crossed and recrossed the most exposed part of the North Sea always in winter, benefitting from darkness but enduring appalling weather. It was indeed the weather that was their chief enemy and their crews' feats of seamanship and pilotage showed that the spirit of their Viking ancestors was very much alive among the fisher-folk of the Norwegian coast.

The decision by British ministers in July 1940 to set up SOE as a separate clandestine service alongside SIS to promote, supply and organise resistance in German-occupied Europe gave rise to considerable friction over clandestine sea transport. In the case of France, for example, SIS, with the backing of the Chiefs of Staff and the Admiralty, progressively assumed control of all such operations and ran them in such a way that SOE came to rely almost entirely on the Royal Air Force for the transport of both men and material. The pattern that evolved in the case of Norway was, as we have seen, very different: there SOE-sponsored sealines operated by Norwegians escaped SIS control and predominated, so that in the last phase of the war SIS found itself using SOE's American-built submarine chasers for most of their operations. The less well-known SIS links are however an integral part of Norway's wartime history.

18 Special Duty Operations in Norway

MARK SEAMAN

BEFORE the outbreak of the Second World War both the British Foreign Office and the War Office had made some rather faltering steps into examining the methods, efficacy and likely uses of subversive or guerrilla warfare. However, neither the Secret Intelligence Service's Section D nor the British Army's GS(R) (later MIR) appears to have given much consideration to air support for clandestine operations. This was to prove a matter of some regret, for techniques had to be learnt under the most demanding of wartime conditions and the Royal Air Force, or at least some of its most powerful and influential commanders, was frequently to prove itself a singularly uncooperative partner.

In the years leading up to the war and even during the 'Phoney War' period, the SIS and Section D had little need of clandestine air transport. The only significant instances would appear to have been special charters to extricate personnel in danger of capture by the Germans. SIS's networks, focused on the organisation's flimsy Passport Control Office cover, were run by officers serving with an ill-defined consular status and using wireless and courier channels for communications. It was through these same avenues that the fledgling Section D managed to build up arms and explosives caches in legations.

But in the spring and summer of 1940 this convenient system of supply and communication was shattered. Apart from isolated neutral countries such as Switzerland and Sweden, Western Europe fell under German occupation. SIS officers were obliged to flee leaving the surviving networks, in the main, directionless and with scarcely any provision for direct communication with London. Consequently SIS was faced with the problem of infiltrating agents into occupied Europe in order to reinforce existing circuits or create new networks to compensate for the recent calamitous reverses.

SIS was quick to develop a naval facility for landing agents. However, for landlocked countries and areas where the coastline was too heavily guarded, aircraft were the only solution. Clandestine air operations also offered speed, relative accuracy of delivery and the opportunity to maintain regular supply drops.

An accurate assessment of the development of clandestine air operations during the Second World War is to a great extent blighted by the general unavailability of SIS records. The situation regarding SOE's papers is (as of 1991) little better. Consequently, even the date of the first clandestine air operation has been a source of some debate. The most recent history of Special Duties Operations in the Second World War describes a Section D attempt to rescue General de Gaulle's family from France on 18 June 1940.[1] Another somewhat anecdotal source maintains that an agent was parachuted near Paris on 20 June but substantial doubts must be cast over the reliability of this account.[2] At this time the RAF had no specialist unit to carry out this type of operation nor was there any significant experience of parachute dropping. In fact, the first trial jumps from Armstrong Whitworth Whitley aircraft did not take place until 13 July at the Central Landing School.[3]

What is certain is that British Intelligence recognized the need for clandestine air transport. In the summer of 1940 SIS approached the Air Ministry with a suggestion that 'experiments' be made to decide whether the landing of light aircraft in occupied territory was feasible and, if so, which type of aircraft would be suitable. At the same time it was suggested that 'beginnings' might be made with the provision of special aircraft for dropping agents by parachute.[4] 'Experiments' and 'beginnings' were quickly transformed into something far more concrete. In late July 1940, Flight Lieutenant W.R. Farley arrived at the RAF's North Weald fighter station to assist in the creation of a specialist unit to implement SIS's request. On 20 August 1940 the Director of Plans at the Air Ministry announced the formation of No. 419 Flight.[5] The aircraft establishment was meagre to say the least, consisting of two Westland Lysanders with two more in reserve. These army cooperation/ tactical reconnaissance aircraft were intended to fulfil the first part of SIS's demands while the parachuting facility soon followed with the arrival of two Armstrong Whitworth Whitley Mark V bombers. It would appear that the unit went operational even before the Air Ministry's announcement of the Flight's formation. On 18 August, an attempt was made to infiltrate an SIS agent, Henri Leenaerts, into Belgium.[6] This early mission is confirmed by a post-war RAF summary stating that 'The first landing operation was attempted in August 1940 on behalf of SIS but for reasons unknown it was unsuccessful and the aircraft was lost.'[7] The first operation carried out by the Flight's Whitleys would appear to have taken place at the end of August when, in the words of one of the aircrew, 'We picked up our 'Joe' at Tangmere and put him into a field south of Paris.'[8] Thankfully, amongst all this uncertainty, at least one operation is clearly on record with an SIS-sponsored agent, Lodo van Hamel, being parachuted into the Netherlands on the night of 28–29 August 1940.

It is a tribute to both the RAF and SIS that operations were taking place so soon after the unit's creation. But storm clouds were gathering. No. 419 Flight was an oddity; a unit employing reconnaissance and bomber aircraft based at a fighter station. Furthermore, the highly secret nature of its activities made it an administrative aberration that was to be a source of irritation to RAF staff officers.

In the first months of its existence, the Flight's commitment was exclusively to SIS. Although SOE had been formed in July 1940, it was in no position to rush agents into the field let alone organise supply drops to resistance groups. It was not until 14–15 November 1940 that the first SOE operation was mounted but it proved to be an inauspicious beginning; having arrived over the dropping zone, the French agent refused to jump.

It soon became evident that a single flight of aircraft would not be sufficient to meet the demands made upon it. While SIS's requirements primarily consisted of the insertion (and occasional extraction) of agents, SOE's remit was far greater, encompassing no less than the creation and supply of secret armies throughout occupied Europe. It was clear that SIS had acquired not merely a rival for the RAF's services but a stablemate whose objectives often ran counter to its own interests. Ominously, senior staff officers at the Air Ministry were quick to regard SOE as, at best, a nuisance and, at worst, a wasteful encumbrance upon their own strategic air offensive. Thus, as SOE struggled to find its feet, it found itself beset by enemies in London, long before its agents got to grips with the German foe. Churchill's oft-quoted invocation to 'set Europe ablaze' was typically colourful but failed to appreciate the logistical difficulties in starting and fuelling the conflagration. In its charter, SOE was instructed to coordinate its activities with guidelines laid down by the Chiefs of Staff Committee and consequently its priorities were geared to specific aspects of Allied strategy. In a general directive of 25 November 1940, addressed to SOE by the Chiefs of Staff and entitled 'Subversive Activities in Relation to Strategy', a variety of tasks and objectives were outlined concluding with a list of operations and regions to be given priority. Ranked in the third and lowest priority category was Southern Norway.[9]

*   *   *   *   *

It is therefore not surprising that Norway was low on the list of priorities for Special Duty operations. Furthermore, communications with the country were deemed to be reasonably good, certainly in comparison with most other countries in occupied Europe. Clandestine sea operations, while indisputably hazardous, were quickly and lastingly established while the long border with neutral Sweden invited exploitation.

Thus the clandestine organisations possessed viable alternatives to air transportation. This was just as well since Norway was, especially in the early years of the war, a particularly difficult objective for Special Duty flights. The official historian of SOE in Scandinavia, having concentrated on naval operations, has claimed that 'of all the European countries in which the Allied air forces served the Resistance Movement, Norway presented by far the greatest difficulty'.[10] This is not an opinion, however, endorsed by Group Captain R.C. Hockey, a member of No. 419 Flight from November 1940, who thought that 'the most difficult country was Czechoslovakia – a long flight, all over enemy territory, much high ground (the Tatras and associated ranges), flights only in the winter to benefit from the long nights, so terrain was often snowbound, and no reception facilities in Czechoslovakia.'[11] Certainly many of the hazards listed by Group Captain Hockey also applied to Norway and in a contemporary (and somewhat understated) appreciation, the commanding officer of No. 1419 Flight (the renumbered No. 419 Flight) wrote to SOE:

Your query regarding flights to Norway, these may be attempted by aircraft of No. 1419 Flight during and after September. September is perhaps the best month as during late autumn and winter bad weather was to be experienced over the North Sea.[12]

Indeed, the weather was to be a major determining factor in Special Duty operations to Norway. Slow-moving bombers required the cover of darkness (albeit during a moon period) to make the long trip across the North Sea. But long nights meant winter flights and this, in turn, increased the likelihood of bad weather and brought the accompanying risks of snow, cloud, icing and the obscuration of dropping zones.

In spite of these inhibiting factors, the first Special Duty flight to Norway was attempted on 13–14 February 1941 when a Whitley Mark V piloted by Flying Officer A.J. Oettle dropped an SIS-sponsored agent, Sverre Midtskau.[13] RAF records are at best sketchy and it is merely recorded that the aircraft on its return trip was obliged to stage through the Orkney Islands in order to receive a replacement tailplane. Almost a year was to pass before SOE completed its first drop, by which time No. 419 Flight had metamorphosed into No. 1419 Flight in March 1941 and expanded into No. 138 (Special Duty) Squadron in August. Operation *Cheese/Fasting*, flown by Pilot Officer W. Smith, took place on 2–3 January 1942 when a Whitley dropped Odd Starheim and Andreas Fasting into Vest Agder.[14]

Apart from some difficulties with an airscrew, the flight seems to have been completed without too much trouble. Another operation, however, *Anvil/Lark*, was not so fortunate. The pilot's report on this endeavour offers a graphic insight into the multiplicity of problems inherent in such operations and merits being reproduced in full:

On the morning of 5th January 3 Group meteorological service forecast clear weather for the Oslo Fiord with convectional cloud in the North Sea. Two aircraft were therefore detailed to fly to Wick with passengers to operate from there. Bad weather was encountered in North Yorkshire. It became evident the weather was deteriorating rapidly in the North and it was decided therefore to return to Linton. Sergeant Jones, the pilot detailed for Operation ANCHOR, pushed through to Wick.

The 4 Group forecast received forecast NNE winds of 60 miles per hour over the North Sea at 15,000 feet becoming slowly NNW towards morning. This was rather unfortunate because it entailed a head wind in each direction. The extra distance also from Linton instead of Wick necessitated replanning of the operation. Accordingly the accompanying officer was informed of this and a conference was arranged after dinner at Linton. The LARK pinpoint had been altered twice and I therefore asked the accompanying officer if it was essential that ANVIL should be dropped on the point chosen pointing out that the difficulties of wind and high cloud (which would necessitate climbing with high supercharger and would therefore ruin the careful consumption figures) might necessitate a shortening of the distance. The accompanying officer

Captain Marks, professed entire ignorance of either operation and pointed out that he was very new to this kind of work and acquiesced willingly to a conference. At the conference ANVIL pointed out that he would prefer to adhere to his original pinpoint. LARK declared that it was immaterial where he dropped provided it was near a railway. As the other aircraft would be using the pinpoint originally selected for LARK it was necessary to avoid this so as not to prejudice ANCHOR operation from Wick, whom we hoped would be dropped on the following night. A final agreement was made for ANVIL to be dropped on his original pinpoint and LARK to be dropped about 30 miles west on point chosen by him. They produced maps, but these were quite useless for navigation and positions were marked on the RAF maps.

Take off was made at 22.30 hours. High convectional cloud was met with over the North Sea, which necessitated the use of supercharger to climb above it. After four hours fixes were obtained by Astro and confirmed by Loops giving us a ground speed of 105 miles per hour. On the winds obtained from this ground speed the round trip was estimated to take 13 hours. This was beyond the safe endurance of the Whitley as base conditions were by no means certain, and accordingly I was forced to point out this fact to the passengers and ask them if they would dare to abandon the trip. They replied in the negative so I was determined to make a pinpoint first on the coast of Norway to obtain another ground speed before making a final decision. Over the coast of Norway convectional cloud gave way to high stratus. The Whitley was unable to climb through it fast enough and heavy icing on airscrew and wings was experienced. Finally so much ice was met with that the aircraft could not climb at all. Attempts were made to get beneath the cloud but at 5000 feet the coast of Norway was seen in gaps to be covered with low cloud. Accordingly the trip was abandoned. On the return journey further icing was encountered, the airspeed indicator and other instruments became unserviceable. A landing was made at Linton at 0604 hrs.

Report by W/Cdr W R Farley Captain and OC 138 Sqn.[15]

While frustration was being experienced operationally, other problems were simmering in London. In spite of the growth of the flight into a squadron, there was still a persistent shortage of aircraft. Appeals to the Air Ministry and Bomber Command for a further allocation, however, not only fell on deaf ears but engendered a distinctly hostile reaction.

Air Chief Marshal Sir Charles Portal, the Chief of the Air Staff, signalled his attitude to SOE's activities when, on 1 February 1941, in a letter to Gladwyn Jebb, SOE's Chief Executive Officer, he opined:

I think that the dropping of men dressed in civilian clothes for the purpose of attempting to kill members of the opposing forces is not an operation with which the Royal Air Force should be associated. I think you will agree that there is a vast difference, in ethics, betweeen the time honoured operation of the dropping of a spy from the air and this entirely new scheme for dropping what one can only call assassins.[16]

With hindsight one can only wonder at such misgivings over moral niceties in the light of Bomber Command's policy of area bombing German cities. However, Portal's ethical qualms also reveal what was to become a persistent RAF belief that SIS and intelligence-gathering were more acceptable than SOE and its 'dirty tricks'. Furthermore, Portal's objections were not solely rooted in moral grounds or a preference for SIS. He perceived SOE's demands for aircraft as constituting a dangerous dilution of Bomber Command's efforts in favour of a speculative strategy. He expressed his opinions to H.N. Sporborg, a senior SOE staff officer, thus:

> . . . your work is a gamble which may give us a valuable dividend or produce nothing. It is anybody's guess. My bombing offensive is not a gamble. Its dividend is certain; it is a gilt-edged investment. I cannot divert aircraft from a certainty to a gamble which may be a gold-mine or may be completely worthless.[17]

Portal was not alone in his antipathy and found an ally and even more vehement adversary of SOE in his deputy and, later, the Commander-in-Chief, Bomber Command, Air Marshal Arthur Harris. Harris's objections to SOE echoed those of his superior. He accused it of trying to create its own air force and did all that he could to ensure that this aim would not be realised by a group of 'panacea mongers'.[18]

Behind these high-level wranglings the work of the Special Duty squadrons continued. As ever, statistics for SIS operations are all but impossible to obtain but those for SOE operations are generally available. No operations were carried out in 1940 or 1941, but in 1942 22 sorties were made to Norway, 11 of them being successful. Twenty-one men were parachuted along with 6 tons of supplies (15 containers and 14 packages).[19] Furthermore, in May 1942 some of the burden of Special Duty operations was taken by No. 1477 (Norwegian) Flight (subsequently No. 333 (Norwegian Squadron). This unit, based at Woodhaven in Scotland, flew Consolidated Catalinas and carried out their first clandestine operation on 1–2 May 1942, landing two agents at Vikten. As part of the RAF's Coastal Command the squadron maintained their regular duties but found the time to complete seventeen special operations, the last of them taking place on 26–27 April 1945.[20]

The variety of methods of transportation into Norway – SOE vessels, SIS vessels, No. 333 Squadron, Nos 138 and 161 Squadrons and the cross-border route from Sweden – ensured that, in spite of the ever-present weather difficulties, there were never the same crises as were encountered with the maintenance of links with France, Poland and Yugoslavia. It must also be conceded that Norway continued to remain a long way down the Chiefs of Staffs' and SOE's lists of priorities. In a COS memorandum of 20 March 1943, 'Special Operations Executive Directive for 1943', it was stipulated that:

The Requirements of SIS should in general be accorded priority over your own operations in Norway, Sweden, France and the Low Countries,' and 'We attach importance to your [SOE's] operations in the following general order of priority: 1. The Italian Islands, Corsica and Crete. 2. The Balkans 3. France. 4. Poland and Czechoslovakia. 5. Norway and the Low Countries. 6. The Near East.[21]

SOE's reply to this directive and especially its limiting of air resources came in an 'Appreciation' to the COS dated 24 April 1943:

It emphasised the importance of the production of adequate transport facilities and pointed out that the demands for transport exceeded the means of delivery by about 200%. Since one of the essential characteristics of Resistance Groups was that unless they were served sufficiently to enable them to retain their dynamic quality they tended to disintegrate, the demand for supplies was progressive and the lack of adequate transport facilities not only retarded their expansion, but threatened their very existence.[22]

The estimated shortfall of aircraft amounted to 117 bombers and Portal inevitably opposed the allocation of the equivalent of four additional squadrons to the existing Special Duties force. Having failed to find a solution, the matter was referred to the Defence Committee on 2 August 1943 for their judgement. No conclusive decision was forthcoming regarding an increase in the number of aircraft. However, responsibility for these operations was transferred from the Air Ministry to Bomber Command. Perhaps sensing SOE's fears that their affairs had been entrusted to a less than benevolent guardian, the Defence Committee put it on record that

(iii) it is open to the Minister of Economic Warfare to appeal to the Defence Committee, if at any time he considers that SOE requirements are not being given a sufficiently high priority.'[23]

Fortunately these altercations had little effect upon SOE's Norwegian activities. Low down the list of priorities, serviced by other means and generally restricted to air operations for only six months of the year (and largely during moon periods), Norway nevertheless experienced a substantial increase in air supply in 1943. Fifty sorties were flown of which twenty-four were successful.[24]

The agents in the field would select a likely dropping zone (DZ) and communicate its location to London. If the Air Ministry's intelligence directorate (AI2(c)), SOE's Air Liaison section, the country section and the Special Duty squadron all approved the DZ, agreed encode confirmation messages were transmitted by the BBC. A reception committee would await the arrival of the aircraft over the DZ, signalling a recognition letter in addition to a group of lights or beacons. On occasion, drops were assisted by the use of the navigational aid, Rebecca/Eureka and, although the system did not meet with universal success elsewhere, in Norway it achieved significant results.

There were any number of reasons why an operation might fail, and men and supplies were dropped in the wrong location all too frequently. However, on occasion the field was able to send a message confirming a success and this report would, in turn, be sent to the Special Duty squadrons' base at RAF Tempsford. The saga of *Goldfinch 4a* offers an insight into the vicissitudes of clandestine air support:

> 14/5.3.44. The field send thanks for 12 containers and one package: The plane dropped on the run in and they congratulate the pilot on his fine work. 23.4.44 The containers and package from this operation were received safely by the Reception and hidden away. It has just been learned that the hiding place was discovered and reported to the Sheriff and the Germans have taken the stores.[25]

The build-up to D-Day did not signal any diminution of the Special Duty flights to Norway, and 17 tons of supplies were dropped in the first three months of 1944 alone. During the same period USAAF Consolidated B-24 Liberators began to participate in these types of operations and completed four successful supply dropping sorties, delivering five tons of material. Their efforts increased immensely during the summer months, supplying 47 tons to the RAF's three. However, the crescendo of operations greatly increased following the liberation of France. Nos 138 and 161 Squadrons were joined by Handley Page Halifaxes, Short Stirlings and Armstrong Whitworth Albemarles from Nos 3 and 38 Groups and the volume of agents and supplies soared. Between October 1944 and the end of the war in Europe, the RAF attempted 921 sorties to Norway, succeeding with 546 of them. A total of 98 agents were dropped and 878 tons of supplies were dropped. However this period also saw the first losses of RAF Special Duties aircraft engaged on SOE Norwegian operations, with 23 aircraft failing to return. During this same period the USAAF made 130 sorties, succeeding with 59 of them and dropping 25 agents and 90 tons of supplies.[26]

Substantial, and often overstated, claims have been made for the efficacy of clandestine operations during the Second World War but perhaps one of the most balanced appreciations has been made by Bickham Sweet-Escott, a senior SOE staff officer. He observed that 'the only hope we had of doing our job in Western Europe lay in the parachute'. Furthermore, he believed that Norway had witnessed the very best of special duty work with the achievement of Operation *Gunnerside*. 'It was the classic proof of our contention that one aircraft which drops an intelligent and well-trained party can do more damage than a whole fleet of bombers.'[27]

References

1   K. A. Merrick, *Flights of the Forgotten* (London, 1989), p. 14.
2   M.R.D. Foot in *Proceedings of the RAF Historical Society*, Issue No. 5, p. 10.
3   Merrick, *Flights of the Forgotten*, p. 18.
4   PRO, AIR 20/8224, 'The Formation of an SD Flight and Early Operations'.
5   *RAF Narrative, Air Historical Branch, Special Duty Operations in Europe*, p. 143.
6   Papiers William Ugeux, No. 56, Centre de Recherches et d'Etudes Historiques de la Seconde Guerre Mondiale, Brussels.
7   'The Formation of an SD Flight and Early Operations'.
8   Merrick, *Flights of the Forgotten*, p. 18.
9   PRO, CAB 80/56.
10 Charles Cruickshank, *SOE in Scandinavia* (Oxford, 1986), p. 6.
11 *Proceedings of the RAF Historical Society*, Issue No. 5, p. 20.
12 PRO, AIR 20/8242.
13 Ivar Kraglund and Arnfinn Moland, *Norge i krig*, vol. 6, (Oslo, 1987), p. 29.
14 Ibid, p.110. It is surprising that although Fasting had been given the operational name 'Biscuit', his real name appears in RAF records.
15 PRO, AIR 20/8334.
16 M.R.D. Foot, *SOE in France*, (London, 1966) p. 153.
17 Ibid, p. 13.
18 Sir Charles Webster and Noble Frankland, *The Strategic Air Offensive against Germany*, vol. III (London, 1961), p. 82.
19 *RAF Narrative* Appendix H.10.
20 Sten Stenersen et. al., *Slipp over Norge* (Oslo, 1982), p. 56.
21 PRO, CAB 80/68.
22 *RAF Narrative, Air Historical Branch, Special Duty Operations in Europe*, p. 19.
23 Ibid, p. 31.
24 Ibid, Appendix H.10 and Appendix H.11.
25 PRO, AIR 20/8363.
26 *RAF Narrative*, Appendix H.10 and Appendix H.11.
27 Bickham Sweet-Escott, *Baker Street Irregular* (London, 1965), p. 114.

19 Norwegian resistance: the Swedish connection [1]

SIR PETER TENNANT

ON 16 June 1990, the Norwegian minister of defence, Per Ditlev-Simonsen, accompanied by several hundred veteran Norwegian police troops trained in Sweden during the war, unveiled a plaque on a giant granite runestone in the presence of the Swedish minister of defence Roine Carlsson at the large country house of Johannisberg in Gottröra Parish in Roslagen as a thank-offering from Norway to Sweden for the training of the Norwegian Police Troops during the war. The local paper, *Norrtelje Tidning*, announced the event with the banner headline, 'Revolver Harry's private army and Johannisberg castle'. The Norwegians had raised the money for the stone and its transport among those who had trained in Sweden. How different from 9 April 1940 after the German invasion of Norway. The Finnish winter war was just over. Many volunteers and much war material had been shipped by Sweden to Finland but it was not to be so with the German invasion of Norway. No Swedes were allowed to volunteer for the Norwegian forces and no war material was supplied. When King Haakon asked for permission for himself and the Norwegian Crown Prince to cross into Sweden to shelter from German attack he was refused by the Swedish King. In June 1940 the Swedes concluded a transit agreement with the Germans, which gave the Germans the use of the Swedish railways for the relief of troops on the Norwegian front, thus providing until 1943, when the agreement was abrogated, protection for over two million German soldiers from Allied attack. In the summer of 1941, after the German invasion of Russia, the Swedes added to the transit facilities by agreeing to the passage of the Engelbrekt division from Oslo across Sweden to Finland. Meanwhile Swedish territorial waters were used by German warships and troop ships on their way to and from Finland; there were also a number of so-called courier planes flying between Finland and Norway and landing in Sweden. But thanks to Revolver Harry, who had a habit of acting first and asking for permission afterwards, a massive operation was built up for the training of Norwegian police troops. It took place first under cover of so-called health camps, organised by some of the remarkable Norwegian doctors who sorted out the sheep from the goats among the streams of refugees. The Norwegian military attaché in Stockholm, Ole Berg, cooperated with Söderman from the start and ended up as Norwegian commander-in-chief.

The demonstration in 1990 of gratitude by the Norwegians to the Swedes was not the first. In 1965 there was a large meeting in the Aula of Oslo University to celebrate the 20th anniversary of the entry of three battalions of

Norwegian police troops into Finnmark. The prime ministers and commanders-in-chief of both countries were present and Harry Söderman was remembered as the hero of the occasion. Then in 1983 the two kings met in Stockholm to celebrate Swedish help to Norway in the war with the unveiling of a great 15-tonne granite memorial from Hallingdal in Norway, which was sited in Djurgården. On June 13th 1983, the Norwegian C-in-C General Sven Hauge laid a wreath on Harry Söderman's grave at Turinge churchyard near Södertälje. A party of Swedish Dragoon Guards and eight men from the Norwegian Royal Guard paraded for the ceremony. So however much the Swedes tend to forget the war and the unneutral behaviour of Harry Söderman, this is not so in Norway.

As head of the Criminal Technical Institute in Stockholm he was throughout the war a friend and ally for whose solid support we were most grateful. I had known him before the war through my brother-in-law Fille Fellenius who had switched from literature and philosophy to psychology and was working with Professor Katz the German refugee Professor in Stockholm's Technical High School (the future university). They co-operated with Söderman on criminal psychology. He became a close friend, a sailing companion on my boat *Valkyrian* and an eating, drinking and singing gastronome who introduced me to the delicacies of surströmming, fermented Baltic herring which stank so pungently that it had to be eaten in a sealed room. He was also an expert on reindeer meat, especially tongues and spare ribs at the time of the autumn slaughter, quite apart from his love of French food and wine as he had lived in Lyon for many years.

Many of my academic friends found it difficult to understand our compatibility. First because Swedish academic snobbery regarded his Lyon doctorate in ballistics as valueless and second, because as a police expert he had investigated the Reichstag fire. He had close relations with the German criminal police, and had been misquoted by the press as promoting the Nazi thesis that it was a Communist plot. I discussed it with him at the time and he was in no doubt that Van der Lubbe was alone responsible and motivated by his burning hatred of Nazism. Recent investigations in the Federal Republic have confirmed Söderman's findings, which were based on his own meeting with van der Lubbe, and the conclusions reached by the German criminal police at the time. His reputation in fact provided a good cover for his pro-Allied activities, for this cheerful, burly, eccentric adventurer with his pock-marked face and cloth cap, stood by us through thick and thin.

Söderman was born in 1902 in Stockholm, studied chemistry in Malmö, went into industry and between 1921 and 1924 studied in the chemical industry in Germany. He became fascinated by the application of science to criminology and carried out a long study journey from Turkey through Asia to China to investigate police methods. He finally returned to Lyon to work under the renowned criminologist Edmond Locard who appointed him his assistant. He returned to Sweden to publish the first of his many books and then went back to Locard's police laboratory in Lyon, taking his doctorate in 1928 with a thesis on small arms entitled 'L'expertise des armes à feu courtes'. This was the origin of the nickname 'Revolver Harry'. He then lectured for a year in Lyon and in 1930 was appointed to lead a government course in Sweden on criminology. Harry became a lecturer (Docent) at what later became Stockholm University and from 1939 to 1953 he was head of the State Criminology Institute. He became well known internationally in police circles and in 1934 had organised and run New York's Police Laboratory. He had close contacts with Scotland Yard and was a friend of Sir Ronald Howe in CID. We flew him in 1942 for discussions with Sir Ronald in London and they seemed to have spent a riotous fortnight together fitting in racing at Newmarket and wartime nightlife in between work.

My amateur pre-war training had at least taught me the elements of security which were singularly lacking in our legation at the beginning of the war. No-one would listen to me so one night, to prove my point, I climbed into the building through a top-floor window and called in on our naval attaché, at that time Commander John Poland. He was working at his desk with a glass of whisky in one hand and a revolver in the other. He pursued me till I surrendered and had caused sufficient commotion to make my point. London was told of our deplorable state of insecurity and at my suggestion it was proposed to ask New Scotland Yard if we might approach Söderman to help us locally if they could not provide the necessary equipment. This was agreed and it was evidence of our government's regard for Söderman that he was called in to advise. He was horrified when he saw the state of our defences, provided us with devices which at that time were far advanced and added the urgent recommendation that we should employ a full-time trained security officer. After some months, much to Söderman's amusement, Scotland Yard sent us a fingerprint expert whom Söderman knew well and did not rate very highly. We all got to like the giant Mr Battley with his tiny head and his Anthony Eden hat a size too small. He kept us in order and set us a splendid example by tip-toeing into our offices to catch us napping. He travelled with diplomatic bags as a king's messenger to Gothenburg like a pantomime clown with chains and handcuffs and leg-irons which were then locked to his sleeping-car bunk.

Having seen to our legation's security, Harry remained in touch throughout the war, except for six months in 1940 when he told me he could not see me until the Rickman affair had been cleared up. This was a bungled attempt by our Section D to blow up the iron ore loading cranes at Oxelösund, an operation in which I was wrongly thought to be implicated. We then resumed our sailing weekends at my father-in-law's house Viksberg, near Sodertälje. Here we fished and shot and bathed and walked and collected mushrooms and talked. As an Interpol official he travelled in and out of Germany and Switzerland and ran a training programme in Finland while we were technically at war with them. One useful by-product of his Finnish activities, was an enormous supply of out-of-bond angostura bitters which I bought off him for the legation. The Finns, who were to be hosts at the Olympic Games when the war broke out, had been left with excessive supplies of various kinds, including drink to satisfy all tastes. They were not familiar with angostura bitters but had bought it in quantities which they imagined would meet foreign demand. They then tried to drink it neat and discovered that in spite of their galvanised stomachs they would be unable to consume the quantities required for many years. So I bought a supply off Harry which met our needs for the whole of the war.

One day I got his help over a strange German refugee who had allegedly been one of Otto Strasser's men. He came to Sweden with the Jewish exodus from Denmark in 1943 and called on me with plans to broadcast on the BBC to subvert German morale. I suspected the man was a German agent and told Harry of my suspicions. I asked him if he could be watched but not arrested, as I had plans if possible to get him over to England. Harry established that he was in contact with the German legation and that he was making radio transmissions at regular intervals. They had not been able to decipher them, nor were they able to find the transmitter, but suspected he was using a converter on an ordinary high-powered radio receiver. He continued to visit me and press for a chance to fly to England and broadcast for the BBC. I suggested to Harry that the Swedes might now be glad to be rid of him and we might be able to find some use for him. So finally he was flown over, well received, installed in a flat and given a radio receiver.

He recorded some tapes for the BBC and was watched. He began transmitting immediately, but it was impossible to find the transmitter. He was followed round London and in the course of a short time no fewer than twenty contacts were identified until one day, their patience exhausted, the Special Branch broke into his flat too soon while he was transmitting. But he was too quick for them and they never found the device he used to convert his receiver. He was subjected to lengthy interrogation and finally sat out the rest of the war in Dartmoor. But that was not the end of the story. After a few months we received a message from Buckingham Palace saying His Majesty was being plagued by letters from a prisoner in Dartmoor declaring he was a refugee from Hitler and had been kidnapped by a man called Tennant in Stockholm who had sent him to London on a spurious invitation from the BBC, and that he had been unjustly imprisoned as a spy. The matter was explained to His Majesty who continued to be his host for the rest of the war.

We sent Harry over to England as the result of a very interesting approach made to him by his old friend the SS General Arthur Nebe, the head of the German Criminal Police whom Harry knew well and trusted. Nebe got Harry to come and stay with him for a week in his house on the Wannsee in Berlin together with the Police President of Berlin, Graf Helldorf to discuss their plan for the overthrow of Hitler which ended with the abortive Stauffenberg plot of 1944 for which poor Nebe was executed. Harry came back to Stockholm with a complete plan of action to be put to the British government which involved the arrest of the top Nazis by the criminal police and the defeat of two SS-Panzer divisions held in readiness by Hitler to quell popular disturbances. The proposal was for the British to land by sea and air and establish a bridge-head near Hamburg. Harry spent a fortnight in London as the guest of Scotland Yard before the proposal was not unexpectedly turned down. However this visit led to Harry's most enterprising exploit, known to us as 'Revolver Harry's private army'.

In the 1930s some 200 Norwegian police officers had been trained in criminology at his Institute. In the spring of 1942 when he was in London, he renewed his close relationships with CID, dating back to 1934 when he lectured at Hendon Police College. He had known Sir Norman Kendall, the head of CID, for many years. As a police official he met Terje Wold, the refugee Norwegian minister of justice, who asked him about training Norwegian policemen in Sweden to take over Norway after the war. This was followed up in Sweden early in 1943 by Olav Svensen, the Norwegian police officer in charge of the legal office of the Norwegian legation, who had the responsibility for sorting out the sheep and goats among the swarms of Norwegian refugees. Over dinner one night they drew up a plan for training fifty Norwegian policemen to replace the Nazi police officers after the German defeat. The Norwegian government in London took a long time to make up its mind but by May, Svensen had 20,000 kroner available to help with training.

Harry then approached Gustaf Möller, the minister of the interior, with his colleague Thorwald Bergquist. They gave their blessing. Harry then got the help of Stockholm's Police Chief, Eric Ros, and G. Biörklund, the head of the State Police College, who provided accommodation and teachers, and started with a three-month course for twenty criminal police officers. The aim was to re-establish law and order in Norway, bring the criminals to justice and avoid the degradation of lynch law. Eight such courses were held and 200 officers were trained.

The next stage was to find a site for the Norwegian Police College and this was discovered in a country house at Gottröra, a deserted and unpopulated area very suitable for exercises and manoeuvres for some fifty men without attracting attention. The whole scheme had to be kept secret and the secret was well kept from everybody, I think, but the Germans, in spite of the fact that the enterprise in the end encompassed some 15,000 men from very different establishments and large quantities of weaponry and motor vehicles. Harry scraped together furniture and bedding with the help of Zeth Höglund of the Stockholm town council who never failed to give practical help. The first instructor was Ewert Trofelt, a senior police officer doing military service as a captain in the military police. This giant figure, six feet seven inches tall, was Harry's right-hand man up to the end of the war and followed him on his dramatic entry into Oslo at the time of the capitulation. He was very popular with the Norwegians and stayed in Norway after the war to organise crash training in police methods for members of the resistance.

The Norwegians were on the whole raw recruits with no sense of discipline so they were given military as well as police training. They were equipped with Swedish army weapons by the middle of the summer of 1943. Captain Helge Gleditch, the Norwegian officer in charge, had responsibility for recruitment. The courses included Norwegian language, criminal law, report writing, police work, criminal police work, exercises, tactics and medical services. The 20,000 kroner provided by the Norwegians soon ran out, even though all Swedish services and manpower and material were provided free.

The next stage was to train a force of some 1,200 men. The Swedish authorities provided the expanded requirements, while the Norwegian government in London produced 7.5 million kroner to fund the project. Harry's Norwegians were officially called 'The State Police Corps' responsible to the

Norwegian Ministry of Justice. They consisted of eight companies, in each of which the men were fully armed with pistols, sub-machine guns, two light mortars and twelve light machine guns. There were six dogs per company and each company was fully motorised with twelve lorries and one staff car and six motor-cycles. Gottröra was expanded with new barrack buildings and in 1944 a new camp was built at Axvall, another at a place known as Torpet and a further location called Stora Fors, which was a dog and dog-handler's training camp.

Then came another sudden expansion of the Norwegian force together with a new Danish one. Harry was put in command of some 10,000 men, with permission to expand to 12,000. He had been given leave of absence from his official post but kept his offices in the Institute which became the hedquarters of the organisations. This expansion started with him and the Norwegian military attaché Ole Berg who later became commander-in-chief of the Norwegian army. They devised a scheme for an additional force to cope with all the possible emergencies arising from a German capitulation and the need to protect the civilian population.

There was also the remarkable Norwegian lung surgeon, Dr. Carl Semb, one of many Norwegian doctors in the resistance, who set up numerous 'health camps' all over Sweden to examine the refugees and get them into first-class physical condition. These camps were combined with the others until there were some fourteen new camps to accommodate 500 hundred men each.

The first of these camps was the 17th-century country house of Mälsåker near Mariefred on Lake Mälar which alas was burnt down early in 1945. I visited it with Harry before the disaster and was impressed by the troops who were shortly due to move to Lapland to enter northern Norway when the time came. The worst constraint on the expansion of Norwegian police troops was the lack of trained officers, most of whom had been caught by the Germans and shipped off to concentration camps in Germany. Officer training therefore had to be carried out in Sweden, much of it with the help of Norwegian officers flown over from England who were fully trained in commando tactics. A late addition to all this was a naval unit started at Mauritzberg Castle where finally nearly 500 sailors and fishermen were trained as harbour police. Another specialised group was trained by SOE-trained Norwegian officers in sabotage and the handling of the latest Allied weaponry.

The huge organisation with all its complicated components had to remain as secret as possible in spite of the tendency of Norwegians to chatter. Security on the whole was remarkably good though some weapons were smuggled over to the resistance in Norway. Swedish insistence on security was not popular with the Norwegians and this was perhaps the worst area of touchy relations between the Norwegian troops and their Swedish hosts. Morale on the whole was high, and the desertion figure of about 1,000 over two years was not too depressing out of a body of over 10,000 men, about a quarter of the Norwegian refugees who escaped to Sweden. Many of these were undesirable characters and quisling spies. Apart from moments of tension between the Norwegians and Swedes there was also a certain animosity among the Norwegians against their own legation, which on one occasion led to a serious crisis when the cooks went on strike. Punishment for indiscipline was difficult but culprits were sent to punishment camps far away from towns and with only heavy work in the woods as relaxation. Much trouble was taken to provide entertainment, films, travelling theatre troupes, concert parties and so forth.

As a result of the total German take-over of Denmark on 29 August 1943, the Danish commander-in-chief took the initiative to ask the Swedes to do the same for them as for the Norwegians. The Danes on the whole were a different proposition from the Norwegians as the groups were smaller, amounting only to about 3,000 men, and very much better trained and disciplined since their own officers had escaped with them. General Knudtzon was sent to Sweden by the Danish Freedom Council to organise a Danish Brigade and purchase arms. Their camp was in Sofielund in Småland, where they housed 500 men. This was followed by other camps to accommodate in the end 3,000 men. The training was more rapid than with the Norwegians as there were many more officers available. In consequence discipline was better and they concentrated more on allied commando military training rather than police work.

With the German capitulation the Danish Brigade crossed over from Hälsingborg to Helsingør, escorted by Swedish destroyers, to be met with no German resistance and a warm welcome by the population. But while street fighting broke out in Copenhagen, the Brigade was held back until the following day when it went into action for the loss of only two men and four dead among the Danish Nazi Hipo men. There was no further resistance and the Brigade was given guard duty on the German frontier in Jutland and elsewhere. The Danes were very popular in Sweden and sorely missed when they left.

The Swedish army, after the departure of the deplorable commander-in-chief General Thörnell, became wholly supportive of Harry's enterprise and made a generous contribution of weapons and manpower for the training of the Norwegian officers. Support came in particular from General C.A. Ehrens-värd, who as a colonel had set up the Swedish Volunteer Corps in the first Finnish war. In December 1944, 4,800 Norwegians were taken on manoeuvres in Dalarna with the help of the Swedish army and among the umpires was no less a person than Prince Gustaf Adolf. The new Swedish C-in-C, General Jung, was also presemt as an observer. The Norwegians were very popular with the local people and as they marched past the schools the children sang the Norwegian national anthem, 'Ja vi elsker'. The manoeuvres revealed weakness in the staff work of the Norwegians in handling large units and the Swedish army set up a series of staff courses to give them more experience. In April 1945 an even bigger exercise took place with some 6,000 men at Järvsö in Hälsingland. The minister of the interior, Gustaf Möller, and the future prime minister, the giant Tage Erlander, were present. I had sent the latter over to London for a period of months on a course in air raid precautions. Prince Gustaf Adolf again took part in these manoeuvres.

The German retreat in Finland southwards through northern Norway was marked by a vicious destruction of everthing that lay in their path in the winter of 1944–45. The Swedes co-operated with Bernt Balchen, the famous Norwegian-American airman, to bring relief to the local population. In December 1944 Balchen arrived with ten Dakotas first at Västerås, where they

loaded a field hospital and Norwegian personnel and then flew on to the airfield
at Kallax near Luleå, where Harry's Norwegian policemen joined the American airmen. After bureaucratic delays by the Russians who by now were in
Kirkenes in northern Norway, Harry got permission to send in his men. From
12 January 1945 and in the following weeks 968 Norwegian police and 917,342
kilograms of material were flown by Balchen to northern Norway from
Sweden. Another base was built at Karesuando, the most northerly inhabited
spot in Sweden. Roads were built through the snow and ice before the early
spring thaw and some of the Norwegian police troops managed to enter
Norway; but the thaw made motorised transport impossible and they had to
resort to walking, riding horse or driving in reindeer sledges. Harry staked out
an airstrip on a lake at Karesuando which Balchen immediately made use of.
By the time of the German capitulation on 8 May all was ready for the
Norwegian troops to march in.

Söderman had entered Norway alone by 8 May but the Allies refused to
allow his police troops to cross into Norway until two days later, much to their
disgust. The final figures were 1,310 men into Kirkenes in March 1945; then in
May after the capitulations 3,915 into Narvik, 2,570 to Trondheim and 4,975
to Oslo, a total of 12,770 men, 792 horses and 600 motor vehicles. There is
never any complete agreement on the total numbers which seem to vary
between 13,000 and 17,000, with a balance of some 2,000 who remained in
Sweden.

The Norwegians were disappointed that they had no chance to fight, but it
was a mercy that the German army behaved in a disciplined manner and that
the quisling Norwegians did not attempt to put up a last stand. Allied fears of a
final campaign in a Norwegian redoubt, the Wagnerian dream of the bombastic German General Boehme were not realised, largely owing to the demoralis-
ation of the German troops who all wanted to go home. The final bill for
Harry's operation is interesting. All the training provided by the Swedish
army and police was a gift, while Sweden wrote off loans of 50 million kronor
to Denmark and 150 million kronor to Norway.

Harry was not content with his own private army; he had to get into
Norway ahead of everybody in order to save the prisoners in the concentration
camp of Grini and the jails of Oslo from reprisals by the Germans or the
quislings. Through his contacts with the German police in Berlin he got in
touch with the head of the Gestapo in Norway, Oberführer Fehlis, to negotiate
the liberation of the Norwegians in Grini and Møllergaten No. 19, as well as
the 10,0000 Russian prisoners of war being used a slave labour in the north.
With the agreement of the prime minister and the foreign minister, and the
Norwegian legation, and with the clearance of our military attaché Reggie
Sutton-Pratt whom he discovered in a yard getting his boat ready for the
summer, Harry took the train to the Norwegian frontier at Charlottenburg on
21 April 1945 and met the Gestapo Chief, Fehlis. They had a picnic and
discussed the whole question of liberating the Norwegians in Oslo and the
Russian prisoners of war in the north. Fehlis did not know that Himmler had
already allowed the Swedes to liberate Norwegians in the concentration camps
in Germany and take them to Sweden and he promised he would get into touch

with Himmler to see what could be done. He kept in touch by telephone and then with no answer coming from Himmler, Harry had a message that Terboven the Reichskommissar in Norway wished to discuss the matter with him in Oslo. So he left for Oslo on 6 May with the agreement of the Swedish prime minister and foreign minister and the Norwegians, but to the annoyance of certain circles in Britain who did not wish to share credit for liberation with an unauthorised neutral civilian.

He was met by the Gestapo at the frontier, driven to Oslo and accommodated by them in a requisitioned Norwegian shipowner's house where he met Fehlis for discussions. Terboven kept on putting him off until just as he was going to see him on Monday the 7th at 15.50 the radio announced the capitulation of Germany. Harry drove to Grini with his faithful Trofelt and a German official detailed to open up the prisons for him. He called the 5,000 prisoners together, handed over the command of Grini to the Norwegians under Gowart-Olsen, made a stirring speech, and asked inmates to remain in Grini till further notice. They all sang the Norwegian national anthem. Then Harry went to Møllergaten No. 19 where all cells were opened. He made them a speech and told them to stay there till he could transport them to Grini where they would all be concentrated for feeding and medical inspection. He released five poor wretches who were condemned to death, then went to the Gestapo headquarters at Viktoria Terrasse, where there were thirty prisoners whom he freed and had transported to Grini. He used these headquarters as his own and with the agreement of the Norwegians took over responsibility for the police. He got the Red Cross to transport all prisoners to Grini and supply rations and medicines. He stopped all sale of alcoholic liquor, occupied the radio station and lifted the blackout. Finally the home front underground emerged and asked him to continue in command. They disarmed the Quisling guard at the Castle and fought off a threat of attack at Møllergaten No. 19 with another harangue by Harry to the crowd. In the meantime Fehlis disappeared and was later found to have committed suicide with the double security of a cyanide pill and a shot in the head with his revolver. On the Wedneday Harry handed over to the Nowegians and drove back to Sweden.

The next day, hoping for a short rest, he was asked to go north to take charge of the release of the Russian prisoners of war. Together with Balchen he filled seven Dakotas with supplies of cigarettes, food and medicine and flew to Bodø which was still occupied by the Germans. A Norwegian underground committee had been formed to look after the Russians and he then proceeded to visit all the camps spread from Mo i Rana to Narvik as forced labour for Hitler's northern Norway railway. The loss of life had been horrific in this brutal Todt Organisation operation. He was stunned by the starvation and illness that prevailed in the camps and by the brutality of the Wehrmacht which had always been so proud of its honour and its discipline. He then had a victory parade in Bodø with his police troops, the Americans and a mixed bag of Ostarbeiter, mainly Russians and Yugoslavs. The Swedish Red Cross came in and nurses took charge of the sick with medicine and food.

This was the last of Harry's wartime efforts after which he returned to his Institution with the new title of Director General. He remained there till 1953 when he left for the United States. After the war he became one of the leading lights of Interpol and when it was reorganised he was made chairman of its European Narcotics Committee. In 1951 he spent seven months in West Germany to help with the organisation of the German Federal Police. We met again then as I was much concerned with police matters as deputy commandant of the British sector of Berlin. Then in 1952 he suddenly moved to an international police appointment in Tangier and sold up his delightful country house, Berga near Södertälje, which he had bought from a mutual friend who was a neighbour of my wife's family at Viksberg. He died suddenly of a heart attack in Tangier on 6 March 1956 aged only 54. He had married for the third time and left a young family of four children in addition to his son Pehr by an earlier marriage. His loss was felt very deeply by his friends around the world not only in police circles. He had had enough experience of the abuse of power by the secret police in Nazi Germany and in occupied Norway and Denmark to have any sympathy for the lack of political control of Sweden's own security police. He was a brave and extrovert adventurer with intelligence and expert knowledge of his profession, together with a love of humanity which endeared him to people in many countries, especially in Scandinavia and Finland.

References

1   Sources: My own private papers; Fru Karin Sköld, Harry Söderman's sister who
now has his archive; Harry Söderman's own account *Skandinaviskt Mellanspel*
(Stockholm, 1945); Ole Kristian Grimnes, *Opptakten til de norske polititropper i
Sverige* (Oslo, 1968).

20 The Spitsbergen operations 1942–3

SIR ALEXANDER GLEN

Editor's Note

TWO participants in the Oxford conference, apart from Sir Alexander Glen, had personal connections with the Spitsbergen operations. One was Sir Robin Maxwell-Hyslop, whose father, Captain A.H. Maxwell-Hyslop, GC, RN, commanded HMS *Cumberland* during Operations *Gearbox 2* and *Gearbox 3* for the relief of Spitsbergen. The other was Colonel Andrew Croft, who had accompanied Sir Alexander on the Oxford University 1935–6 Expedition to Spitsbergen, and who was serving in 1941–2 as assistant military attaché in Stockholm. In his memoirs *A Talent for Adventure* (Hanley Swan, 1991, pp. 164, 168–9), Colonel Croft describes one remarkable aspect of the background to the Spitsbergen operations:

Two Norwegians in particular distinguished themselves at about this time by a daring exploit on a train. Certain German Air Force Generals were in the habit of making regular visits to northern airfields in Norway, and with teutonic discipline their movements were apt to be predictably timed. Invariably they lunched in the VIP dining car, happily leaving their briefcases behind. The two agents slipped silently into the carriage, seized the briefcases and jumped from the train as it slowed down with the connivance of the driver. Within forty-eight hours I had those briefcases on my desk . . .

In June 1942 I was summoned to London much to my surprise and told to report to the Admiralty. The briefcases ... contained important details about German Meteorological bases in the Arctic. On arrival I was instructed to join Sandy Glen and leave forthwith in a Catalina flying-boat for Akureyri in Northern Iceland; there was barely time to learn what it was all about. . . .

In fact the Royal Norwegian government, with the Admiralty and Coastal Command, had already taken action and despatched the *Fritham* expedition, with Glen among its members, to Spitsbergen. The tragedy that struck the expedition in May 1942 is described in Sir Alexander's paper. The task in June for Glen and Croft was 'to map the southern limits of drift ice between Greenland and Spitsbergen so that our convoys could choose a more northerly route and avoid as far as possible those punishing German bombers.' That task accomplished, both men moved on: Croft back to Stockholm and thence to

Corsica to undertake 52 sea operations to the coasts of north-west Italy and south-east France, followed by a sizeable parachute operation to southern France; Glen to Albania and Yugoslavia. It was not the end, however, of operations on Spitsbergen.

★　★　★　★　★

Germany's attack on the Soviet Union in the summer of 1941 opened up a vast new battleground and it imposed an equivalent new problem of supply upon the Western Allies. The land route through Persia was both remote and limited in capacity, Japan blocked any communication from the east. The only remaining possibility was by the northern seas, the long exposed route from Iceland through the narrow Bear Island Channel between north Norway and Spitsbergen to Murmansk and Archangel.

Over the winter of 1941–2, German confidence in speedy and total victory in Russia was such that little effort was made to interrupt the Allied convoys on this route. The Red Army's dogged resistance in winter warfare, however, changed Berlin's strategic appreciation and, by the spring of 1942, heavy ships and U-boats together with torpedo bomber squadrons of the Luftwaffe were being concentrated in north Norway, with the purpose of cutting the northern route and of threatening the North Atlantic as well.

The Arctic had a further significance for Germany. Deprived of weather information from the west, the Arctic islands including Spitsbergen, Greenland and Baffin Island provided scope for manned stations to be established by U-boat and Luftwaffe. The logistical effort was massive, involving at certain periods over twenty U-boats and more regularly three or four squadrons of JU88 and HE111 specialised in weather reporting. The tactical need behind this was compelling, in its immediate influence on operations on the eastern front and later in the west, notably on the dates chosen for the Ardennes offensive.

It is difficult today to remember that up to 1940 flying operations in the Arctic beyond 80 degrees north had been limited to a few pioneer flights by Norwegian, American, British and Russian explorers. It is equally difficult to recall that prior to the delivery in 1941 of the first Consolidated PBYs, the Catalina, the Allied air forces lacked any aircraft capable of the 2,500-mile return flight to the Spitsbergen area, the critical point on the sea route to north Russia. But this was not all. While the Luftwaffe were accumulating experience in high latitude operations, the RAF were discovering that existing maps extended only to 70 degrees north latitude and that little was known of navigational problems beyond. It was at this time that an enterprising, perhaps foolhardy operation of minor significance was to become a catalyst, forcing the allocation of the first VLR Catalina with a selected aircrew for special and top secret operations over the Arctic Seas. The catalyst was the approval by the Chiefs of Staff for a small Norwegian force, *Fritham*, to occupy, in April 1942, Spitsbergen deep in enemy air and sea space. The approval had its conditions.

As to means of transport, two aged, tiny ships, with a top speed of 5 knots, one a coal-burner, belching black smoke, had to creep 1,200 miles north-eastward unobserved along the ice edge from Jan Mayen. The second condition, more reasonably, was that we in this operation under Lt. Colonel Sverdrup's command knew we were expendable. There was a reassuring caveat however, that prior reconnaissances would be flown by the Catalinas and that Sverdrup and I would fly as special observers.

Well, the two little ships covered 1,198 out of 1,200-miles undetected. Then, when already icebreaking into Green Harbour, they were clobbered on 13 May by four FW200 bombing from 50 feet. Both ships were sunk with the loss of seventeen men including Colonel Sverdrup and Colonel Godfrey, but over forty survived on the bay ice, where we quickly learnt that bombs dropped at such low level on ice, bounce two or three times, giving a moment or two to move to right or left, and that aerial gunnery is reassuringly inaccurate. Fortuitously, it was only a couple of miles across the sea ice to the deserted Russian coal mine at Barentsberg, evacuated nine months before by the Royal Navy. At that time thirty pigs had been killed and left in a snow drift. As we expected, they were perfectly preserved nine months later and, with loads of dried mushrooms from the steppes, and nearby masses of new-laid gulls' eggs, we lived all right. These Norwegians were Spitsbergen men, they were at home in an environment they knew, and no enemy was going to evict them. All we needed was to get our wounded to safety, and enough weapons to resume the fight.

We were confident that the Catalina with Flight-Lieutenant Tim Healy and his determined crew would make contact. When, we could not know for, at that time, we had no knowledge of Bletchley or that the German reports of the sinkings had already been deciphered. Nor could we guess that our small operation was already part of much larger events, including the need to provide VLR Catalina escorts to the convoys as the protection of winter darkness gave way to 24-hours daylight. We did know, however, that frequent surveys of the limits of the sea-ice were already accepted as a vital requirement in determining the amount of open sea available to the convoys, especially in the narrow confines of the Barents Sea, for it was these surveys that the early Catalina flights had already pioneered.

This was indeed a hectic time for 210 Squadron at Sullom Voe, and especially for Tim Healy and Ernest Schofield his navigator, who had been given virtual total authority by AOC-in-C Coastal Command. Help came from the Astronomer Royal, from Professor Debenham at Cambridge, from the Director of the Royal Geographical Society over the most appropriate methods of polar navigation, and from the Hydrographer at the Admiralty for the immediate preparation of high latitude projections ('charts, not maps, my boy' as the Admiral gently chided Schofield). All this on a top secret basis and all concluded within ten days, together with the provision of a special aircraft. P for Peter was fitted with three overload tanks in the centre bay to provide over thirty hours endurance, an astro-compass with four mountings, and three magnetic compasses adjusted for polar navigation (one a distant reading gyro magnetic serviceable up to 85 degrees north) and specially balanced P9 and P4s.

Otherwise, the aircraft was stripped of all possible equipment. Wireless silence, dead-reckoning navigation, flying much of the way little above wave top height over 24-hours of sea and ice. Ernest Schofield in *Arctic Airman* has described the tremendous personal support given by Air Chief Marshal Sir Philip Joubert and his SASO, Air Vice Marshal G.B.A. Baker, not forgetting SASO's last remark, 'You have 100% support from here but remember, no rescue services up there, you'll be on your own, good luck'.

So it was that only twelve days after the *Fritham* ships were sunk, on 25 May, Catalina P for Peter took off from Sullom Voe. Much of the 1,200-mile flight to Spitsbergen was at between 380 and 600 feet, with a low cloud base not unwelcome in the cover it gave. After 10.23 hours flying, radar picked up South Cape, 35 miles distant, and after a brief period of heavy icing at zero temperature, cloud lifted giving an exact landfall at South Cape, Spitsbergen. Some sixty minutes later contact was made with the *Fritham* survivors at Barentsberg. Signals were exchanged by Aldis lamp over a sixty-minute period, making clear that there were wounded to be evacuated but that what the survivors insisted upon were weapons and, if possible, reinforcement but positively not evacuation.

The support flights were delayed by a period of appalling weather over the Barents Sea but on 1 June P for Peter again slipped mooring at 07.05 at Sullom Voe. After 11.30 hours flying and after sighting one HE111, Spitsbergen was picked up, but fog and snow flurries covered the entrance to Icefjord and it was only Healy's skill in following the shore a few feet from the water that brought the aircraft into Green Harbour. Once inside, a southerly wind improved visibility, arms and supplies were dropped and then suddenly Healy took advantage of an ice-free strip of water in the middle of the fjord to make a perfect landing. Despite drifting brash ice which had to be fended off, the dinghy was launched and in the next two hours or so the wounded were brought safely aboard through the blisters – no easy job, with the point-5 Colts necessarily armed against enemy intervention.

Reports of Proceedings for the Admiralty were taken, jars of rum and tobacco sent ashore and at 20.07 Healy took off. A few minutes later the first huge plate of eggs, sausages, beans and bacon was being handed through by Schofield to the wounded, and, as he turned for a moment to hand on a knife and fork, an empty plate was handed back with, behind, a beaming Norwegian face and gloriously grease-enmeshed beard.

So followed three further 24-hour flights by P for Peter over the next ten days to build up supply and arms and to co-ordinate plans for the reinforcement of Barentsberg by Operation *Gearbox* with the cruisers HMS *Manchester* and HMS *Eclipse* in early July.

Already Tim Healy's achievements had been recognised by an immediate DSO coupled with a DFC for Pilot-Officer Schofield and a DFM for Sergeant Kingett. Theirs was the true pioneering of RAF Polar flying, which was to make such a major contribution to the successful maintenance of that harsh and difficult supply route to north Russia throughout the rest of 1942 and until the end of the War. Of Healy himself I should like to recount one incident. When briefing Admiral Bonham-Carter immediately prior to the sailing of

Gearbox from Iceland, the Admiral asked for some bridge-height photographs of Barentsberg. 'What is bridge height, Sir?' asked Tim. '62 feet' the Admiral replied. Upon which, Tim with a smile said 'I think we can just make that height, Sir.' Two months later, on 25 September, between Murmansk and Spitsbergen, his last operational flight, P for Peter was intercepted by a JU88 off Cape Kamin. Tim was killed instantly, the only casualty.

The Luftwaffe and the Kriegsmarine by their exploitation of their northern Norwegian bases had effectively cut the Allied supply route to North Russia in the summer of 1942, and were representing a potentially deadly threat to the North Atlantic convoys as well. Had *Bismarck* not been squandered on her lone mission a year earlier, her addition to *Tirpitz*, *Scharnhorst*, *Gneisenau* and the heavy cruisers and pocket battleships could well have been overwhelming.

But the lessons learnt in the disaster of Convoy PQ17 were being applied by the Allies and had their first impact in September 1942 on PQ18. HMS *Avenger*, with her Fleet Air Arm Sea Hurricanes, altered the odds while the imaginative and exceedingly difficult Operation *Orator*, with its deployment to North Russian bases of 36 Hampden torpedo bombers and six PRU Spitfires, together with the cross-over patrols by two squadrons of Catalinas off North Norway, materially assisted the Royal Navy to bring the greater part of the convoy to its destination. In this, the pioneering flights of Coastal Command in the previous spring and early summer had made their esential contribution.

As to Spitsbergen itself, the new Norwegian comnmanding officer Captain Ernst Ullring, DSO RNN, provided his own particular Nelson touch. The offensive was his creed. Whether fighting German aircraft with a point-5 Colt from a motorboat or hunting U-boats with, as the Captain of HMS *Sheffield* reported, a tin-opener, he was on the attack. He made life particularly difficult for the German weather stations, forcing them to ever more remote areas and to the use of automatic instead of manned units.

Spitsbergen was held without major incident until at 02.43 hours local time, on 8 September, 1943, the Norwegian sentry on duty at Kap Heer suddenly saw a dark shadow at the entrance of the Ice Fjord. It revealed itself to be *Tirpitz*, followed by *Scharnhorst*, escorted by ten fleet destroyers and carrying a landing force of 300 Brandenburg Commandos. All this against a Norwegian garrison of some eighty men, who put up a spirited defence and then, as the German landing forces made ground, succeeded for the most part in retiring in good order into the mountains behind. Quite a compliment! The German forces were back in the safety of North Norway little more than 36 hours later. Within three months *Scharnhorst* was sunk, within six *Tirpitz* destroyed by the Lancaster bombers. And this remote outpost of Spitsbergen continued under Norwegian control.

Discussion

Mr Arthur Sclater, commander of the Shetland base from 1942 until the end of the war, commented on the paper by Sir Brooks Richards. He said that SOE

and Chaworth-Musters[1] got the whole thing going in the Shetlands, but that
the framework was established by a regular SIS man, L.H. Mitchell, who
remained in command until about November 1942 when Sclater took over. *Mr
Sclater* went on: 'I only got to Shetland accidentally because I was a trained
Royal Marine and fluent in Norwegian. My mission was to try to have a few
simple rules to keep the civilian volunteer crews in order. I learned at once
from Mitchell that I was on loan to the secret service. Our job was to keep a
good shipping line going for passengers and, every now and again, stores.
Mitchell said "Keep well clear of politics", by which he meant people in
London. None of us ever worried about what was going on, or not going on,
between SIS and SOE. As a layman, I would say that our base couldn't have
worked at all without endless cooperation from C-in-C Home Fleet down-
wards, and from the RAF.' Mr Sclater ascribed this success to Mitchell: he had
the knack of getting on with anyone in uniform by making them laugh against
himself. Moving on to Leif Larsen, Mr Sclater said that the only trouble
Mitchell and he had was that they had too many people pestering them to join
Larsen's crew. In response to a remark about David Howarth, Mr Sclater
replied: 'Howarth was full of good ideas. But I always gave the order: "Don't
let Howarth brief crews!"'.

Mr Leonard Pagliero commented on the papers by Mark Seaman and
Joachim Rønneberg. He confirmed the low priority attached by the RAF to
missions to Norway: 'We were given the aircraft that Bomber Harris didn't
want. We trained in Whitleys ('flying coffins') and flew Stirlings with a ceiling
of 10,000 feet. We flew over sea at low level to avoid radar and had to rely on
dead reckoning. Training was good; we did succeed in getting into Norway
without aids of any kind. We were helped by the fact that all the lighthouses in
the Skagerrak were in operation; and the intelligence we received before our
flights was first-class. We had to make sure that we crossed the Norwegian
coast *between* lighthouses. If we got too near a lighthouse we knew we wouldn't
get back for our eggs and bacon the following morning. Having come in at a
very low level, we climbed to 10,000 feet, hopefully to get out of the range of
guns, because that was as high as we could go, and we went in.' *Joachim
Rønneberg* said that he was not criticising the RAF or the pilots, but felt that
the people responsible for briefing might have done both the RAF and SOE a
great service by letting Norwegians participate in discussing the way in. 'The
RAF said "Just follow procedure; just be there; it's not our problem".'

References

1   *Colonel Andrew Croft* remarked that in April 1940 Chaworth-Musters had escaped with him from Bergen cross-country to Nesttun, but was then too exhausted and decided to surrender. However, he was reasonably fluent in Norwegian and was persuaded by friends to await the availability of a boat to take him to the Shetlands. His peace-time pursuit was the study of mice in Afghanistan.

PART V

The Liberation and after

21 Planning the Liberation: the Norwegian contribution

PAAL FRISVOLD

A S early as the beginning of 1943 it was clear that the liberation of Norway would in all probability not come until the final phase of the war, after the total collapse of the German war machine. The Casablanca meeting in January of that year resulted in the first Allied planning for the liberation of Western Europe, in which Operation *Overlord* was to be the decisive campaign against the European centre of German power and impose 'unconditional surrender'. Planning, and subsequently the execution, of *Overlord* was always accorded the very highest priority. As Chief of Staff to the Supreme Allied Commander (COSSAC) the British general Sir Frederick Morgan was given the entire responsibility for the planning. But even if *Overlord* was the Allied planning staff's chief concern, the staff was also instructed to prepare an alternative plan to meet the eventuality that the enemy came to show serious signs of weakness in the occupied countries before *Overlord* could be launched. This reserve plan, which was to include Norway, was code-named *Rankin*. It was drawn up in three variants: *Rankin A*, *Rankin B* and *Rankin C*. The difference between these three versions was, briefly:

Rankin A: Reconquest of the occupied areas.

Rankin B: Of his own accord the enemy abandons parts of his north-western frontier line in order to concentrate his forces in more central parts of the front. This might apply to part or all of Norway.

Rankin C: A complete collapse of Germany's military machine and unconditional surrender.

The *Rankin A* variant was soon set aside as an improbable alternative. *Rankin B* was to prove a difficult alternative for the planning staff, not least as applied to Norway. Sending expeditionary forces to liberate Norway would cost a good deal in terms of land, sea and air resources as well as creating major transport and supply problems. From a purely strategic point of view Norway was not on the road to Germany but was rather to be regarded as a blind alley. Nevertheless, COSSAC's recommendation for *Rankin B* was to prepare a brigade group for North Norway and a division for South Norway, in order to 'secure the necessary naval and air bases and assist the Norwegian Army in the work of reconstruction.'

For *Rankin C* the goal was to occupy as soon as possible some suitable areas to secure compliance with the demand for unconditional surrender and to reconstruct the occupied countries. At first, COSSAC reckoned on having such forces for Norway, as mentioned under *Rankin B*. These forces were to be sent to Norway 'as soon as the situation permits' and, together with the Norwegian Army based in the United Kingdom, take control of Norway, reconstruct the country and secure the disarmament of the German military forces.

At the same time the draft plan emphasised that guidelines would have to be drawn up for an Allied military government in the occupied areas and for the reestablishment of the national administrative apparatus. The latter challenge was satisfactorily met through the preliminary Civil Affairs Agreement between the UK and Norway signed in 1943 and the final treaty of 16 May 1944 between the UK, the USA and the Soviet Union on the one side and the Norwegian government in exile on the other.

In July 1943 the Norwegian Chief of Defence was given a first informal briefing by General Ismay regarding how the Allies envisaged the liberation process, without the *Rankin* plans being mentioned directly. This brings me to the thinking about the liberation of Norway that had already begun on the Norwegian side.

The most important task of Forsvarets Overkommando (FO), established in London in February 1942, was to prepare as well as possible from the Norwegian side for the work of liberation, by coordinating the forces and resources available, acquiring the necessary basic materials and, not least, ensuring Norwegian access to the planning of the liberation. FO would thus ensure that maximum account was taken of Norwegian interests by exploiting the Norwegian contribution to the liberation process.

As an internal Norwegian matter – and before any regular channels for collaboration with our allies had been properly established – FO drew up a number of plans, proposals and reports describing how the Norwegian side expected the liberation to come about and what form the Norwegian contribution would take. Much of what had been done laid the groundwork for internal Norwegian activities, but it was also vital that the result of this work was known to our allies – that is, first and foremost to our British friends.

In time, what we may call a liaison and cooperation channel was established between FO and the Planning Committee of the British Chiefs of Staff Committee (COS). Early in 1942, that is, before the Allied planning work following the Casablanca meeting had got under way, this Planning Committee was given reports concerning the organisation of Norwegian staffs during the reconquest of Norway, not only in the Allied units but also in the Allied staffs. After discussions with the British planners, a provisional draft was drawn up, assigning to the Norwegian commander-in-chief the role of the chief liaison officer with a close relationship with the Allied C-in-C Norway. It was also envisaged that the Allied commanders of sea, air and land operations would each have attached a chief liaison officer from the equivalent Services. In addition, Norwegian liaison officers would probably be needed at every army staff down to brigade level, at every RAF station and at every port where there were Allied naval units.

In August 1942 FO sent the British Planning Staff a report entitled 'General Principles of Norwegian Cooperation During Operations in Norway'.

This emphasised once again the support and liaison functions at which the Norwegian military contribution to liberation aimed – including the Home Forces. Special attention was drawn to the importance of providing weapons and equipment to both the Home Forces and for the creation of regular military units in the occupied areas, so as best to enable these Norwegian forces to perform their tasks. At length, in September 1942, FO submitted a complete and final organisational plan for Norwegian liaison attachments to an Allied land forces command for Norway. In consequence of this, the green light was given for Norwegian officers to serve in British units.

FO was thus quite active in 1942, before Allied planning for the liberation of Europe had started. Understandably enough, the British reaction to the Norwegian plans was courteously non-committal. The British were not very enthusiastic about involving themselves in negotiations that had necessarily to be mainly theoretical until such time as Allied planning could take more concrete forms – and as we have seen, this did not take place until 1943.

Contact with the Allies had hitherto gone through the Planning Committee under the British COS Committee. In September 1943 FO was informed that in future it should report direct to COSSAC. Before they had managed to establish this new channel, however, COSSAC decided that responsibility for the reconquest of Norway should be transferred to Scottish Command in Edinburgh, under Lieutenant-General Sir Andrew Thorne. For the rest of the war, it was to be Thorne who was responsible for leading all planning for the liberation of Norway, directly under the newly established SHAEF (Supreme Headquarters Allied Expeditionary Force). This change in the channels of communication between FO and the Allies must be seen in relation to the fact that Norway, even in the context of *Rankin C*, was something of an 'appendix', without much direct relevance to the planning of the offensive against the enemy's hardcore, the German military machine on continental Europe. This remained increasingly true throughout the war, and was to create major problems for General Thorne.

In November 1943 Scottish Command asked FO to appoint a military committee for joint consultation on operational plans. This committee, chaired by General Strugstad, became the embryo of what was later to be called 'the Norwegian Military Mission', the permanent liaison between FO and Scottish Command. From the autumn of 1944 that part of Scottish Command which had the responsibility for operations in Norway was called 'Force 134' and based at Riccarton House seven miles outside Edinburgh. At the same time, a small Norwegian staff was permanently attached to Force 134, called 'Norwegian Military Mission, Advance Element at HQ 134'.

Scottish Command had inherited the plan for *Rankin C* from COSSAC. At a meeting in Edinburgh on 2 and 3 December 1943, General Strugstad was given an oral briefing on the plan as it was then. At the same time Scottish Command was informed of the arrangements for Norwegian command and staff bodies, and of the Norwegian views as to how British-Norwegian cooperation should be organised. As the Norwegians began to get wind of the Allied plans for the liberation of Norway, they found them highly unsatisfactory. Both militarily and politically, a principal objection was that the plan did not include provision for the sending of Allied troops to North Norway. British and American forces in North Norway would mean that the two Western Powers would guarantee Norwegian territorial integrity vis-à-vis any intentions the Soviets might have. Another complaint was that the Allied plans for Norway were based on forces that were far too small for the challenges they would encounter.

On 11 January 1944 the Norwegian Chief of Defence, General Hansteen, had a meeting with the chief of the COSSAC staff, General Morgan. At this meeting Hansteen expressed in strong terms, his dissatisfaction with the fact that Norway was now relegated to liaising with Scottish Command, an organ at a lower level of the military hierarchy which had to work within rather narrow limits laid down by directives from higher staffs. For Norway it was vital to get in on the ground floor: 'We knew more about Norway than the British, and it is our country, so we should be enabled to comment at an early stage', insisted General Hansteen. The Norwegian Chief of Defence made it clear that the *Rankin C* plans were unsatisfactory at several points. As mentioned before, it was not intended to send liberation forces to North Norway at all, and the other forces intended for Norway were quite inadequate. To this General Morgan replied that the plans had to be based on the forces available in the British Isles at any given time. Future events were to show that this very question was to be a major and permanent problem for General Thorne.

I should make it quite clear, however, that the Norwegian dissatisfaction at having to go through Scottish Command was based on matters of principle, and had nothing to do with General Thorne personally. Norwegian political and military authorities always had great respect for General Thorne as a man of honour. He looked after Norwegian interests as far as he could within his scope and without betraying the loyalty he owed to his principal, SHAEF.

On the basis of information on *Rankin C* that FO received from Scottish Command in March 1944, a detailed summary of the plan was drawn up. It was now laid down that the plan in question aimed at a German capitulation and therefore did not count on any opposition worth mentioning to the Allied liberation forces. Nor was it planned to send forces further north than Trondheim. For this limited mission was envisaged a force composed of the Norwegian brigade in Scotland, a British division (52 Lowland) and an American infantry regiment reinforced by the Norwegian-American 99 Infantry Battalion. Air support would be provided by two Norwegian fighter squadrons, the two Norwegian seaplane squadrons, and two squadrons of lightbombers and a transport unit from the RAF. The bottleneck would be the transfer of the force to Norway. According to the plan, it would take from six weeks to three months after the German capitulation before the whole force was landed on Norwegian soil. This was a conclusion that Norwegian authorities could not accept. Norway was a blind alley in the strategic picture, but the Norwegian authorities were of the definite opinion that the liberation of North Norway was also an Allied responsibility. Norwegian protests led in the end to this responsibility being accepted. Thanks to developments in the Arctic theatre, however, northern Norway rapidly became of great interest. In the autumn of 1944 Russian forces broke through the German front and on 24

October reached Kirkenes in Finnmark. This led to the transfer of a Norwegian military mission with a reinforced mountain company from the Norwegian brigade in Scotland to Finnmark via Murmansk, being then placed under Russian operational command. As far as the Western Allies were concerned, this Operation *Crofter* was the purely logistical responsibility of Force 134.

Right up to the war's final phase, the main problems facing General Thorne and Force 134 were to obtain the forces that would be necessary to implement the *Rankin C* plans, and to acquire the means of transport to move these forces. These problems were only to get worse. The American and British forces originally earmarked for Force 134 were one after another transferred to the west European theatre. Most serious was the redeployment of the British 52 Division, which after a couple of years' collaboration with the Norwegian brigade was trained for mountain warfare in Norway, but which in 1944 was committed below sea level on Walcheren!

To illustrate how bad the situation was, I might mention that in the summer of 1944 Eisenhower's chief of staff, General Bedell Smith, told his boss that because of the lack of forces he did not know what he would do if the German garrison in Norway fell apart. In reality, most people on the Allied side, including General Thorne, knew that any Allied forces and other resources to supervise even a relatively orderly German capitulation in Norway would pretty much have to be a matter of eleventh-hour improvisation. All Allied forces had to be concentrated now on the offensive against the German heartland, because it was firmly believed that this was the most rapid route to the goal of Norwegian liberation.

In the last year of the war, a major concern of the Norwegian authorities was to seek to influence the Allies towards adapting their plans and their preparedness so as better to meet Norwegian needs and interests. At the same time, the question arose whether the Norwegians could contribute resources outside the UK that could to some extent compensate for lack of Allied forces. Two factors thus came into the picture: Milorg and the Norwegian police troops in Sweden.

From the autumn of 1941 Milorg had been subordinate to FO in London. In the course of 1943 Milorg had worked out an organisational form that was well-suited to the missions it could be expected to be assigned in the country's liberation. Its weakness was lack of weapons and equipment. That in the course of 1944 Milorg more and more won the confidence of FO and our allies, was perhaps due most of all to the fact that its leader visited the UK twice that year. Between the head of Milorg, Jens Christian Hauge, and General Thorne, representing SHAEF, a friendship grew up that was to have great significance for Milorg's future development. Following directives from SHAEF and in collaboration with FO, early in 1944 SOE began to supply Milorg by air with enormous quantities of weapons and other equipment. No fewer than 1,200 sorties were flown from British airfields to Norway in the last year of the war. The missions assigned Milorg in connection with the liberation included protection of Norwegian industrial and power plants against any attempts at scorched-earth tactics by the Germans, maintenance of order vis-à-vis surrendered German troops and of public order in general, and securing Gestapo documents upon German capitulation. At its leader's request, Milorg units were also to take part in sabotage attacks on communications before a German capitulation to prevent transfer of forces to the continental theatre.

As is well known, Sweden gradually 'revised' its neutrality policy in the course of 1942, from originally being strongly pro-German to being pro-Allied. Among other things, this resulted in many thousands of young Norwegians who had fled to Sweden being allowed to organise as so-called police troops whose missions were officially to be of a purely police character. In reality this was a force of about 14,000 fully-trained field troops, ready at short notice to advance into Norway in the event of a German collapse. A couple of these field battalions were airlifted to Finnmark at the beginning of 1945 in order to reinforce the Norwegian troops there.

In the last year of the war the Norwegians in the United Kingdom continued to work on organisation and exercises for the staffs, liaison units and so forth who were designated to accompany Allied forces to Norway – the Civil Affairs personnel, district command staffs corresponding to the Allied zonal commands, and liaison personnel at all levels.

In the winter of 1944–5 Scotco – Force 134 – continued to work on its plans for the liberation of Norway, in the autumn of 1944 renamed *Apostle*. Later came Operation *Doomsday*, a supplementary plan to *Apostle*. But all plans were still afflicted by shortage of resources and the fact that it would take a long time from the German capitulation until Allied forces could land on Norwegian soil. It was therefore a prime task for Norwegian military and political authorities to exert pressure on our allies to correct this state of affairs.

In the spring of 1945, as total German collapse on the Continent approached, the fear grew that the German forces in Norway would continue the struggle in their '*Festung Norwegen*'. There were no plans for coping with such an event. King Haakon VII and his government thus raised the matter at the highest Allied level. On 5 April the King gave a lunch for prime minister Churchill and foreign secretary Eden. The Norwegian side included Crown Prince Olav, who was Chief of Defence, and the prime and foreign ministers. At this lunch the King took the initiative personally and expressed grave misgivings as to what might happen if the 12 or 13 German divisions believed to be in Norway, together with parts of the Kriegsmarine and Luftwaffe, continued to fight on after the Allies had gained control over Germany. The King asked first if the Allies would postpone their celebrations of victory over Germany. Churchill rejected any such idea on account of the British people's need, after all they had suffered, for a national celebration of VE Day. During the lunch the Norwegians maintained that the Norwegian people could easily come to feel themselves betrayed by the Allies, and might draw comparisons with the situation in 1940, when the British retreated from Norway. Churchill could only promise that the Allies would continue the war until Norway was free. Asked directly whether he would send Allied forces to Norway if the Germans continued to resist, Churchill refused point blank: there were neither troops nor ships for such a situation. Nor did he show any interest in an Allied campaign through Sweden. Not until the Norwegian foreign minister mentioned that Sweden might be willing to assist such an enterprise, was Churchill's reaction positive. He nevertheless returned several times to what he emphasised was the most probable outcome: that the Germans in Norway would surrender at the same time as their defeat in Germany. We may add here that shortly after this an Allied campaign through Sweden in conjunction with Swedish troops was being seriously considered by the Allies, and that staff discussions between SHAEF and the Swedish defence staff – in which Norwegian officers were to take part – were under preparation when the Germans capitulated.

After these rather depressing statements by Churchill, the conclusion had to be that in the event of fighting in Norway after a German defeat, the Swedish alternative would have to take first place. Two days after the lunch with Churchill the matter was raised by Crown Prince Olav. He pointed out that the danger of continued German resistance in Norway was more and more acute. Even Eisenhower had now said that no orderly and universal German capitulation could be expected, and that Norway was one of the areas in which fighting might continue. Reports from Norway also indicated that the Germans were making preparations that might create a '*Festung Norwegen*'. It seemed clear, the Chief of Defence said, that the Germans would be able to establish a strong redoubt in Norway. And even if the Germans were not to fight to the last man, they could at any rate not be expected to capitulate until the call to surrender was backed by a sufficient military force. Given such a situation, FO had to note that, firstly, the Allies had neither planned nor prepared a fighting liberation of Norway; secondly, that the forces of the *Apostle* plan did not remotely approach what would be necessary to convince the Germans of the wisdom of surrendering; and thirdly, these forces were not even strong enough to master the situation that would be created by a German collapse in Norway.

All this made the Allied contingency preparations for the liberation of Norway even less satisfactory than it they had hitherto been. The Chief of Defence proposed that a new attempt be now made to prepare against the increased threat of a really critical situation in Norway. This must be set in motion at once and in earnest. For his part, Crown Prince Olav demanded – to begin with via Force 134 and General Thorne – that SHAEF should without delay plan a rapid Allied intervention, even if sufficient forces could not be provided at first. Since Eisenhower's SHAEF was subordinate to the Allied joint chiefs of staff in Washington, the matter had to be raised through diplomatic channels. The Chief of Defence then considered a Swedish intervention. Particular emphasis was laid on the fact that operations could be mounted from Sweden at much shorter notice than from the West, and that a combined preparedness from both the West and Sweden would have the best chance of convincing the German garrison in Norway that further resistance would be futile.

The Chief of Defence's approach to the Norwegian government resulted a few days later in a note to the Swedish government, with a copy to the Foreign Office. The Norwegian note went a good deal further than the Chief of Defence had suggested. After explaining how the altered situation could lead to continued German resistance in Norway, the government stated that it felt certain that Sweden would be prepared for armed intervention in Norway 'if it should prove necessary to save the Norwegian people from suffering that would cast dark and enduring shadows over the whole of the North.' For Sweden to be ready for action as soon as the Allied had declared victory over Germany, however, measures would have to be taken immediately, so that the Germans in Norway understood that further resistance would be pointless. 'It is known that the Swedish Government has already made preparations necessary for defensive purposes, but the Norwegian Government is convinced that its object will only be attainable if the Swedish army is as far as possible put on a full war footing.'

Even for a Swedish government that had softened its neutrality policy, this was hard to swallow; and the Swedish reaction was not only negative, but a sharp rejection. We may, however, add that the Swedish defence staff had already been instructed in complete secrecy to plan for a Swedish invasion of Norway, and that the plan had been approved by the defence minister on 5 April 1945.

At the same time, the Norwegian Chief of Defence had sent General Thorne a sharp memorandum in which he painted Norwegian prospects in gloomy colours and stated that the Allies had no plans to meet continued German resistance, despite its being public knowledge that General Eisenhower himself considered this alternative to be not improbable. 'The Norwegian High Command must therefore urgently request the immediate obtaining of approval from the Allied Supreme Command in Europe for a plan to liberate Norway on the assumption that the enemy will resist.'

In the meantime, Norway's diplomatic offensive vis-à-vis the Allies was in full swing. It opened with a conversation on 12 April between the Norwegian foreign minister, Trygve Lie, and Sir Laurence Collier of the Foreign Office, in which Lie used the Norwegian note to Sweden as the point of departure for a passionate appeal to the Allies to take the threat of German resistance in Norway seriously. The note to Sweden must be seen in the light of Churchill's discouraging attitude during his lunch with the King on 5 April, which had created a climate of some bitterness in the Norwegian government.

It should be added here that Eisenhower had by this date already started work on new plans for a liberation of Norway against German resistance, based on Swedish assistance. On 12 April Churchill had also floated the idea of Swedish armed intervention in Cabinet, as foreshadowed by his remarks during the Royal lunch a week previously.

Nothing came of this operation. But even though the Swedish government had rejected the idea of engaging the Germans in Norway with its own military forces, it was exceptionally positive in its support for Norwegian preparations on Swedish soil. As we have seen, it backed the creation and training of the Norwegian police troops and their preparations for an advance into Norway. Similarly, in the course of April 1945 the Swedes permitted the establishment of Norwegian staff units on Swedish soil, for example for the three district commands whose districts bordered on Sweden, so as to expedite the advance. The mission of these district command staffs was to coordinate all Norwegian military activity in their districts, including Milorg, the police troops and the formation of new national forces. They were also to see to regional and local cooperation with our allies, as regards both the Germans and liaison with Norwegian civil authorities. In this way they were virtually opposite numbers of the Allied zone commanders.

Then came the collapse of the German war machine and unconditional surrender, also in Norway. Milorg were in place first and carried out the missions expected of them. From Sweden came the district commands and the police troops, and at the eleventh hour Allied troops and transports were made available to General Thorne, led by the First Airborne Division. In the course of a few months control, disarmament and evacuation of the German forces, repatriation of Allied prisoners of war and displaced persons were all accomplished under the superb leadership of General Thorne. I would therefore conclude this account by quoting from the letter the prime minister sent General Thorne when he left Norway, his mission accomplished:

> Before you leave our country, I feel a great need to convey our thanks and tribute to you for your work for Norway. Great and difficult problems, which had previously filled us with unease and anxiety, have under your leadership been happily resolved in the space of a short time. The disarming and interning of the enemy was achieved without conflict; the evacuation is nearly completed; and the import of supplies has saved Norway from hunger and privation.
>
> You are today leaving a country, General, which is deeply grateful to you and your country and will not forget what it owes the United Kingdom.

22 Andrew Thorne and the Liberation of Norway[1]

SIR PETER THORNE

NORWAY was excluded from the surrender of the German armies to Montgomery on Lüneburg Heath on 5 May 1945, which covered only Holland, north-west Germany and Denmark. This may explain why so little has been written about it in English. The official history devotes effectively only a footnote to it.[2] Neither volumes V and VI of the Grand Strategy series nor volume 3 part 2 of the British Intelligence History mentions the liberation. There is however an extensive literature in Norwegian.[3] It was left to Sir Andrew Thorne, GOC-in-C Scottish Command, to secure the surrender of some 350,000 Germans with a body of troops that never amounted to more than 30,000 men. Since the task was obviously impossible by force of arms, he had to rely on his own powers of persuasion and negotiation, backed by the *Fortitude* deception plan and such intelligence on conditions in Norway and the morale of the German troops there as was available.

This paper is based largely on my father Andrew Thorne's 1951 Report on the Liberation of Norway, but it also deals with several aspects of his involvement which are not explicit in that report. I did not see it until after my father's death, and it seemed virtually unknown in the UK – not even the Imperial War Museum having a copy.[4] This must be due to the fact, as stated on the covering letter from the War Office on the Cabinet Office's copy, that it had been written 'at the request of the Norwegians and with the approval of the British and U.S. Chiefs of Staff . . . [with] permission to translate and publish it in Norway. It will not be published in this country'. Unless otherwise stated, all quotations are from this report.

One of Thorne's main problems during the run-up to the Liberation was the Allied High Command's sudden attack of jitters, in early 1945, about the possibility that elements of the Wehrmacht in Norway might continue to resist after the armies in Germany had surrendered. This was probably triggered by the shock of the initial success of the German Ardennes offensive, reinforced by two rather ambivalent reports from the Joint Intelligence Sub-Committee (JIC) on the likelihood of continued resistance in Norway.[5] It led to the production of a radically 'Revised Plan for Norway' which – if General Boehme, the Wehrmacht commander there, had not obeyed Doenitz's order to surrender – would have involved an invasion via Denmark and Sweden, with Swedish cooperation, and a seaborne assault on Stavanger mounted by Scottish Command.

When Thorne left Norway after the liberation some very remarkable tributes were paid to his achievements. They included a letter from King

Haakon to King George VI[6] and another from Trygve Lie, the minister for foreign affairs, to Ernest Bevin, the foreign secretary,[7] as well as a most glowing account of Thorne's success in Norway in an official report from the British ambassador in Oslo (who almost exactly a year earlier, as ambassador to the Norwegian government in exile, had written to the Foreign Office about Thorne's unsuitability for the job, recommending his removal).[8] There was also a rather surprising presentation to Thorne by the Swedish general staff of an elegant glass decanter with his name and the date of his visit to Stockholm engraved on one side, and on the other, rather enigmatically, a centaur cantering off clasping a protesting nymph: perhaps this was a reminder of how perilously close Sweden had come to losing its neutrality. But probably the tribute that Thorne found most rewarding was the farewell letter from prime minister Gerhardsen which is quoted at the end of General Frisvold's contribution to this volume.

The *leitmotif* and favouring factors

This last tribute confirmed that the Allied Expeditionary Force had succeeded in observing the warning – quoted by Thorne in the foreword to his Report – given by the Crown Prince in a speech to Allied commanders and staff officers in Edinburgh in August 1944, 'that in re-establishing an old Government . . . developed by the people themselves . . . you will get much further in every stage with cooperation and direction than with command'. Thorne comments that 'Every endeavour was made to base Allied assistance on this *leitmotif*'; the corollary was that the success of the Liberation would be judged by the Norwegians by the speed with which the soil of their country was freed of enemy and Allied personnel – and at times it must have seemed almost inevitable that the latter would out-stay their welcome.

Thorne starts the report by describing how 'in the summer of 1943 [he], as GOC-in-C Scottish Command, was instructed to begin planning to liberate Norway in the event of a German surrender'. The plan, originally code-named *Rankin Case C Norway* and subsequently renamed *Apostle* was 'laid down in a directive from SHAEF issued in October [1943] when it first seemed possible that aerial attack would compel a German surrender'. In June 1944 Scotco was also ordered to plan for Operation *Rankin Case B* Norway which envisaged a German withdrawal from that country. There were to be several changes in the designation of Thorne's appointments and commands, rather in the manner of those Central Asian rivers that alter their names every hundred miles or so: from GOC-in-C Scottish Command, to Military Joint Commander Force 134, to C-in-C Allied Land Forces, Norway and Head of the SHAEF Mission to Norway, and finally to C-in-C British Land Forces Norway.

The penultimate paragraph of Thorne's foreword summarises the principal factors on which the success of the plan was to depend. As regards the Germans in Norway, he believed, justifiably as it turned out, in two seemingly contradictory aspects of the Wehrmacht's reactions to a collapse of the armies in Germany – the inevitable disappearance of the will to fight on and the ability nevertheless to carry out the capitulation terms in a prompt and disciplined manner. He also had confidence, equally well founded, in the ability of Milorg to turn itself in a surprisingly short time into a credible and highly effective 'protective' force that could perform quasi-peacekeeping tasks in the extremely dangerous period between the preliminaries to the capitulation and the time that (a) the 1st Airborne Division – the spearhead of Thorne's minuscule Allied Expeditionary Force – could establish themselves at Oslo, Stavanger and Kristiansand and (b) the destroyers carrying the 'Herald Parties', who were to supervise the enforcement of the capitulation provisions, could arrive at other Norwegian ports.

Order of battle problems

The almost ludicrously small size of Force 134 was, as Thorne pointed out in his report (page 7), 'because the Liberation of Norway was rated so low by the Allies, from the point of view of allocating formations, shipping, etc.' This was due to the fact that 'strategically the recapture of Norway could not possibly lead to the defeat of the German forces . . . all resources available to the Western Theatre must be concentrated in Germany' – although Hitler thought otherwise, describing Norway in 1942 as the 'Zone of Destiny of the War', and Churchill long hankered after *Jupiter*, an Anglo-Russian assault in northern Norway. Thereafter – even before D-Day – Thorne had to promise to release various formations within a month of their landing so that they could be re-allocated to the war against Japan.[9]

> The Order of Battle . . . for Force 134 [had] been based on the provision
> of one British Division, a U.S. Infantry Regiment (reinforced), the
> Norwegian Forces and various Administrative units, but one by one
> these British units, provisionally earmarked and highly trained, were
> engulfed in North Western Europe as the U.S.Regiments had been.

It must have seemed ironic to Thorne that at the same time that his Order of Battle was becoming ever more attenuated he was figuring in the *Fortidude North* deception traffic – as readers of Michael Howard's *Strategic Deception* will be aware – as the Commander of the (bogus) Fourth Army. As early as April 1944 an Abwehr control had asked one of the double agents: 'Please state exact number of Divisions, etc., belonging to Fourth Army under General Thorne'.[10]

I will return later to the role played indirectly by Deception in the actual capitulation proceedings, but it is a sad reflection on Force 134's Order of Battle that, after the Norwegian Brigade had been committed to Operation *Crofter* (the reoccupation of northern Norway under Soviet operational control), the combat strength of Force 134 was reduced to one Norwegian parachute company, thereby making Thorne briefly the commander of two notional or nearly notional armies, the bogus Fourth Army and the virtually non-effective Force 134. It was not only in combat troops that Force 134 was woefully deficient: Thorne warned that his signal resources were so weak that he might not be able to find enough W/T operators to accompany the disarmament 'heralds' to Norway.[11]

'It was not surprising therefore that [he] should look elsewhere for help . . . towards what Special Force H.Q. had been able to build up in the way of wireless communications and Norwegian confidence'. Liaison through Special Force HQ with the resistance movement was continually being strengthened, especially after a meeting in Scotland between Thorne and Jens Chr. Hauge, the leader of Milorg.

Thorne's growing confidence in Milorg does not appear to have been shared by the Foreign Office or the Joint Planning Staff. On 22 December the FO wrote to the Cabinet Office: 'The Norwegian Forces of all kinds to deal with this problem [of a German collapse] including the "Police" trained in Sweden, seem likely to be totally inadequate';[12] and a JPS paper of 14 January describes the Norwegian resistance movement as being 'too scattered, lightly armed and inadequately trained to be profitably used in action'.[13] Thorne's respect for Milorg was, however, shared by General Boehme, who reported to Doenitz on 1 May 1945 that it had 'good human material' and was 'formidably armed'.[14]

Quite apart from inadequate numbers, Thorne's 'main problem was [how] to avoid or at least reduce the time lag of 10–14 days before formations based in the U.K. could arrive in Norway'. This time-lag would be as much as 30–40 days if the formations involved were already in north-west Europe. Even the Foreign Office kept hammering away at this,[15] but the War Office seems to have done little about the problem until SHAEF sent a 'signed Eisenhower' signal on 5th April pointing out the 'danger of leaving large German forces uncontrolled in Norway' for possibly up to six weeks, and urging 'would it be possible for 1 Airborne Division to be earmarked for this operation? It will be ready for operations on May 1st and 21st Army Group are not pressing for it.'[16] In the event, SHAEF had to signal on 3 May: 'Units for Doomsday [the code name for the actual landing of the *Apostle* troops in Norway] must now be assembled in U.K. 1 A/B Div is not now available.'[17] But on 5 May SHAEF was able to allot 1st Airborne Division for Norway. On 6 May the commander and his staff arrived in Edinburgh, and by the afternoon of 8 May the Division was ready to fly to Norway. Even at this last moment the Division's Parachute Brigade was detailed for a task in Denmark, and an *ad hoc* Brigade to take its place was formed from the Divisional Artillery. (All of which shows that the praise that Thorne gave his planning staff in his foreword was not unjustified).

The revised plans for Norway

Whereas the planning for *Apostle* had proceeded on the assumption of a complete cessation of hostilities in Norway after the German capitulation, this had to be modified at the beginning of 1945. Perhaps as a result of the shock to Allied optimism after the Ardennes counter-offensive, there was much speculation in Allied and neutral countries as to the reality of the existence of the so-called German *Festungen*, and Thorne points out on page 4 of his report that 'the Wehrmacht's actual dispositions . . . were adequate for a long campaign'. This naturally caused great anxiety, not least to the Swedes, with the possibility of war coming closer to their frontiers. SHAEF prepared plans to deal with post-capitulation resistance in Norway by an overland advance on that country via Denmark and Sweden, on the assumption that Swedish troops would intervene in some strength. The first high-level warning of possible pockets of German resistance after the collapse of the Wehrmacht in Germany seems to have been in a Chiefs of Staff paper of 18 January.[18] (The JPS paper of 14 January (note 13 above) appeared to discount the likelihood of 'the worst case' – i.e. continued German resistance). The paper of 18 January said 'it was quite possible that the German Divisions in Norway under the command of a Nazi fanatic might give a great deal of trouble'. A similar warning was given in the final paragraph of a letter from Hollis to Sargent at the Foreign Office on 22nd February:[19]

> For your information, we are examining the present plans for the Allied occupation of Norway in the light of the latest appreciations of German resistance continuing in isolated pockets after the collapse of German resistance in general.

On 20 March the JPS produced 'Revised Plans for Norway',[20] basing their belief in continued enemy resistance on the two recent reports of the Joint Intelligence sub-committee (note 3 above). They recommended that 'the most economical course' would be an overland advance through Sweden to capture Oslo, using Gothenburg as a base, 'possibly with the cooperation of the Swedish armed forces'. The plan included a draft directive to Supreme Commander Allied Expeditionary Force from the Combined Chiefs of Staff which envisaged two US or British divisions being used, in addition to four or possibly more Swedish divisions: 'This plan to be prepared as soon as possible'. Thorne's reactions to these alarums are not known, but presumably they would have been extremely sceptical. The 'signed Eisenhower' telegram of 5 April about 1st Airborne Division might have been some sort of a promise from SCAEF that he had not forgotten about *Apostle* in the current excitement about the 'Revised Plans for Norway'.

On 13 April Montgomery cabled the Chief of the Imperial General Staff: 'There are all sorts of possibilities looming ahead . . . I have even heard it stated that 21st Army Group may have to go through Denmark and via Sweden into Norway and clear up that country'. According to Hamilton, Montgomery was 'dumbfounded' at that prospect,[21] and it certainly seems strange that nothing should have leaked out from SCAEF about the 'Revised Plan's' implications for 21st Army Group. Montgomery told the CIGS on 20 April that he had had discussions with Eisenhower and had recommended that 'the troops to go into Denmark should be the ones which will go right on to Sweden and Norway'.[22] Eisenhower did not dissent, but said 'he would think it over'. Hamilton says (page 488) that SHAEF's 'controversial plans for the Liberation of Denmark and Norway were simply shelved', but on 28th April SHAEF produced an appreciation by the planning staff for 'Assault operations on Norway'.[23] This included the following paragraphs:

(a) 'opposed amphibious operations are practicable only in the Stavanger area', and

(b) 'the operations should be commanded by 21st Army Group/2nd TAF under the overall direction of SCAEF, with Scottish Command mounting the amphibious forces and supplying the SHAEF Mission to Norway . . . Should *Apostle* conditions arise prior to the entry of Allied forces into Sweden or before an amphibious assault to Stavanger is mounted, Scottish Command should relieve 21st Army Group of all responsibilities for Norway'.

The Eisenhower version

Although the SHAEF appreciation of 28 April laid down the division of responsibilities as between 21st Army Group and Scotco in the event of an assault operation, there is still some mystery about the reference to Thorne in the last chapter – 'The Final Phase' – of Eisenhower's *Supreme Commander's Report*.[24] After discussing the impending collapse of resistance on 'the North German Plain', he goes on to say:

it was possible that some withdrawal might be attempted into Denmark and Norway with a view to make a last stand in those two countries, while "Fortress Holland" would continue to hold out behind the water barriers. The prevention of such a withdrawal, by means of a rapid Allied advance to the Baltic, thus became the primary objective of our operations in the northern sector.

He then says, 'For the subsequent reduction of Norway in the event that the German garrison there continued to hold after its isolation had been effected, a task force was assembled in Scotland under the command of Lt-General Sir Andrew Thorne'.

There appear to be a number of inconsistencies and uncertainties in this paragraph about the roles to be played by 21st Army Group and Scottish Command:

1 Eisenhower's phrase 'for the subsequent reduction of Norway' suggests he was making his final dispositions before the expected collapse of the Wehrmacht in Germany; and the reference to 'Fortress Holland' still holding out suggests that these plans were being made during the last week in April.

2 What was Eisenhower's intention about Jutland? Was it to use it as a base for subsequent operations against Wehrmacht resistance in Norway as in 'A Revised Plan for Norway' (the SHAEF appreciation for the assault operation on Norway was dated 28 April)? Or did he consider the Revised Plan as a complete waste of time and intend to seal Jutland off against Nazi last-ditchers

fleeing north, as stated in his Report, or against the Russians advancing rapidly westwards towards Denmark?

3   How realistic was the final sentence about a task force being assembled in Scotland to tackle German resistance in Norway? As Eisenhower was aware (see his request for an airborne division for *Apostle*), Thorne did not have enough strength even to carry out an unopposed liberation, let alone one resisted by up to eleven divisions.

Planning for the Wehrmacht

One of the essential preliminaries to the surrender was the preparation of the so-called 'Herald Parties' to supervise the execution of the disarmament terms at various German subordinate HQs. These sprang from Thorne's conviction that Wehrmacht discipline would survive even when morale crumbled, and they were his solution to the most difficult problem facing the planners: how to disarm, intern, guard and administer the 350,000 Germans with the small forces available. Thorne decided with SHAEF approval that the Germans should be left as an army in being under their own system of command and administration – but with himself in control as the commander-in-chief. This policy was completely at variance with the Allied aims elsewhere, which were to destroy the cohesion of the German forces and to belittle the prestige and authority of their commanders. Thorne also realised it would conflict with the *leitmotif* of the Crown Prince's warning, because it was bound to be unpopular – if not downright incomprehensible – in Norwegian eyes, as they would expect to see every German behind barbed wire at once.[25]

To the casual observer the disarmament and internment plans seemed wonderfully simple: the Wehrmacht were to march out of the towns and villages that they had been occupying; before entering the various designated Reservations where they were to be interned, they were to stack carefully all their weapons of 20 mm calibre or less under Allied supervision; once inside the Reservations they were to administer themselves until the time came for them to be repatriated, and – unless specially exempted – they were not to move more than one kilometre from the reservations. But all these plans depended on the Wehrmacht's acceptance of military facts and on German discipline and, in the last resort, on the soundness of Thorne's belief that this discipline would survive the trauma of the surrender and the necessarily harsh capitulation terms.

How far was Thorne justified in believing that his forecasts about Wehrmacht morale and discipline would be proved correct? For this he had not only the normal sources of intelligence available to a commander, but also the knowledge he had acquired about the German military mind. Readers of Donald Lindsay's *Forgotten General: A Life of Andrew Thorne* will remember that in the four years of World War I he had had as much opportunity as anyone to study the strengths and weaknesses of the German fighting man.[26] In Berlin, as military attaché from 1932 to 1935, he had watched the rebirth of the German army,[27] and in 1940, as commander of a newly formed division, he had succeeded in blocking a series of German armoured thrusts against the Western side of the Dunkirk perimeter.[28] *Forgotten General* gives two examples of his skill as a forecaster about the Germans. The first was in a letter to his wife in the winter of 1914, explaining that she had to give up any hope of seeing him 'home by Christmas' because, he insisted, 'Germany has to be totally defeated whatever the cost . . . otherwise [their three sons] Sandy, George and Peter will all be doing the same as I am in another twenty years or so'.[29] Actually it was some twenty six years later that the three sons were evacuated from Dunkirk with their father. The other forecast – shorter-term and more public – was in the report by Thorne which the ambassador in Berlin sent to the Foreign Office in July 1934: 'that, after some five years, the Reichswehr of some 21 infantry and 4 mobile divisions in peace will be capable of expansion into some 70 divisions on mobilisation, supported by a very strong airforce and backed by a carefully organised industry.'[30]

Guessing the Lillehammer enigma

The 'normal sources' of intelligence on which Thorne depended for the Liberation do not seem to have included much Ultra. On the other hand the flow of information was helped both by a land frontier – which could never be completely sealed – with Sweden, a neutral power with access to the Allies, and by a highly organised resistance movement with its own W/T links. The key question that they had to answer in March–May 1945 was how the Wehrmacht would react to the expected collapse of the armies in Germany. There was every reason for German morale in Norway to be low: although they might claim to be an undefeated army, they had been indulging in the soul-destroying task of waiting for an invasion that never came (other than the odd commando raid), and they were receiving continually depressing news from home of military defeats and aerial destruction.

But whatever the spirit of defeatism throughout the HQs and units spread along the long coastline, their leaders appared to face the future defiantly – anyhow until Doenitz ordered the General Surrender. On 1 May – after Hitler's death – Boehme reported that he had a strength of eleven divisions and five brigades: 'In Norway we can fight any battle'.[31] On 3 May at Flensburg 'Boehme, Lindemann [C-in-C Denmark] and Terboven [the Reichskommissar in Norway] spoke up for the continuation of war'.[32] On 6 May, at the meeting on the Swedish – Norwegian frontier between the German minister in Stockholm and Boehme's representative, the former was told 'that the forces in Norway were quite intact and would be able to hold out without any difficulty for a couple of months longer'.[33]

It might have appeared that this readiness to fight on was of a somewhat limited nature and was not to the last ditch, being designed to provide the Doenitz Government with a bargaining counter in their negotiations with the Allies, as indicated by von Krosigk's telling Schellenberg on 1 May 'that Norway is still a pawn in the game',[34] and Boehme's Order of the Day:

'Norway must be a pledge in the hands of the Wehrmacht until Germany's and Europe's freedom is secured'.[35]

A surprising source

One of the sources best placed to report on Wehrmacht morale was 'Edel', who had contacts in the HQ at Lillehammer and who was, for instance, able to predict on 28 April that Doenitz *most probably* would be appointed successor to Hitler and Head of State if the latter died – i.e. two days before Doenitz heard of this himself.[36] Not all his reports contained such newsworthy items, but through Milorg's secret radio transmitter he provided a flood of reports in April and May giving London very valuable insights into the developing situation in the HQ at Lillehammer. (Edel, when not engaged in intelligence work, was Jens Chr. Hauge, head of Milorg. I understand that Thorne was not aware of this inspired but horribly dangerous form of moonlighting.)

Among other reports, on 19 April Edel informed London: 'Happy to report that German Nazi Leaders have decided to go to Bavaria repeat Bavaria not to Norway, which was seriously discussed two weeks ago. Conditions in Berlin obviously confused.'[37] Hauge quotes another report – which he says 'is not confirmed otherwise, but may be correct':

> There is also a report that Terboven in the middle of March summoned Boehme and Ciliax [the] Naval Commander, and asked if they could guarantee the loyalty of the troops in Norway in the case of German collapse on the continent. Terboven was then apparently playing with the idea that Hitler, Himmler, etc, should come to Norway. The two commanding chiefs could not guarantee the loyalty of their troops.[38]

Hauge describes his contact as a Major H. 'in a central position in the high command who thought that I was a humanitarian Norwegian with some sort of influence in Home Front circles and had some sympathy for the new Germany to come. He had no idea that I was a Milorg man'.[39]

It is interesting to note that on 24 April Special Force HQ, when passing to the Foreign Office Edel's cable of 19 April, commented: 'Personally I do not wish to over-emphasise the opinions expressed. There is always the likelihood that the contact which Milorg has with the Germans is used for two-way traffic'.[40] This phrase suggests that Special Force HQ thought it possible that the Wehrmacht was using Major H. to pass deception material to the Allies.

Swedish uncertainties

Thorne devotes over a page of the pre-VE Day section of his Report to relations with Sweden: these were always likely to be a problem, and they became increasingly so with the prospect of 'post-capitulation resistance' and with the directive to SHAEF to start the production of the 'Revised plans for

Norway' on 22 March. Nearly a month later it is clear from a Combined Chiefs of Staff telegram of 21 April that the negotiations about Swedish involvement had not got very far: 'We are in general agreement . . . that [the] moment for entry of Sweden into the war must be carefully judged. At this stage we want to avoid frightening Sweden into a downright refusal in [the] belief our military requirements will be far greater than will in fact be the case'.[41]

Two days earlier Churchill had fired a broadside in a minute to Ismay about Sweden's unhelpful stance, particularly in view of the possible continuance of the menace of the U-boats based on Norwegian ports: 'I regard this as the last opportunity for the Swedes to save their name before the world. Up to a few months ago they could plead they were frightened. Now they have no excuse except a calculating selfishness, which has distinguished them in both wars against Germany.'[42]

On 29 April Mallet, the British minister in Stockholm, informed the Foreign Office that he had heard via the Crown Prince that the minister for foreign affairs 'would rather welcome the arrival of a small SHAEF mission'.[43] This was officially confirmed by the minister himself on the next day, thereby indicating that Sweden was preparing to end her century-long neutrality.[44] Its impending loss was viewed with mixed feelings in Stockholm, but the government seems to have embraced the prospect with some enthusiasm. The Combined Chiefs of Staff apparently felt that it was necessary to warn SCAEF that there could 'be no intention of undertaking any major commitment for re-equipping Swedish armed forces. Swedish demands should be kept to a minimum . . .'.[45] This hope of getting arms on the cheap was to reappear in the later offer to intern the Wehrmacht in Sweden.

The threat to Sweden's neutrality began to lift with the arrival of Schellenberg in Stockholm with – according to Mallet's telegram of 5 May – full powers signed by Doenitz to negotiate with the Swedish government for the cessation of the German occupation of Norway. The Swedish government therefore pressed for the despatch of another SHAEF mission to Stockholm for this purpose and were prepared to fall in with any proposals by SHAEF for the temporary internment of Germans.[46] The following day Mallet sent a further telegram, stating *inter alia*: 'It would seem almost certain that Schellenberg would surrender the German troops in Norway to such a mission' and – almost pleadingly – 'The Swedes only desire to do whatever SHAEF thinks most helpful and they are anxiously awaiting guidance'.[47] Later that day SHAEF sent Mallet a telegram indicating that negotations in Stockholm were a poor option, and on 8 May they signalled him: 'It is not the intention that any Germans should enter Sweden, and General Thorne is already in contact with the German Command in Norway'.[48]

Doomsday

Thorne's negotiations with the German Command were entrusted to Brigadier Hilton. Sad to relate, pages 13 and 14 of Thorne's Report, dealing with the acceptance of the surrender terms and the arrival of the Crown Prince and

Thorne himself, are masterpieces of understatement, echoing at somewhat greater length his remark in the foreword: 'In the event the liberation went smoothly and expeditiously'. So much could have gone wrong. 'If, for example', as Hauge writes at the end of *The Liberation*, which gives an absorbing account of the scene at Lillehammer, 'Doenitz had not established a form of government in North Germany that the German military in Norway had to obey; if Terboven, Boehme and Hoelter [his Chief of Staff] had been left to themselves in Norway; if the allied leadership had not acted with a happy combination of firmness and human insight; if the government and Home Front had not cooperated; if Milorg had not managed its part of the task; if the German discipline was not deeply rooted; if the Norwegian people had let emotions carry them away from prudence – then the liberation of Norway might have turned out quite differently. It could have been necessary to defeat *Festung Norwegen* by force of arms. Or the liberation might have developed into a long-drawn confused transitional period with scattered fighting and destruction.'

Mercifully the good sense of the Norwegians prevailed, and there was no serious outbreak of violence. Hilton formally presented SCAEF's surrender terms at 10 p.m. on 8 May, and Boehme notified their acceptance the following morning. Whatever he may have thought earlier about continuing the fight, the ground was cut from under his feet by Doenitz's General Surrender on 8 May. He was not to know that the Allied Expeditionary Force was barely one tenth of his own. It was a most fortunate spin-off from the *Fortitude North* deception plans: he never doubted that Thorne's forces would have been of an adequate size to enforce the surrender terms.

Thorne had in fact had the utmost difficulty in establishing W/T contact with Boehme and eventually had to route his messages through General Dewing's HQ in Denmark.[49] The three paragraphs at the bottom of page 13 deal with what was probably his most pressing requirement on landing in Norway: the establishment of a proper system of communications, which could only be achieved by taking over wholesale German signals personnel and equipment. That and the gradual build up of the Allied forces, which was completed by mid-June with the arrival of the US Task Force of one infantry regiment and the last two British brigades, allowed Thorne to concentrate on the remaining two great tasks of his assignment – the full restoration of Norwegian sovereignty and the repatriation of the Wehrmacht.

Envoi

These two problems were linked: Thorne could not terminate the Military Phase and re-establish the Norwegian government until the progress of disarmament and internment had effectively removed any threat from the German forces; and he and the Allied forces had to stay in Norway until the greater part of the Wehrmacht had been repatriated. As he explains on page 15, the Liberation had gone so well and so peacefully that it 'was impossible for any Norwegian, particularly the Home Front Leaders, to realise that there was any risk'. He had pointed out to the British ambassador that it would have been quite wrong to have handed over responsibility to the government while, for instance, the tanks of a panzer battalion could enter Oslo virtually unopposed – yet he could not announce that publicly.[50] Eventually by the beginning of June the situation had improved sufficiently for him to obtain SHAEF agreement to restore full sovereignty to the Government (other than the powers needed to control and evacuate the Wehrmacht) in time for the King to return on 7 June, five years after had been forced to leave Norwegian soil.

There were to be a number of disappointments and delays before repatriation of the Wehrmacht began, and each delay affected Thorne adversely in two ways: it increased the danger of his overstaying his welcome, and it lowered morale in the Reservations and therefore made it more difficult for the German commanders to maintain discipline there.

There were two other areas of potential discord. The first was the replacement of the Crown Prince as Commander in Chief by General Ruge – though Thorne could not of course show his regret. The general had spent the years 1940–5 in captivity and had not acquired the ability of those who had served with the Norwegian forces in Scotland to understand the British military mind, and Thorne disapproved of his plans for the reorganisation of the Norwegian army.[51] Fortunately this was more than counterbalanced by the appointment as prime minister of Gerhardsen, who had likewise spent many years in captivity but who soon proved himself a staunch ally. The second difficulty was the unpopularity caused by the disposal of German war material. This was always bound to be a tricky problem; it became a bone of contention between Thorne and the Norwegians, and he felt strongly enough about it to spend almost a whole page on it at the end of Part 2 of the Report. Inevitably he took his share of the blame, in particular for not having alerted SHAEF earlier to the outrage that the seemingly wanton destruction of expensive weapons and equipment would arouse. It is obvious, however, that he considered that his efforts to get SHAEF's policy altered received only very tardy recognition and that he was left unsupported for too long.[52]

As regards Boehme and his forces, the 1951 Report describes some of the earlier difficulties, particularly with the 'arrestable categories', but thereafter Boehme carried out his side of the capitulation impeccably, perhaps because he sensed that Thorne could be expected to behave in a chivalrous manner. But any hopes of a speedy evacuation were destroyed when it became obvious that conditions in Germany were so appalling that a further influx of over 300,000 ex-Wehrmacht personnel could not be accepted for an indefinite period.[53] Hopes were then raised by the Swedish offer to hold the 300,000 temporarily in their country, only to be dashed when the offer was withdrawn. Thorne's reactions to this let-down are for once almost uncharitable; but he did eventually succeed in getting the US Zone to take some Germans to keep up the hopes and therefore the morale and discipline of those awaiting repatriation in the Reservations. It came to light during Trygve Lie's visit to Stockholm in July that one of the reasons for the Swedes' original offer to let the Wehrmacht intern themselves in Sweden was their belief that they would be able to acquire the weapons that the Germans would be carrying with them.[54] The plan became less attractive when it was discovered that the Allies would make the Wehrmacht dump their arms on the Norwegian side of the frontier; the Swedes had probably been misled by the procedure followed in Denmark, where the Wehrmacht were allowed to cross the frontier into Germany carrying their weapons before handing them over. Nevertheless Thorne was invited to Stockholm by the Swedish commander-in-chief.[55]

Thorne's hopes of a timetable for the evacuation which would avoid the need for providing his troops and the Germans with winter clothing became once more attainable with a change of heart later in July at USFET and 21st Army Group. This made possible an adequate flow of Boehme's troops into the British and U.S. Zones and thus enabled Thorne to keep his promise that the Liberation would be virtually completed by the end of November. Thorne wrote in his final weekly letter to the CIGS on 14 October:

> Boehme and Bechtolsheim [a corps commander he had known in Berlin] leave Norway by air on 16th October. Both . . . have carried out my instructions and orders most loyally and efficiently, and I could not have asked for better support in the very difficult task of controlling and administering a disintegrating army. I am arranging to see General Boehme before his departure to thank him for his cooperation.[56]

Two years later Boehme was to commit suicide in the war criminals' prison at Nuremberg.

Thorne himself left Norway on 1 November to a moving farewell from the Crown Prince and the government. The official history of the Second World War subsequently recorded: 'Perhaps the greatest tribute by the Norwegian Government to the work and attitude of the Mission and to the trust they felt in its Head was paid some five years later',[57] when the Norwegian government asked for General Sir Andrew Thorne to return from retirement to serve as an adviser to the Ministry of Defence on the organisation of the Norwegian Army. But the most immediate tribute was the final paragraph of Gerhardsen's letter: 'Dear General, you leave today a country that feels a deep gratitude to you and to the country you represent. We will not forget what we owe to Great Britain.'

References

1 In preparing this paper I received magnificent help from the staffs of the Library and Records Department, Foreign and Commonwealth Office, and the Army Historical Branch, Ministry of Defence, and the Imperial War Museum. All documents cited are in the PRO unless otherwise stated.

2 L.F.Ellis, *Victory in the West*, vol. II, *The Defeat of Germany* (London, 1968), pp 339–40.

3 e.g. Jens Chr. Hauge, *Frigjøringen* (Oslo, 1970); Olav Riste *London-regjeringa: Norge i krigsalliansen 1940–1945*, vol. II (Oslo, 1979).

4 A copy is now available in the National Army Museum.

5 JIC (45) 55 (Final), 18 February 1945, 'German Situation after Capture of Berlin and Loss of Ruhr'; JIC (45) 76(0) (Final), 3 March 1945, 'Resistance in Norway after the Capture of Berlin and the Loss of the Ruhr'.

6 *The Scotsman*, 8 November 1945.

7 FO 371/47528.

8 FO 371/43253.

9 WO 205/333.

10 Michael Howard, *Strategic Deception* (London, 1990), p.118.

11 WO 219/282.

12 FO 371/43254.

13 FO 371/47505.

14 Marlis Steinert, *Capitulation 1945* (London, 1969), p.142.

15 COS (44) 1047 (0).

16 WO 219/282.

17 WO 205/347.

18 COS (44) 1047 (0).

19 FO 371/47507.

20 JPS (48) 43 (Final).

21 Nigel Hamilton, *Monty the Field Marshal* (London, 1986), p. 479.

22 AD/2046.I C-in-C 21st Army Group Plans, 20 April 1945.

23 WO 219/255.

24 Eisenhower, *Supreme Commander's Report*, 1946, p. 137.

25 Andrew Thorne's 1951 Report, p. 11.

26 Donald Lindsay, *Forgotten General: A Life of Andrew Thorne* (London, 1987), chs. 6–7, passim.

27 Ibid, pp. 98–114.

28 Ibid, pp. 136–7.

29 Ibid, p. 73.

30 FO 371/17695 X/M/02867.

31 Steinert, *Capitulation 1945*, p. 142.

32 Ibid, p. 144.

33 Folke Bernadotte *The Curtain Falls* (New York, 1945), p. 127.

34 Steinert, *Capitulation 1945*, p. 229.

35 Hauge, *Frigjøringen*, p. 69.

36 Ibid, p. 68.

37 Ibid, p. 75.

38 Ibid, p. 75.

39 J. Chr. Hauge, personal letter to Peter Thorne.

40 FO 371/47509.

41 FO 371/47508.

42 Ibid.
43 FO 371/47509.
44 Ibid.
45 N4962/158/G (FO).
46 FO 371/47509.
47 Telegram from Stockholm to FO, No. 820, 6 May 1945.
48 FO 371/47509.
49 WO 205/333.
50 FO 371/97511.
51 National Army Museum 8703–31 unscheduled, Thorne papers, copies of letters from General Sir Andrew Thorne to Chiefs of Staff to SCAEF and CIGS. A copy of A.T.'s letter to Ruge is enclosed in the letter to CIGS of 20 September 1945.
52 Ibid, Statement in the Norwegian Press of 8 September 1945
53 N 7622/158/30 (FO).
54 N 9746/158/30 (FO).
55 FO 371/48036.
56 National Army Museum [note 51 above], Letter to CIGS of 14 October. 1945.
57 F.S.V. Donnison, *Civil Affairs and Military Government in North-West Europe 1944–1946* (London, 1961), p. 170.

23 The Western Allies, the Soviet Union and Finnmark 1944–5

MALCOLM MACKINTOSH

Introduction

THE aim of this chapter is to add a Soviet political and military dimension to Anglo-Norwegian relations during the Second World War. Its main emphasis is on the brief entry of Soviet troops into Finnmark in October–November 1944 in what the Russians officially call 'Victory in the Arctic'. The chapter opens with a section recalling the German plan to use the military occupation of Norway in April–June 1940 to deploy troops to the far north of Norway and Finland in the area of Kirkenes, with the aim of advancing eastwards into the Kola peninsula and the capture of the port and naval base of Murmansk and Polyarny. Some consideration will be given to the role of the Royal Norwegian government in London during the campaign. Finnish-German operational planning for the war in the north will also be discussed. Soviet attitudes to Norway as an ally in 1941–5 will follow an account of the Soviet campaign in the autumn of 1944 on Soviet, Finnish and Norwegian territory; the final surrender of German troops in Norway; and Finnish operations in the north under Soviet orders – which ran well into 1945.

War comes to Scandinavia

In historical terms, the involvement of the Soviet Union in Scandinavia and, indeed, in northern Norway, began with the Soviet invasion of Finland on 30 November 1939. The 'peace' agreement which followed the Red Army's disastrous campaign against the Finns – the 'Winter War' – included the incorporation of part of Finland's Arctic coast near Petsamo (Pechenga to the Russians) into the Soviet Union, and brought Norway's defences close to the military power of the Soviet Union. This treaty, signed on 13 March 1940, was followed less than a month later, on 9 April, by the German invasion of Denmark and Norway. The Norwegian government left for Britain, but a regional capitulation agreement between the Germans and the remaining Norwegian forces, signed on 10 June 1940, allowed certain Norwegian forces to stay in Finnmark to act as border guard units. This meant that the first German troops to be stationed in Finnmark, with their headquarters in Kirkenes, did not arrive until late June of that year. On the Soviet side of the border, under the command of the Leningrad Military District, was the Fourteenth Army, based in Murmansk, which had participated in the Arctic operations of the Winter War.

With Hitler's decision to attack the Soviet Union – the date of his directive for Operation *Barbarossa* was 18 December 1940 – planning included an attempt to persuade Finland to participate in the war in order to recover her lost territories and restore Finnish losses caused by the Soviet aggression of the Winter War. Finland's strategic and economic position had worsened after the Soviet annexation of the lost lands and of the Baltic States in June 1940. Later in the year, the Germans approached the Finns with offers of economic help in return for military cooperation. On 16 May 1941, the first official German-Finnish military talks opened in Berlin. These were continued in Helsinki and led to an agreement on joint operations against the Soviet Union. A plan, code-named *Silver Fox*, was drawn up which defined the roles of German and Finnish forces; Finland formally agreed to take part in Operation *Barbarossa* on 11 June 1941, with parliamentary committee approval given three days later.

The concentration of German troops for the Arctic campaign against the Soviet Union was a complex operation of major proportions. The plan agreed with the Finnish High Command involved the creation of an Army – originally named 'Army Command Norway', and later the 'Twentieth Mountain Army' – with a strength of four German divisions and two Finnish divisions. The northern strike force, 19 Mountain Corps, was made up of troops already deployed in Norway, including the 2 Mountain division stationed in Kirkenes and the 3 Mountain division which was brought to the area by road from Narvik. These divisions were reinforced by the SS-Kampfgruppe Nord which came through Sweden to strengthen 19 Mountain Corps. The southern column of the Army, the 36 Army Corps, came to Finland by sea – officially to facilitate the rotation of German troops garrisoning Finnmark in Norway. Its headquarters was in the Finnish town of Rovaniemi, from where it was planned to attack the Soviet 42 Rifle Corps covering the White Sea port of Kandalaksha. Of particular relevance was the definition of a line across the 'waist' of Finland – between Oulu on the Gulf of Bothnia and Luojarvi on the Soviet-Finnish frontier. All troops to the south of this line were to be under Finnish command, while the Germans controlled the forces to the north, including the two Finnish divisions subordinated to them by the Finns early in June. Partly due to administrative complications and partly to the official 'excuse' for the movement north of the 36 Army Corps, this Corps did not reach it deployment area by 22 June 1941 – 'Barbarossa Day' – and the main offensive by the German and the Finnish forces in the Arctic was, in fact, launched on 29 June 1941.

Military and Political developments, 1941–44

The details of the military campaign launched on that day are outside the scope of this chapter. The 19 Mountain Corps' task was to advance towards Murmansk, and to capture the town by 4 July, while the 36 Army Corps tried to cut the Leningrad-Murmansk railway and reach the White Sea at Kandalaksha. In the initial phase, the Fourteenth Soviet Army, commanded then by Lt.-General V.A. Frolov, consisting of the 14 and 52 rifle divisions and the 23 Fortified Zone (in the 'Fisherman's' (Rybachi) peninsula) put up determined resistance. With the help of naval infantry of the Northern Fleet in Polyarny, who landed small detachments along the coast behind the German lines, it succeeded in halting the enemy offensive on the River Zapadnaya Litsa by the end of July. A similar situation developed on the Kandalaksha sector, where the two divisions of 42 Soviet rifle corps, commanded by Major-General R.I. Panin, the 104 and the 122 rifle divisions, held the Germans and the Finns about 140 kilometres from the sea.

In the autumn of 1941 Soviet forces, combined with ships of the fleet, attempted a counter-offensive from the lines of the Zapadnaya Litsa and Lake Chapr, but the German defences held and a planned amphibious landing behind the German positions was abandoned. The Germans, conscious of the growing logistical importance of the far north to themselves and to the Russians, especially as British and other Allied convoys succeeded (though with heavy losses) in reaching Murmansk and delivering weapons, aircraft and supplies to the Soviet Army, increased their sea and air strike capabilities in 1942 and 1943. Early in 1943, the German Navy deployed the pocket battleships *Scharnhorst* and *Tirpitz* and the heavy cruisers *Hipper*, *Lützow* and *Scheer* into north Norwegian waters and ports for operations against Allied fleets and convoys in the North Atlantic. The German air force based at Norwegian and northern Finnish airfields amounted to over 500 planes in 1943, compared with the 200 available to the Soviet Northern Fleet.

Indeed, as the ground war developed into a kind of stalemate in 1942–3, the conflict in the north and the Barents Sea assumed increasingly large naval proportions. The Germans sought unsuccessfully to seize the two peninsulas – Rybachi and Sredny – covering the entrance to the Kola inlet by land and amphibious operations, while the Soviet Northern Fleet sought to interdict German supply convoys and communications passing in both directions along the Norwegian coast as far south as Tromsø and Narvik, and also the entrance to Varanger Fjord. This fleet tried to play its part in limiting the movements of the powerful German naval units in Norwegian waters against Allied vessels and convoys, though German superiority at sea in the area significantly reduced the Soviet contribution in this direction in this period of the war.

The Norwegian government in London: a dilemma in the north

While military and naval operations were under way in the Arctic, and especially against the background of declining German fortunes in the war as a whole, the Norwegian government faced growing dilemmas about the policies it should adopt towards the eventual liberation of Norway from German occupation. In the first place, it was unclear what the Germans might do as Allied victory in the north approached: would they capitulate, try to withdraw their forces into another country, or make a last stand in a kind of 'Fortress

Norway'? In planning for the liberation of the country by Norwegian and other Allied troops, Norwegian concerns were particularly related to the very limited Allied forces which could be deployed to Norway, and to the fact that early Allied plans did not include the despatch of any forces to northern Norway or Finnmark. As far as Soviet intentions were concerned, the Norwegians in London believed that the Russians were in favour of Norwegian forces taking part in the liberation of northern Norway, but it proved impossible to discover what the Soviet Union intended to do about this theatre of war or whether, at this stage, Moscow planned to pursue the Germans in the north on to Norwegian territory.

The Norwegian government in London was in a difficult situation. It wanted to achieve the liberation of the homeland as soon as possible, including some involvement of Soviet troops, if appropriate, but was afraid of possible problems in persuading the Russians to leave once the war was over. In May 1944 the government did sign a Norwegian-Soviet jurisdictional agreement accepting, in fact, that in principle Norway's northern territory could become a 'Soviet area of military operations'. But it was even more anxious to use Norwegian forces in the liberation; at sea, the Norwegian Navy and its merchant counterpart were playing a major role in supporting the war effort. On the other hand, the ground and other forces established in Britain were inadequate and not at all well trained or suited to take part in the liberation of Finnmark. Neither the British nor the Americans were able to provide the essential transportation or even emergency supplies for such an operation, or to support the population of Finnmark if operations were undertaken. The government was still in the throes of this critical debate when events on the ground took over, and attention turned to a major Soviet strategic offensive against Finland which ultimately brought Soviet troops on to Norwegian soil in the Arctic and changed the course of the war in that region.

The decisive battle in the north: 1944

By the summer of 1944 the Soviet high command had in place a series of strategic offensives westwards, known mainly as Operation *Bagration*, which were to take the form of 'rolling' attacks from north to south during which the main German armies would be destroyed and as many of Germany's allies as possible forced out of the war and overrun or occupied by Soviet troops. Not unexpectedly, the strategic plan was aimed first against Finland on Russia's northern flank. For some time, the Finnish government under President Ryti had been seeking ways of disengaging from the German war effort without losing the territories it had recovered in what the Finns call the 'Continuation War'. In February and March 1944, Finnish representatives had been in touch with Madame Kollontai, the Soviet minister in Stockholm, about her government's terms for an armistice and an end to the war; but these contacts had come to nothing, and the Finns decided to continue the war in accordance with a defensive strategy.

On 9 June 1944, the Soviet offensive against Finland opened with a massive land and air attack on the Karelian Isthmus where most of the hardest fighting had taken place in the Winter War. Two Soviet armies of the Leningrad Front under Army-General Leonid Govorov, supported by artillery and air bombardments, and totalling 260,000 men, the heavy guns of the Baltic Fleet, and over 530 aircraft, attacked the Finnish positions – roughly along the old 'Mannerheim Line'. By 16 June, the Finnish defences had been breached, and on 20 June, the strategic city of Viipuri (Vyborg) had fallen to the Russians. Almost immediately, the Red Army opened up a second front in Karelia to the north of Lake Ladoga – along the line of the River Svir between that lake and Lake Olonets – on 21 June. Here, two lower-strength Soviet armies of the Karelian Front under the command of Army-General Kiril Meretskov, the Seventh and the Thirty-Second, crossed the river and recaptured the town of Petrozavodsk on 29 June. As the Russians approached the Soviet-Finnish frontier of 1940, their offensive halted while further assaults were made westwards from Viipuri, where Finnish defences held. Fighting went on from 25 June to 10 July without significant Soviet gains; and on 12 July, the Soviet high command called off the offensive against Finnish forces, transferring some of its main formations to the south of the Gulf of Finland ready for the next stage in the 'rolling attacks' – against German forces in Estonia and Latvia.

The severe losses of this campaign resurrected in the minds of Finland's rulers the need to withdraw from the war, and on 1 August 1944 President Ryti resigned, handing over his office to Marshal Mannerheim, the legendary hero of the Winter War. On 25 August, the Finnish minister in Stockholm formally asked Madame Kollontai for Soviet agreement to armistice talks in Moscow, which was granted by the Russians. A ceasefire was proclaimed on all sectors on 4 September, and on 19 September an armistice was signed, with the diplomatic agreement of Britain and the United States. Officially the war between Finland and the Soviet Union had come to an end.

There remained, however, two major problems to be solved, one of which directly concerned Norway. The armistice terms agreed with Moscow included a Finnish undertaking to break off relations with Germany at once and order the departure of all German troops from Finland, if necessary expelling them by force or handing them over to the Allies as prisoners of war. In fact, the German Twentieth Mountain Army with headquarters in Rovaniemi in north-west Finland, still had over 220,000 men on Finnish, Soviet and Norwegian soil in the far north – in the area assigned to the Germans in the demarcation agreement of June 1941. The Soviet high command took on the operation to drive the 19 Mountain Corps from Soviet territory west of Murmansk, crossing, if necessary, into Norway – with the agreement of the Norwegian government in London. The Finns were ordered to turn their arms against 36 Army Corps in Finnish Lapland: both operations contributing to the main military campaign in the Arctic region.

The Petsamo-Kirkenes operation: October–November 1944

The Soviet high command ordered the command of the Karelian Front, which was responsible for operations against the Finns and the Germans between Lake Ladoga and the Barents Sea in the north, to prepare for an attack on German forces in the Petsamo area on 26 September, and for the destruction of the Twentieth Mountain Army under the German Generaloberst L. Rendulic, before the onset of the Arctic winter. The commander of the Front, Army-General Kiril Meretskov, an unsuccessful Army Commander on the Karelian isthmus in the Winter War, and his Chief of Staff, Lt.-General A.N. Krutikov, decided to use the existing army deployed for the defence of the Kola peninsula and Murmansk, the Fourteenth, under Lt.-General V.I. Shcherbakov, reinforced by three Corps, two from the Seventh Army recently engaged in the Svir River campaign, and one from the Nineteenth Army protecting the town and port of Kandalaksha on the White Sea; both of these armies had ceased active operations following the Finnish armistice. Two new types of Rifle Corps, the 'Light' Corps, composed of ski, mountain and marine brigades specially trained for operations in the Arctic, were added to the Army: the 126 'Light' Corps and the 127 – the latter having seen service in the Svir operations. The full Fourteenth Army thus consisted of three regular Rifle Corps and two 'Light' Corps: a total of eight divisions, four brigades, one independent guards tank brigade, a mobile infantry group in reserve, and three naval infantry brigades in the Rybachi peninsula under the command of the Northern Fleet of Admiral A.G. Golovko. General Shcherbakov's 97,000 men, 2,103 guns and heavy mortars, 126 tanks and SP guns and over 1,000 air force and naval aircraft greatly exceeded the strength of the 19 Mountain Corps, although the Germans' defensive positions were well prepared and supplies and ammunition stocks were reported to be adequate. The whole German group consisted of 53,000 men, 770 guns and mortars, 160 aircraft and over 200 naval vessels blocking access to the northern fjords.

General Meretskov and the Army Commander, General Shcherbakov decided to launch the main attack towards Petsamo (Pechenga) from the south-eastern direction in the area of Lake Chapr. It was to be led by the 99 and 131 Rifle Corps and the Guards tank brigade, with the 126 'Light' Corps covering the left and the 127 the right. In immediate reserve would be the 31 Rifle Corps and the Mobile Group. Preparations were also made to deal with the specific problems and obstacles of the planned advance. One was whether the heaviest tank of the Red Army, the KV, could operate in Arctic terrain on the approach of winter: in the event, only one KV tank regiment was assigned to the army, though it, reportedly, performed well. A second problem related to the number of fjords and arms of the sea over which the army would have to pass in their advance. This was solved by setting up of three 'special service' engineer detachments which operated behind the German lines, reconnoitring routes and suitable sites for temporary ferries or bridges over these geographical obstacles in the path of the advancing army.

The 'Petsamo-Kirkenes' operation began on 7 October 1944 with a powerful air and artillery bombardment of the German positions, after which the two forward Rifle Corps, 99 and 131, went into attack. In the first day, the 131 Corps reached the River Titovka, and both formations broke through well-prepared German positions on the road to Petsamo, the German Corps HQ, and pushed ahead steadily. On 9 October, Meretskov ordered Admiral Golovko to land his three Naval Infantry brigades from the Rybachi peninsula on to the coast north-east of Petsamo, a task which was carried out successfully. The Mobile Group was then brought into action in support of 99 and 131 Corps, and, in heavy snowstorms, the main force reached the town of Luostari. This enabled the Army Commander to detach the 126 'Light' Rifle Corps and send it south-westwards to cut the important Petsamo-Salmijarvi road. On 13 October, an amphibious operation by 72 Naval Infantry brigade captured the port of Linakhmari, north of Petsamo, and two days later, the 10th Guards and 14th Rifle divisions of 131 Corps entered the town from the south.

Surviving German units from Petsamo retreated towards and across the Norwegian frontier, and, while the Soviet Army re-grouped for further operations on Norwegian soil, 31 Rifle and 126 'Light' Corps turned south along the frontier to attack a German concentration around the industrial centre of Nikkeli. This grouping, made up of troops from Luostari and from the rest of the German army retreating northwards under Finnish pressure (see below), had the benefit of an 80-kilometre defence perimeter designed to protect the valuable ore-producing plants. With assistance from Soviet artillery, this fortified zone was attacked by the 31 Rifle Corps on 22 October and captured. The accompanying 127 'Light' Corps then sped southwards to seize the vital town of Nautsi on 27 October. The Fourteenth Army, meanwhile, had closed up to the Norwegian frontier and had begun to pursue the remainder of the 19 Mountain Corps on Norwegian soil.

General Meretskov launched the main attack towards Kirkenes in Finnmark from Petsamo with 131 Rifle Corps and the Guards Tank brigade through Tårnet, where they faced extensive minefields and broken bridges, and well as evidence of a 'scorched earth' policy inflicted by the German forces. Practical help, say Soviet sources, was given to the Soviet Army by the local Norwegian population, particularly by fishermen who provided boats to units trying to cross rivers, lakes and fjords. With this assistance, the Soviet army entered Kirkenes on 25 October, where they found that near total destruction of the port facilities and much of the housing had been carried out by the Germans. Most of the garrison of 5,000 men had stood and fought, and almost all were killed. Small units of the 19 Mountain Corps retreated westwards towards Neiden Fjord, pursued by 99 Rifle Corps and 126 'Light' Corps; when the town of Neiden was taken on 22 October, the Karelian Front commander, General Meretskov, reported to the Soviet high command that the campaign was, in effect, over. The operation in the Arctic closed with an 'Order of the Day' on the 'Final clearance of the Petsamo area' issued by Stalin on 2 November 1944.

Norwegian Military Planning for Finnmark

As the Soviet campaign in the Arctic progressed and reached its climax in November 1944, the Norwegian government in London intensified its planning for the operations in northern Norway and for the post-liberation needs of the people in that area. A military mission and an Independent Mountain company of 230 men were despatched to the headquarters of the Soviet force in the north, where they were well received by General Shcherbakov, the commander of Fourteenth Army. The Norwegian prime minister then suggested to the Allied Command that an expeditionary force might be landed on the coast of Norway somewhere north of Mosjøen in order to help to cut off the German retreat. The British Chiefs of Staff replied that, unfortunately, no forces were available for such an operation, owing to commitments elsewhere. In January 1945, the Norwegians came up with another plan, involving a naval task force designed to send part of the Norwegian Army Brigade in Scotland, supported by a Royal Air Force squadron, to Finnmark, mainly for humanitarian aid to the population – which had suffered grievously from the German scorched earth policy. This plan gained some support from the Allied Command, but British military reaction was negative, due, it was said, to lack of resources; and the expedition never set sail. It has to be admitted, in looking at relations between the Western Allies and Norway during the war in the north in 1944–5, that these difficulties caused some dissatisfaction in Norway with their British allies: difficulties which the successful choice of General Sir Andrew Thorne to command the Allied Land Forces in Norway after the German capitulation fortunately went some way to solve.

The Finnish Lapland campaign, September 1944 to April 1945

Returning now to the final military operations on the Arctic Front – primarily between German and Finnish forces – it will be recalled that the second provision of the Soviet-Finnish armistice agreement was that which required the Finnish Army to disarm, force the surrender of, or destroy any German troops still deployed in Finland after the armistice who refused to leave of their own free will. This referred to the bulk of the Twentieth Mountain Army deployed, under its headquarters in Rovaniemi in Finnish Lapland, in the area at the head of the Gulf of Bothnia around Kemi and Tornio. They had been joined by some of the troops from the Petsamo area already liberated by the Soviet Army, and by 36 Corps retreating from west of Kandalaksha when Finland withdrew from the war. This reinforced German Army amounted to 167,000 men with 8 – 12 months' supplies and ammunition, and showed no intention of leaving Finland without a fight. Indeed, they reinforced the demarcation line of June 1941 with about two divisions, and awaited a Finnish attack. Initially, neither the Finns nor the Germans wanted to go to all-out war, and informal contacts were even made on the ground between Finnish and German commanders under which the Germans withdrew northwards towards the Norwegian frontier as the Finns 'attacked' the 'retreating' units.

The latter even left 'prisoners of war' behind to convince the Allied Control Commission, then sitting in Helsinki to supervise the armistice and chaired by the Soviet Party leader, Andrei Zhdanov, that the terms of the agreement were being carried out.

This 'play-acting' was soon detected, and the Commission ordered the Finnish Army to go over to a full-scale offensive. One problem for the Finns was that while they were expected to obey this order, the Commission had also decreed the demobilisation of the Finnish Army, which meant that the only troops available were raw recruits. In October 1944, Zhdanov sent a menacing letter to President Mannerheim threatening that if he did not take 'immediate measures' to drive the Germans out of the country, the Soviet Command would take action on its own: the threat to the future of Finland was obvious. A Finnish force of four divisions and two brigades was sent by land and sea to the north, where severe fighting began early in October. The Germans fought hard, and accompanied their actions by a scorched earth policy in the area of the fighting which turned the local population against the German Army and gave the young Finnish soldiers a motive to fight.

By 8 October 1944, the Finns had gained control of the land at the head of the Gulf of Bothnia, capturing both Tornio and Kemi, and passing through a devastated countryside. A week later they took Rovaniemi, after which the German General Rendulic split his force into two parts: one, with orders to retreat northwards towards Lake Inari near Nautsi in the hope of linking up with 19 Mountain Corps – of whose movements and approaching defeat Rendulic had no information. Eventually, this group disintegrated in the wilds of Lapland after causing widespread destruction in the area. The second part of the German force retreated north-westwards through the Finnish 'panhandle' into the Norwegian mountains along the valley of the Tornio and Muonio rivers. On 30 October the Finns captured the town of Muonio on the Finnish-Swedish frontier, and in mid-November, an important German fortified position in the mountains of the 'panhandle' was taken. Individual German units actually held on to mountain passes leading into Norway near Saana, where small numbers remained until late April 1945. Finnish troops finally forced them over the Norwegian frontier, where they surrendered and were disarmed. This ended the final chapter in military operations in northern Scandinavia, on Norwegian, Finnish and Soviet soil, for which the Soviet invasion of Finland in November 1939 and the German invasion of Norway in April 1940 and of the Soviet Union in June 1941 must bear the political and military responsibility in historical terms.

Soviet-Norwegian relations 1944–5: the diplomatic picture

Once the Soviet Union had entered the war as an ally of the West in 1941, Moscow gave full recognition to the Norwegian government in exile. The Russians treated Norway as an allied power under enemy occupation – with the added factor of extensive German use of Norwegian territory and ports in Finnmark for operations against the Soviet Union and Allied convoys in the

North Atlantic and the Barents Sea bringing valuable aid to the Soviet war effort. But when military victory in the north was achieved by the Soviet army, the Soviet Union exploited its success – and its popularity with many Norwegians at home and abroad – to put forward diplomatic claims for a change in the status of, and sovereignty over, the islands of the Svalbard (Spitsbergen) archipelago to the north of the Barents Sea.

This large island group which, in strategic terms, could dominate the Barents Sea and maritime approaches to the Soviet north and the Kola peninsula, and had great economic value, had been the subject of an international treaty in 1920, leading to recognition by the major powers and regional states that the islands belonged to Norway. The Soviet Union refused to adhere to the treaty until 1935, (when the Soviets wanted to embark on mining operations in the islands) although it independently accepted Norwegian sovereignty over Svalbard in return for full *de jure* Norwegian recognition of the Soviet government in 1924.

In the wake of the Soviet victory in the north, the Soviet government presented Norway with new demands over Svalbard. In a meeting with the Norwegian foreign minister, Trygve Lie, in November 1944, Vyacheslav Molotov, the Soviet foreign minister, asked Norway to renounce her sovereignty over Svalbard and accept a revision of the treaty of 1920 to allow for joint Soviet-Norwegian rule, or condominium, over Svalbard and all its islands. A new treaty should be agreed allowing the Soviet Union and Norway to station troops and built fortifications on Svalbard on an 'equal basis', and to guarantee joint Soviet and Norwegian defence of the archipelago. The Russians also asked for the annexation of Svalbard's southernmost island – Bear Island – in the centre of the Barents Sea to the Soviet Union outright, claiming that it was historically Russian. This series of claims, which had its parallels in Soviet demands to Turkey to re-negotiate the Treaty of Montreux governing entry to, and exit from, the Black Sea, and interest in freedom for Soviet naval vessels to leave the Baltic, was based partly on the war situation of 1944 and partly on a desire by the victorious great power to have indefinite unrestricted access to the world's oceans. In the wartime situation, the Norwegian government, while underlining the prohibition in the treaty of 1920 of defence installations on Svalbard, did agree to discussions with the Soviet Union on the future of the islands. It pointed out, however, that any new Norwegian-Soviet treaty would have to be approved by the Storting, which could only meet in full session after the liberation of the country, and by those other signatories of the original treaty who were either on the Allied side or neutral in the war.

Nothing came of this Soviet approach at the time; but their foreign ministry raised the claim again in 1946. On this occasion the Norwegians, responding to public opinion, rejected any agreement with the Russians on defence issues relating to Svalbard, but did negotiate with them over mining interests and other economic prospects. The Soviet government abandoned their defence initiative, and reverted to their original demand on Svalbard, with extensive economic, and some diplomatic, presence in the islands, which Russia still regards as commercially and strategically important.

Conclusions

The involvement of Norway and Finland, traditionally neutral states, in the European balance of power during the Second World War clearly owes its origins to the determination of Germany under Hitler and the Soviet Union under Stalin to extend the power of their states, militarily or politically at will, according to their strategic and ideological aims as the war progressed. The occupation of parts of northern Finland in the Winter War and their annexation to the Soviet Union, followed by the German occupation of Norway, including the positioning of troops in Finnmark and Finnish Lapland made warfare in the Arctic sector inevitable when Operation *Barbarossa* was launched in June 1941. Climatic conditions on land and sea and in the air, and the great distances between Finnmark, Lapland and the Barents Sea from the massive battles on the central fronts combined to limit significant operations in the region to the period 1944–5. Stalemate appeared to be the rule throughout 1942 and 1943 on land – although operations at sea increased steadily with the Arctic convoys and the ocean 'raids' of the German battleships and cruisers into the North Atlantic in those years. Nor should the contribution of the Norwegian resistance be minimised; their activities kept the German garrisons nervously holding on to their positions, and interdiction of supply routes was of vital importance, as was the military and logistic intelligence they provided for the Allied war effort in the north.

When the brief but intense battle came in the autumn of 1944, the military superiority of the Red Army carried the day in the 'Petsamo-Kirkenes' operation, which brought Soviet troops on to Norwegian territory. Here, and in Finland, much suffering was caused by the scorched earth tactics ordered by Berlin. The use of the Finnish army, then in the process of demobilisation under Allied orders, to complete the destruction of the German Army in Lapland caused very high casualties: up to 4,000 young Finnish recruits were killed or wounded in that campaign. While historians rightly give pride of place to Norway and the Norwegian people for their resistance effort, some thought may be spared for the tragic dilemmas forced on Finland by the actions of others in the war which engulfed Europe and most of the world beyond in 1939–45.

24 Between the lines: North Norway 1944–5

TØNNE HUITFELDT

Introduction

Malcolm Mackintosh has written a comprehensive, accurate and well balanced account of the Western Allies, the Soviet Union and Finnmark, with its main emphasis on the brief entry of Soviet troops into Finnmark in October 1944. He states that the initial German plan was to use the military occupation of Norway in April 1940 to deploy troops on the then Soviet-Finnish-Norwegian frontier in the area of Kirkenes with the aim of advancing eastwards into the Kola peninsula and the capture of the port and naval base of Murmansk and Polyarny. Mackintosh's 'prelude' may in this respect be a little ahead of time. In the regional capitulation agreement between the German and the remaining Norwegian forces signed on 10 June 1940 it was allowed that certain Norwegian forces could stay in Finnmark, to act as border guard units. This decision was subject to quite some criticism after the war. In any case, one of the results was that the first German troops did not arrive in Kirkenes until late summer 1940.

The concentration for the German attack on the Soviet Union in the north was in itself an undertaking of major proportions. The 3rd Mountain Division had to move from Narvik to Kirkenes by road, whilst 199th and elements of 702nd Infantry divisions together with various supporting units had to be brought in from South Norway. The 2nd Mountain Division was already in the Kirkenes area, whereas SS-Kampfgruppe Nord came through Sweden and had to be transported from Narvik to Kirkenes. The main force of XXXVI Corps was brought to Finland by sea transport. The troop movements were were carried out under the guise of relief operations for North Norway. Because of the movement restrictions it was not possible for XXXVI Corps to draw up to the Finnish eastern border in time to open the offensive on 22 June 1941, 'Barbarossa Day'. On 22 June the 2nd Mountain Division executed an unopposed occupation of Pechenga and Linihamari, and the 3rd Mountain Division took up a line extending further south to include Luostari (these former Finnish areas had been returned to the Finns by the Soviets after the Winter War). The German attack across the Finnish-Russian border was ordered to take place on 29 June and 1 July 1941. Staggered time was used to make air support available for the initial assault in each Corps sector.

A short time after the initial assault, the Gerrnan attack was halted at the Litsa River in front of Murmansk and Polyarny, and about 140 kilometres east of the White Sea in the direction of Kandalaksha. And in these locations the front lines were to remain on the frozen tundra for the next three years until the Soviets opened the tenth battle of the 'Great Patriotic War' on 7 October 1944.

The Norwegian government in London: a dilemma in the North

As the liberation of Norway from the German occupation became a more realistic possibility, the Norwegian government faced a growing dilemma in the face of Allied plans and preparations for the liberation of Norway which were drawn up in the light of various contingencies: a German capitulation, withdrawal or even a last stand in '*Festung Norwegen*'. Norwegian concerns were particularly related to the very limited Allied forces which could be deployed to Norway, and the fact that the early Allied plans did not include any forces at all to be deployed to North Norway. As regards the Russians, it became evident that they were very positive towards any participation by the Norwegians in the operations in the North from an early stage, but it was not possible to find out what the longer-term Soviet aims were as regards Norwegian territory.

In this situation it appears that the Norwegian government in London had two partially conflicting goals. On the one hand, they wished to contribute to an early liberation of Norwegian territory; on the other, they must avoid contributing to a situation where they would have difficulties getting rid of the liberating forces after the war was over. In fact, as Olav Riste has pointed out, the Norwegians increased those difficulties in May 1944 by concluding a Norwegian-Soviet jurisdictional agreement (approved by the Western allies) which accepted that Norway was in principle a Soviet area of operations. This was the first clearly negative result of Norway's decision to have its own liberation agreement with the Soviet Union.[1]

The Norwegian government was in a difficult situation even though its constitutional and political basis was solid and well recognised, and it was able to pay for the maintenance of the Norwegian forces in Great Britain through the earnings of the Norwegian merchant navy. Norwegian efforts to take an active part in the military planning for the reconquest of Norway were hampered for obvious reasons. Operational planning at the grand or strategic level was a jealously guarded prerogative of the great powers who provided the bulk of the armed forces to be employed. Secondly, the need for secrecy called for a very restrictive interpretation of the 'need to know' principle. Lastly, it was becoming increasingly clear as the war went on that the liberation of Norway would be a side-show and a dead end in terms of the decisive battle to defeat Germany. Forces nominally earmarked for Norway would therefore be subject to recall at the last minute if required in other and more important theatres.

Exercise *Crofter*

One particular problem which became apparent in the winter of 1944–5 was that the Norwegian forces which had been established in Great Britain, particularly as regards the army, were totally inadequate and not at all well suited for the tasks entailed in the liberation of Finnmark. Another difficulty was the inability of the government to get the British and American leadership to provide essential transportation and even emergency supplies for the population in Finnmark which had defied the German order to evacuate and remained in the scorched area.

The Soviets had, as mentioned, been positive towards Norwegian participation in the operations in the high north. But when the Norwegian contribution was finally fixed at a military mission and an Independent Mountain Company of 230 men, this was not well suited to impress the Russians, even if the number was twice what had been originally prescribed by SHAEF! I believe that Mr Churchill may have unintentionally contributed to the Russian misgivings, when he wrote in a letter to Stalin on 23 October 1944: 'At Moscow you said you would let me know whether there was any way we could help you in Northern Norway. I understand that a token force of 200 Norwegians will be sent. Please let me know if you have any other requirements and I will immediately make enquiries whether and to what extent they can be met.'[2] At that time, The Soviet 14th Army had committed *96,806 men* against the German forces on the northern front. Colonel A.D.Dahl, then commander of the Norwegian Military Mission at Kirkenes has described his first meeting with the Commander of the 14th Army, where Lt Gen I.V. Shcherbakov expressed his surprise and disappointment at the small size of the Norwegian contribution. Still, the Norwegian contingent was well received and supported by the Russians.

The Finnmark plan

At a later stage of the events in Finnmark it became crucial for the Norwegian government to try to prevent the Germans from completing their policy of 'scorched earth', and to bring humanitarian assistance to the remaining population. On 15 November 1944, the Norwegian prime minister had arrived at the conclusion that the only thing which could help was if the Allies landed somewhere north of Mosjøen to cut off the German retreat. The prime minister proposed to ask Britain and the USA if they could mount such an operation at short notice. This idea was raised with foreign secretary Anthony Eden, who answered that the Norwegians 'ought to know that there were no British soldiers available for such an expedition'. The British Chiefs of Staff stated on 13 December 1944 that it would be impossible to carry out such an action, because the forces which would be required could not be trained and equipped for Arctic operations before February, which was set as the final date. The real reason was, however, that the Western allies had no army forces to spare at all, but the Chiefs of Staff asked that this was not made known![3]

Early in January 1945 the Norwegian navy and the Joint Defence Command came up with a new plan for a naval expedition to Finnmark. The purpose was mainly to provide humanitarian assistance for the civilian population, but it also had a wider aim: to recruit forces locally and to insert forces from the outside to achieve sufficient strength to occupy the areas which had so far been liberated, and to extend this westwards as the enemy either withdrew or left behind only small units. The Norwegian forces to be used were the remainder of the Norwegian Brigade in Scotland and the Mosquito section of 333 Squadron (the Catalina section was to come later), as well as personnel and equipment for an air base at Kirkenes. The Norwegian proposal was subsequently raised with the British and American governments. The Norwegian Chief of Defence, Crown Prince Olav, went to the USA in January to negotiate directly with the Combined Chiefs of Staff in Washington. The Crown Prince was also a personal friend of President Roosevelt, and he had good opportunities of supporting the Norwegian proposal outside formal command channels.

The reason why the Norwegian authorities chose to by-pass SHAEF and went directly to the Combined Chiefs of Staff was that the inter-allied committee for civilian supplies in Washington had refused to approve a SHAEF authorisation for providing 6,000 tonnes of civilian supplies for Finnmark, since the area was not occupied by SHAEF forces. The Norwegian Finnmark plan required at least 1,500 tonnes of civilian supplies in addition to the 6,000 tonnes approved by SHAEF. It is evident that the Norwegian government at the time believed that the cause of the supply problem rested with SHAEF, while the difficulties in reality came from the inter-allied organs in Washington. Before the end of January 1944 the Combined Chiefs of Staff in Washington had received two different recommendations on the Norwegian plan: one positive from SHAEF and one negative from the British authorities. The final British recommendation was disapproval, but with the addendum that a 'minimum plan' with respect to a rescue mission for the civilian population in the 'vacuum' would be regarded with greater goodwill.

Riste concludes that the handling of the Finnmark plan by the Allies was one of 'systematic delay in all quarters, as regards both substance and procedure'.[4] He doubts whether a straight refusal of the plan would have created greater irritation on the Norwegian side than what followed from the delaying tactics; but once this tactic had been chosen, it was carried through with firm resolve, assisted by the Yalta meeting (February 1945) which neutralised the decision-making process in Washington for a month. The negative handling of the Finnmark plan added considerably to the cooling of relations between Norway and Great Britain at the end of the war. And the bitterness of the people of North Norway, having felt abandoned and seemingly forgotten by both their own government and the Western allies during that winter lives on to this day.

The end

In the final phase of the war, everything seemed to come out even 'better than deserved'. The Russians never advanced in strength beyond Kirkenes and Neiden, and they left Norwegian territory in North Norway quietly and peacefully in September 1945, even before the last of the Germans! And the Germans did not chose to make a last, desperate stand in *'Festung Norwegen'*. They could possibly have done so if they had known how few forces the Allies really had at their disposal to safeguard the liberation of Norway, and the disarming of the more than 300,000 German troops there. It was good fortune that the Allied deception plan *Fortitude North*, which operated with the non-existent British 4th Army with 350,000 men in Scotland and the American 15th Corps, which did exist but belonged to another army, helped to convince the Germans that a last stand would be futile.

With respect to the happy end it is also of interest to note the importance of personalities and personal contacts for solving problems and arriving at workable solutions. The personal visits of the Milorg leader Jens Christian Hauge to England during the war, and his talks with the designate Chief of the Allied Land forces to Norway, Sir Andrew Thorne resulted in General Thorne gaining sufficient confidence in Milorg to give it an instrumental role in securing a peaceful take-over from the German forces on 8 May 1945. We may also be grateful that it was a personality like Sir Andrew Thorne who was given the task of commanding the Allied expeditionary forces after the German capitulation, and to direct the events which led to a smooth and almost painless reinstatement of Norwegian control of the country. It was also no coincidence that General Sir Andrew Thorne was asked by the then Defence Minister of Norway, Jens Christian Hauge to come back to Norway in 1950–1 to give advice on the reconstitution of the Norwegian Army after the War (even if the idea of Allied advice was not particularly appreciated by the then Chief of the Army, General Wilhelm v. Tangen Hansteen!).

References

1   Olav Riste, *'London-regjeringa'. Norge i krigsalliansen 1940–1945*, vol. II, *1942–1945: Vegen heim* (Oslo, 1979), p. 184.
2   Quoted ibid, p. 195.
3   Ibid, p. 211.
4   Ibid, p. 223.

25 The lessons of war: Norway in post-war Allied strategy

CLIVE ARCHER

THE title of this chapter might suggest that the position of Norway in post-war Allied strategy had something to do with the lessons learnt from the Second World War. In fact, the thrust of the paper is that, while the conduct of Norwegian politicians may have been affected by some of what they considered to be the lessons of World War Two for Norway, Allied strategy – insofar as it affected Norway – was also determined by other and more immediate factors. The Second World War strongly affected the operational environment within which Allied decision-makers functioned – particularly in the five to ten years after 1945 – but it also helped shape the psychological environment of the Norwegian government in the immediate post-war period. This paper will examine the response of Norwegian decision-makers to the post-war strategic situation and how this was affected by what they may have considered to be the lessons of the War. Finally, it will look at the position of Norway in post-war Allied strategy.

First, a note should be entered about terms. 'The Alliance' – that created by the North Atlantic Treaty – did not come about until April 1949, and the Organisation that accompanied it – NATO – only began to be formulated in the early 1950s. However, the term 'allied' can be used in a slightly different context in the case of Norway. It can refer to the United Kingdom, the traditional ally of Norway, and to the United States, the United Kingdom's post-war replacement in the North Atlantic area. This provides a certain continuity when considering Norway in post-war Allied strategy: it will be seen in the context of US strategy, with some reference to that of the United Kingdom.

Post-war strategic situation: the Norwegian response

The strategic world that Norway emerged into in 1945 was quite different from that of 1939. During much of 1939 there was the clear and present danger of war in Europe but there was the intention and the hope on the part of the Norwegians that their country should stay out of any conflict. Indeed, when war finally came, the Swedish, Norwegian and Danish monarchs and the President of Finland met to declare the neutrality of their countries. They hoped to repeat the experience of the First World War which the Scandinavian states had successfully seen out as non-belligerents, albeit ones that had occasionally been drawn closer to the fires of conflict. By 1939 the strategic situation of the Nordic area had changed: the rise of air power had placed its capitals within the radii of both the Luftwaffe and the RAF, and the importance of submarine warfare had been realised after the First World War. War came to the region in November 1939 with the Winter War between the Soviet Union and Finland but Norway, together with Denmark and Sweden, managed to stay out of this conflict, and Norway and Sweden helped to limit involvement in the Winter War by refusing France and the United Kingdom transit rights to aid the Finns.

The German attack on Denmark and Norway on 9 April 1940 confirmed the transition of the Nordic region from the 'quiet corner of Europe' to a potential power vacuum vied over by the Soviet Union, the United Kingdom and the German Reich. While Norway received military attention from the United Kingdom after the German invasion (and, of course, before), the British commitment there was withdrawn to concentrate effort in France and the Low Countries. The Scandinavian states may have been drawn into the theatre of war, but they still remained in the wings.

The end of the war thus brought a new strategic situation for Norway. Technological advance, especially in air power, had altered its geo-strategic position: it was now more accessible and more vulnerable. A major armed power that had indeed turned out to be a threat to Norway – Germany – lay defeated. The United Kingdom, Norway's traditional ally, had helped with the process of liberation, but it was clear by 1945 that the real power to the west was the United States. Furthermore, the first liberating forces on Norwegian soil were those of the Soviet Union, a power that had extended its sphere of influence into east and central Europe by the presence there of the Red Army, and which had obtained a common frontier with Norway. The international political context had also changed. Peace in 1945 saw the transformation of the strong wartime coalition into the institutional form of the United Nations Organisation with its apparent capacity to meet any new threats to international security. This contrasted strongly with the latter part of the 1930s when the League of Nations had all but collapsed and responses to breaches of the peace depended upon whether the British and French governments considered it to be in their interests to initiate action. Thus the world that Norway emerged into in 1945 seemed to be safer than the one it had left in 1939. Added to this, the Norwegian government's view of the world had developed as a consequence of the 1940–5 experience. What had it learnt?

Olav Riste has described the three cornerstones of pre-war Norwegian foreign policy as being a perception of security provided by geographical remoteness, the belief in automatic protection by the United Kingdom, and 'a determination not to jeopardise this fortunate position through ventures into foreign policy'.[1] The first of these had been eroded by the aerial warfare and blitzkrieg of the Second World War; the second had been shaken by the events of 1940; and the third factor was shown by the war to be much more contingent on foreign perception of Norway's strategic position than on Norwegian determination. Nevertheless, Norway, in 1945, tried to rescue something of this inter-war policy. Norway could do little about the change in its geo-strategic position, but it could try to replace the other two cornerstones.

During the Second World War, the Norwegian government in exile was resident in the United Kingdom, thereby bringing it literally closer than ever before to the British government. However, this geographical proximity was not necessarily reflected in policy terms. At first, the Norwegian government was reluctant to tie itself to any formal alliance, but by May 1942 'new thinking' within the government circles had manifested itself in a paper entitled 'Main Principles of Norwegian Foreign Policy' which recommended closer ties with the North Atlantic nations such as the United States, Britain, France and the Netherlands. Eventually these states might enter into a 'binding and committing military agreement on the defence of the North Atlantic'.[2] This broadened out the range of countries on which Norway might rely for future assistance and, in contrast to its previous relationship with the United Kingdom, more than hinted that Norway should have a formal alliance with these states.[3]

Although this policy orientation seemed to foreshadow later membership of NATO, it should be remembered that it was accompanied by the desire not to entertain 'ventures into foreign policy' and, in particular, by caution towards the Soviet Union. The Norwegian government, both in exile and back home in Oslo in 1945, was aware of the new situation whereby the USSR had become a direct neighbour of Norway in the north and had liberated Northern Norway. Norway was thus anxious to become 'the bridge for a reliant co-operation between the Soviet Union and the Atlantic powers'.[4] Arne Ording, adviser to the Foreign Minister, was well aware of the dangers of doing otherwise:

> We may find ourselves faced with the following choice: either to provide
> bases only for the British and the Americans, which the Russians may see
> as a threat, or to give also to the Russians, which will create both
> strategic and internal problems.[5]

It has been suggested that the 'Koht Doctrine' view of Scandinavia best typifies Soviet-Norwegian relations at the end of the Second World War. This doctrine held that Norway should not cling too closely to the West, as the main interest of the Soviet Union in the area was a desire to prevent the West from acquiring strategic bases from which they could threaten Mother Russia.[6] Certainly the presence of Soviet troops on Norwegian soil and the continued Soviet *démarche* over Svalbard pointed to caution in Norway's dealings with Moscow.

The continued existence of the wartime alliance in the form of the United Nations Organisation allowed Norway to follow its optimal policy of keeping bridges open to east and west for at least a short period after the end of the war. The external objectives of Norwegian government policy during the immediate post-war period have been described as '(i) to strengthen the international system and make collective security work by facilitating Great Power cooperation, and (ii) to keep Northern Europe free from Great Power tension and rivalry', a description that could well cover Norway's inter-war stance (at least for much of the time). Perhaps the lesson of the war that had been digested was just how easily the Nordic region could become involved in great-power disagreement.

The period from 1945 to 1948 saw another change in Norway's operational environment that led to its decision-makers to adjust their views of the world and, ultimately, to changes in security policy. The foundations of the immediate post-war policy started to shudder as cooperation between the wartime allies turned into the beginnings of the Cold War. The collapse of Norwegian 'bridgebuilding' policy came in early 1948, following the break-down of the Four-Power Council over Germany in December 1947, the sign-ing of the Brussels Pact in February 1948, the Communist coup in Prague and Stalin's request to Finland for a defence agreement in the same month. The change in Norway's defence situation led it to consider first the prospect of a Scandinavian Defence Union and then to reject this in favour of the North Atlantic Treaty.[7]

Norway's signature of the North Atlantic Treaty in April 1949 following the traumas of the previous year can be seen as a turning point in Norwegian security policy whereby the country finally joined an alliance aimed at collective defence against a specific potential enemy. With this understanding of the situation, 'Never again 9 April 1940' becomes the watchword of the Norwegian decision-makers and the necessity for alliance is the lesson learnt.

Perhaps this is too simplistic. As Professor Riste has pointed out, the move from a seeming neutrality to one of alliance by Norway in 1949 was not a sudden reversal of policy. He has typified the Norwegian signature of the Washington Treaty as 'merely the formalisation of an existing, but until then implicit, assurance that the control of Norwegian territory by a hostile power would be intolerable to the West'[8] and another Norwegian author points out that, even by 1948, Norway was shifting its policy of dependence on the UN to one of establishing a regional balance of power. That the policy of 'bridge-building' endured until late 1947 demonstrates that, for the Norwegian government, there was no one policy option that arose naturally from the 'lessons' of the Second World War. Their range of choices was determined more by the international situation – which changed dramatically from 1945 to 1948 – and the willingness to accept one solution rather than another was determined by a number of factors such as internal politics, Scandinavian and British-American pressures, and economic factors, rather than any particular conclusion drawn from the war experience.

What perhaps is noticeable is the enduring element in the basic tenets of Norwegian policy pre-war, 1945 to 1948 and from 1949. There was the assumption of assistance from the West (whether from Britain, the USA or NATO) should Norway be attacked; and a propensity to deal diplomatically with threatening great powers in the region (whether Germany or the Soviet Union) and to reassure them that Norway would not be used as a springboard for an attack. Thus Norwegian governments have continued with reassurance of the Soviet Union – for example in Norway's Base and Ban policies[9] – even while being full members of NATO.

Lessons for the Allies

The main point learnt by the Allies from their wartime experience with Norway was well expressed by the Norwegian minister of defence in the immediate post-war period, Jens Christian Hauge, when he quoted Marshal of the Royal Air Force Sir John Slessor:

> What good does it do us to hold Scandinavia if Western Europe falls? In the first place, the Allies could not hold Scandinavia in the long run if the rest of Western Europe were to be lost. In the second place, they could not mount a counter-offensive against the Russians from Scandinavia. Strategic interests in Northern Europe were in themselves considerable, but in a desperate situation where the available military means scarcely stretched to saving what was absolutely necessary to avoid losing the war, the strategic interests in Western Europe would loom much larger and Scandinavia would then draw the short straw.[10]

Various American and Allied war plans of the late 1940s and 1950s considered that the Soviets would occupy Scandinavia fairly early on in any war, though perhaps not at the start.[11] The experience of 1940 demonstrated only too well to Norway that, even if the campaign on their territory was going well, the demands of the battle on the continent of Europe would have priority. During the Second World War, there were no major separate campaigns after 1940 in Scandinavia – it only provided sideshows – and there was little belief that the situation would differ in a Third World War fought between the Atlantic Alliance and the Soviet Union.

The second lesson – or confirmation of existing wisdom – drawn from the war experience in Norway by the Allies can be seen in the above citation of Slessor by Hauge. It was that the Scandinavian region should not be used as a springboard from which to launch a counter-attack on Soviet-occupied positions in Europe. As can be seen from other papers, the idea of launching an invasion of the Continent from Norway was rejected during the Second World War. The same considerations were taken into account in the post-war period as had weighed on the minds of planners during wartime: action in Scandinavia would sidetrack the main effort on the continent of Europe and would spread valuable resources dangerously thin. The main concern of the Allies in their immediate post-war strategic planning as it affected northern Europe was that the area should be denied to Soviet use. It was hoped that a foothold might be kept on the Norwegian coast – perhaps Stavanger, maybe Trøndelag – whereby supplies might be taken across from the United Kingdom.[12] However, by 1950 there was some sign of Allied planning allowing for operations in the Scandinavian region – these appeared in the Himmerød Memorandum of October 1950 and in Eisenhower's 'Continental Strategy' – but in the end the notion was not accepted.[13]

A third possible lesson involved the value of deterrence. In post-war Allied strategy, the possibility of Soviet occupation of Norway was accepted with a certain amount of equanimity: the area was less exposed than the Continent, its occupation did not offer a life-threatening situation to the Allies, and it was not the most suitable bridgehead for the re-conquest of Western Europe.[14] However, North Norway was an important area to deny to any potential adversary of the Atlantic Alliance because of its position as a stepping-stone from North America to Europe. Perhaps another lesson learnt by Allies and Norwegians alike from the Second World War was that a modest amount of preparation by both might deter an attack. Norway could no longer suppose that its neutrality would keep it out of great-power conflict, or that if it were to be involved, the United Kingdom would come to its rescue. A more positive indication of support from the British – and the Americans – was required, and this was obtained in the form of guarantees in the the North Atlantic Treaty and post-war assistance with materiel from the two Allies. There was also shared intelligence and plans for stay-behind forces (*Gladio*) – both perhaps born of hard wartime experience. But anything else was problematic, especially in the period immediately after the signing of the North Atlantic Treaty.

By the early to mid-1950s there was more of a discussion as to what assistance the Allies might be able to afford Norway in the case of an attack. Naturally, the Norwegian government tried to manoeuvre debate within NATO's councils to favour a greater commitment by the US and Britain to the North. This seems to have been the case over the establishment of NATO's command system – whereby Norway tried to 'nail' the British and the Americans to the defence of the region – and with Norwegian attempts to get the Allies to accept the likelihood of a sudden grab of North Norway by the Soviets as a war scenario.[15] The basic Allied response was to encourage Norway to do more itself and also to place some pressure on the Norwegian 'base' policy.[16] Though Norway resisted such moves, the tension remained between the Norwegians' limited capability to defend themselves, their dependence on outside assistance in any conflict and their diplomatic requirement to limit great-power presence in Norway in peacetime. In a way, the arrangements made in the late 1970s and early 1980s for the Allied reinforcement of Norway, the pre-stocking of Allied materiel in Norway and the running of collocated bases helped to square this particular circle.[17] The implementation of the lesson of the value of deterrence had taken some time to get fully into place.

The wartime lessons for Allied post-war strategy – especially as it affected Norway – were perhaps quite simple. They were that Norway would remain peripheral to Continental Europe in their war-planning scenarios; that Norway would not be a suitable place from which to launch the liberation of an occupied Western Europe; and that preparation – by Norway and its allies – against hostile action might just deter an attack. However, that these 'lessons' dominated Allied dealings with northern Europe perhaps had less to do with any conscious learning process by politicians and planners from the experience of the Second World War than with the immediate operational situation in which the decision-makers found themselves. The bulk of Soviet forces *were* in central and eastern Europe after 1945 – and it was against this solid mass that the Allies eventually had to deploy their defences, not in the north. Likewise both political and military factors determined that any fight-back would be primarily conducted on the continent of Europe. Finally, the United States was aware, at least by 1949, that a 'Musketeers' oath', materiel and US troops and aircraft could act as a deterrent to Soviet action against western Europe. However, the US administration was not then prepared militarily to re-engage itself in Europe. It took the Korean War rather than any lesson of the Second World War to change American minds, and the US presence in Europe was still to be a selective one.

Conclusions

The Second World War was of course a traumatic time for the leadership of a small state such as Norway which had hoped to remain on the sidelines of the conflict. The political leaders understood that the country's strategic significance had changed but the wartime experience did not determine the policy options open to them – these were more a product of the evolving post-war situation. Perhaps what the war had affected was the outlook of Norwegian ministers, giving them a greater propensity to consider and accept options (such as defence agreements and alliance) that might otherwise have been rejected.

The Second World War moulded the strategic framework within which the Allies had to act after 1945. But events after May 1945 – the American and Soviet nuclear programmes, the division of Germany and the descent of the Iron Curtain in Europe, US demobilisation, the economic aftermath of war, the retreat from empire – were crucial to the development of Allied strategy. Experience of the Norwegian campaign only confirmed what anyhow was the consensus – that Norway would be peripheral to the main battle in Europe, if it came. Despite this, Norway has some strategic value to the Allies and, in the decades which have elapsed since the formation of NATO, Norway and its allies have worked out how these interests can best be safeguarded.

References

1 Olav Riste, 'The Historical Determinants of Norwegian Foreign Policy', in J.J. Holst (ed.), *Norwegian Foreign Policy in the 1980s* (Oslo, 1985), p. 13.
2 Olav Riste, *'London-Regjeringa'. Norge i krigsalliansen 1940–45*, vol. II, *1942–45: Vegen heim* (Oslo, 1979), pp. 277–8.
3 Olav Riste, 'Frå integritetstraktat til atompolitikk: Det stormaktsgaranterte Norge 1905–1983', *Forsvarsstudier III 1983–84* (Oslo, 1984) ,pp. 17–21.
4 Olav Riste, 'Nord-Norge i Stormaktspolitikken, 1941–1945', *FHFS notat*, No.4, 1986, p. 5.
5 Cited in Olav Riste, 'The genesis of North Atlantic defence co-operation: Norway's "Atlantic Policy" 1940–1945', *NATO Review*, No. 2, April 1981, p. 27.
6 Tom Hetland, 'Då Moskva sa nei til Norden: Sovjets syn på Norden og NATO, 1948–1952', *FHFS notat*, No.4, 1984, pp. 2, 50.
7 This period is dealt with in Magne Skodvin, *Norden eller NATO* (Oslo, 1971), pp. 314–17; Nikolaj Petersen, 'Danish and Norwegian Alliance Policies, 1948–49: A Comparative Analysis', *Cooperation and Conflict* 14 (1979), pp. 207–8; Geir Lundestad, *America, Scandinavia and the Cold War, 1945–1949* (New York, 1980), pp. 309–19; Howard Turner, *Britain, the United States and Scandinavian Security Problems 1945–1949*, PhD thesis, Aberdeen University,1982, pp. 427–32.
8 Riste, 'The Historical Determinants Of Norwegian Foreign Policy', p. 20.
9 For an explanation of these policies of not allowing foreign military bases or nuclear weapons on Norwegian soil see Clive Archer, *Deterrence and Reassurance in Northern Europe*, Aberdeen: Centre for Defence Studies, Centrepiece 6, Winter 1984, pp.7–14.
10 Cited in Rolf Tamnes, 'Norway's Struggle for the Northern Flank', in Olav Riste (ed.), *Western Security, The Formative Years. European and Atlantic Defence 1947–1953* (Oslo, 1985), p. 233.
11 Ibid, pp. 216–218.
12 Olav Riste, 'Was 1949 a Turning Point? Norway and the Western Powers 1947–1950' in Riste (ed.), *Western Security*, p.145; Rolf Tamnes, ibid, pp.217–9; Walter Poole, *The History of the Joint Chiefs of Staff. The Joint Chiefs of Staff and National Policy.* vol. IV, *1950–1952*, Historical Division, Joint Secretariat, Joint Chiefs of Staff, December 1979, p. 308.
13 Tamnes, 'Norway's Struggle', p. 219.
14 Ibid, p. 216.
15 Ibid, pp. 225–234.
16 Ibid, pp. 234–240.
17 Johan Jørgen Holst, 'The Contribution of Allied Reinforcements to Norwegian Security' in Ellmann Ellingsen (ed.), *Reinforcing the Northern Flank* (Oslo, 1988), pp. 12–16.

Discussion

Ralph Bennett asked whether there was any evidence that the Germans were preparing to make a last stand in *Festung Norwegen*. *General Frisvold* replied that the underground movement in Norway certainly had the impression that the Germans might continue resistance in Norway and knew that there were nearly 400,000 troops there, with supplies for up to seven months. On the other hand, as General Thorne had anticipated, morale among German soldiers was very low; they would not have fought. *Edward Thomas* said that London had no information either way about *Festung Norwegen*. They did not accept the information from the Norwegian resistance but had no positive evidence on the other side. They had no knowledge of General Boehme's attitude but thought he would comply with any instructions he was given. London thought that the morale of forces in Norway was very low but that discipline would probably hold. Low stocks of oil in Norway would make resistance very short-lived, if it was attempted at all, but the immense investment in new submarine bases in Bergen and Trondheim *might* lead them to try to hold on.

Professor Skodvin said that in February–March 1945, according to German documents now available, two trains of thought existed. One was to go on fighting to the last. The SS, curiously, did not agree. They had contacts with Harry Söderman and talked very freely about Reichskommissar Terboven's 'last stand' attitude. The SS were the only ones who *dared* to go over Terboven's head. The civilian home front leadership were worried. A report sent to Stockholm by Hans Engen (later ambassador to the UN and very active in gathering information) begins with the usual phrase: 'Sources with good connections in the Castle [i.e. Akershus Castle in Oslo, the residence of part of the Reichskommissariat] report that there has been a meeting where they discussed what to do when (not if, *when*) . . .' According to this report there were even military units that felt like resisting. One source of uncertainty was that in January–February 1945 the headquarters of the Gestapo and SD had moved out of central Oslo to Furulund – less of a suburb than it is today – while the military command moved to Lillehammer. 'One of Falkenhorst's staff officers, Bernhard von Lossberg, told me, in 1952 I think, that this was done partly with a view to organising a last stand (*Alpenfestung*) in South Germany and in Norway: "We could have fought for three months fighting a war like the one *you* could have fought in 1940." – i.e. walking around in the mountains and shooting as long as you had ammunition. He was quite sure (and he was an able man) that they had supplies available and that the logistics could work for a couple of months; and they were aware that it would be a long time before the Allies could bring up any force that could cope with them.' However, there was to be no last stand. The die-hard Terboven was called to Flensburg on 3 May and deposed by Doenitz. He went back to Norway and, before committing suicide, left the administration in the hands of Dr Koch. But some small German units did not agree and in the confusion of 5–6 May a battalion of police troops barracked near Frognerparken apparently offered their assistance to Quisling personally: they would march to his residence in Bygdøy to give him protection if he wanted: 'I am not sure how seriously to take this'.

On the wartime lessons for post-war NATO planning, *Group Captain Madelin* noted that Allied Command Europe (ACE) Mobile Force was created to deal with the rather vague questions of confrontation which could arise on the flanks. It is true that the main threat was in the centre, but here the Soviets could not try anything on and pretend it was merely a little local difficulty. The same was not true of eastern Turkey and northern Norway. Those were the days when NATO's strategy was massive nuclear response; and even in the early 1960s McNamara and others saw that this was quite unrealistic. In Finnmark a minor local incursion might become a *fait accompli*, but it could still be represented as something very local. The ACE Mobile Force still exists. Seven nations are represented in it, each of only brigade group size, and its purpose is more political than military. It is made up of nations which are not normally there – e.g. Italians on the northern flank – and is an important addition to NATO deterrence policy in remote regions. *Professor Archer* agreed. The main aim of the mobile force was not to fight, but to tie the defence of Norway in a political way.

Mats Berdal also referred to wartime lessons. He agreed that Norway was peripheral to Allied strategy. But the notion of *denial* was important – denying the area to another power. He pointed to an example of *not* considering the lessons of the war, when in 1953 the Standing Group told the Norwegians that major ground operations north of the Arctic Circle were 'not logistically possible'. Dr Berdal suggested that it was necessary to look at the differing perceptions of countries like Great Britain and the United States, as well as of the different branches of the armed services. The Royal Navy was the service most interested in Norway throughout the 1950s. In discussions on, for example, the carrier programme, it refered to the wartime experience in northern waters, as well as to the experience of submarines. *David Brown* developed this point. For the navy, Norway was part of the maritime, not the continental theatre. The Norwegian Sea had traditionally been regarded as neutral ground. This changed in the early 1950s when the Russians acquired cruisers. The American strike fleet, supported by the Royal Navy, was driven into the Norwegian Sea. The knock-on effect was that the Russians now felt threatened, so that ships they built in the next two decades were primarily defensive, and thus *not* able to come south. It was therefore a victory of the Cold War that the Russians were pushed on to the defensive. But in consequence the Norwegian navy gradually became less important. It was a strong force in the 1940s and early 1950s. Today its frigates are very old, under the US umbrella, and powerless against the Russian fleet. *Dr Berdal* responded that in the 1950s the Norwegian navy did not know what sort of role it was to have. In the 1960s there was a fleet construction plan with massive US aid. By that time they had decided on an inshore navy, but before then they were toying with ideas of having destroyers or even a cruiser. *General Zeiner-Gundersen* agreed with David Brown that the significance of northern Europe must not be seen in context of the UK alone but of the whole alliance and whole of the North Atlantic. The answer to the question why there were no big ships in the Norwegian navy was simple: budgets. Big ships are expensive.

Index

Printed in the United Kingdom for HMSO.
Dd.298170, C12, 3/95, 3400, 5673, 316821.